J. P. Donleavy's
IRELAND

In All Her Sins
And in Some of Her Graces

J. P. Donleavy's
IRELAND

In All Her Sins
And in Some of Her Graces

MICHAEL JOSEPH / RAINBIRD

First published in Great Britain by Michael Joseph Ltd
27 Wrights Lane, Kensington, London W8 5TZ in association
with The Rainbird Publishing Group
who designed and produced the book

© J. P. Donleavy 1986

British Library Cataloguing in Publication Data

Donleavy, J. P.
    J. P. Donleavy's Ireland in all her sins and
    in some of her graces.
    1. Ireland——History——1922–
    I. Title
    941.5082'092'4   DA963

ISBN 0–7181–2723–4

All the photographs in the book are from J. P. Donleavy's Archives
with the exception of the following: Ernest Gebler (page 121 above);
Stephen Hyde (page 220); The *Irish Times* (page 116 above and
page 136); E. Barrett Prettyman Jr (page 189); and photographer
Richard Simmonds (page 210) who the publishers would like to thank
for permission to reproduce their photographs.

The text was set by Wyvern Typesetting Ltd, Bristol
Mono origination by Butler & Tanner Ltd, Frome, Somerset
Printed and bound by Butler & Tanner Ltd, Frome, Somerset

To my Galway Mother

and

To my Longford Father

The latter whose comment upon Ireland

was

'They haven't got a pot to piss in'

I

The ocean beats pearl white against its high dark cliffs and spills a green tinted water on its sallow beaches. To look down from the skies, the tiny fields below are soft, silent and green in their innocence. From brown bogs and purple brighter moorlands, its streams and lakes shine silver. Upon the land that long knows how to tolerate suffering.

But to many of its native born winter non shivering inhabitants, it is a shrunken teat on the chest of the cold Atlantic. From which little of life's bare necessities and less of its joys or juices can be squeezed. And whose grey skies and sodden winds, force the mind to dream. Of other realms and to communicate with an almighty Gaelic god for whom this land alone is worthy of his blessings. And where, if only a horse could speak, we would know most about this citizenry.

Still, to more than a few, Ireland remains a glowingly sweet emerald vision having the fifteenth beer over some bereft bar counter at three a.m. in some outskirt corner of San Francisco, Hawaii, Boston or the Bronx. As patriotic and sentimental songs croak from drink sodden throats celebrating its heroes who fought and sometimes died for its flag. But rarely would it ever be a once bog trotter remembering his summer sweat in the seldom sun, pausing to spit again upon his hands, cutting turf back in a bog in that land. Or a once poor boy on a poor farm, who would at three hours past midnight, drive cattle ten miles through foggy darknesses to market and stand cold through a damp day to drive them back home again, unsold. It is a rare brogue whose vowels still purr lovingly commemorating the land of his birth, for all its saints, its absence of sinners and its abundance of scholars.

But for many an innocent visiting foreigner, its once unspoilt green shores now enclose unsightlinesses of such stupendous multiplicity to be cited as an example to the rest of the world. Ruined cities with their ancient buildings toppled in decay. Street after street unloved and smashed to smithereens by the gombeen man. Plumbing, detergents and soft toilet paper have come. To leave a debris and litter strewn nation, already long past beginning to spew poisons all over its once clean grey skies. Of this, the land of the welcomes. But now of the packaged tourist. Who finds himself happily fleeced in the biggest clip joint in Western Europe. Ah, but this latter is only because the unsimple minded Erse need your money more than you do, and firmly believe you won't miss it, if they take more than they are entitled to.

The Irishman's faith in his own perennial poverty is as deep and unshakable as his belief in the foreigner's eternal wealth. For how could that latter stranger, across an inclement ocean and sea, afford to get here in the first place. But unlike most of the indifferent French or exacting Germans, the Irishman as he attempts to mulct you, will not infrequently murmur a compensatingly humorous turn of phrase or pretend to grin a smile that is on the lips but not in the heart. But at least such gladsome shallowness has made this island universally known for the friendly if not honest, disposition of the people. Who in recent years, since the advent of visual images beamed across the sky and landing to be seen and heard uncensored by the native naked eye, have become subject to one of the most astonishing social and cultural revolutions ever to hit and wreak near havoc upon any people of any nation on earth.

It all must have begun on one innocent day. In England. Where there is a corporation called British Broadcasting. This organization is the most amoral and to some large degree, fair minded, disseminator of information the world has ever known. And the Irish knowledge of the English language provided ready ears and eyes to see and hear the news of freedom of the flesh and mind. And the young, the eager and the frustrated set this conflagration of upheaval alight. Human nakedness had come. Along with aesthetic ideas out of the minds of agnostic men. Gods, other than the Irish god, made known. Four letter words and four letter deeds. In all their graphic technicolour splendour. Forcing many an aesthete who still lurks sheepishly in this land, and whose sensibilities outrage enough, to incite the founding of societies, not only for the prevention of cruelty to innocent grassland, trees and buildings, but also the prevention of cruelty to the spirit of Irish human beings.

And who am I to talk. Or explain. Or raise a finger to admonish, point or accuse. Or cast a first stone. Or say this land is not what it could be. Or should remain what it was. Or even murmur about the cunning gombeen man who might desecrate and sell off this nation and bring it to its derelict sorrowful knees. It is my nation. Mine. Where I am a citizen. Both by blood and convenience. Who became so, entitled as I always was by virtue of the Irish birth of my parents. I was for seven years educated here. While sheltering between times in the cloistered peace of Trinity College Dublin, I took my degree in drinking and harlotry out in the better pubs, at many an abysmal party, or in an occasional elegant restaurant, or even at an occasional stately home, where someone was usually being hammered on the head down the main staircase by a bottle of stout. Punishment given for having split an infinitive. And from this I then vanished. With my ill and random got credentials. To be in cities and places like Boston, London and New York. Or isolated on the Isle of Man. And then, years later, having walked into Fortnum and Mason's in London for tea one afternoon, my wine adviser Mr Young said in some surprise, 'Mr Donleavy what are you still doing here when authors have just become tax free in Ireland.' And only weeks later I found myself speeding up a pollution haunted highway from London to Liverpool. To take the mail boat and land in Dublin. Hopeful, in spite of all my history here, and what they did to *The Ginger Man* in Dublin, that I would upon returning to these emerald pastures, become a resident, and be tax eternally free for my future and past creative scribbles.

Not only from that above do I assume my right to speak, especially against those who would assume I have no such right. But knowing too, that my authority to so utter, is not only warranted but greater and more than most, descending as I do on both parental sides from ancient bog trotters back into the dawn of ages. And hold the name of such tribes for proof. But my privilege arises, too, from a voice oft banned and shunned within these shores but which has already spoken for more than thirty years, saying a song of at times bitter love, yet of love for this land.

I am a 'narrowback'. This I was early called by the novelist, poet and revolutionary, Brendan Behan upon first reaching these shores. It was a term learned by Behan from one, A. K. Donoghue, who like myself, had come to Trinity College Dublin following World War II. Donoghue, a Harvard graduate in Classics, was Boston Irish. And 'narrowback' was a term used by Irish born immigrant Americans to

My four Irish grandparents standing in front of the Donleavy barn in Co. Longford. It became a Donleavy tradition to be photographed in front of one's barn instead of the house. Alas most of the Donleavys had no barns in America, but most did at least have their pots to piss in.

refer to the first generation of Irish born in America of Irish born parents whose backs, broad from the old country, now toiled to rear the narrower backs of their children in the New World. Never having heard the term before, Behan relished the word, and I, as one then quite self consciously American, took it to be derogatory. Behan, then recently released from prison, and I, were that afternoon's joke being played upon us when we were introduced to each other as writers. A term, when then said in our conspicuously unpublished circumstances, was equally meant derogatorily. And not that many moments later, outside Davy Byrnes pub, Behan, his shirt open to his navel and the tongues of his shoes hanging out like a panting dog's, and I, in grey herringbone tweed, were facing each other to fight in the middle of Duke Street. As we squared off, Behan suddenly lowered his fists, and at his most carefully diplomatic put forth his hand to shake mine. To say, 'Why should we give them dirty eegits back sitting in there in the pub, who wouldn't even leave their drinks to watch us fight, the fucking satisfaction of thinking we had.' Behan and I, thereafter, if we did not ever become firm trusting friends, we certainly at least always remained close enemies.

Ah, but let us go back. To where I first ever became conscious of this land. It was inside a cinema at the foot of one of the highest hills in the Bronx, an area extending north of New York City, with pot holed streets and an odd large manor house, around which were still retained open space, and the neighbourhood was known as Wakefield. My very first awareness of Ireland came in the shadowy scenes of a film of Liam O'Flaherty's *The Informer*. To me, a small boy, Victor McLaglen the actor seemed massive, powerful and invincible. His shoulders heaving up under a great weight. And later, being shot by many bullets he went staggering undying along the street displaying a feat of endurance as his life ebbed away in death. And he then, and all these years since, reminded me of my own father. Who could throw a young bull down on its side or lift gracefully in the palm of his hand, a full grown man above his head.

I cannot remember another impression of Ireland until, having

This house was where I lived until the age of six in America. On top of one of the highest hills in New York and with the exception of a German family living on a small estate next door, most of the remaining immediate neighbours were Italian. But it was at the foot of the hill upon which this house stood where I saw the film of Liam O'Flaherty's The Informer.

In Van Cortland Park, The Bronx, my father, myself and my younger brother Thomas (T. J.) who latterly became a resident of Greystones albeit mostly secretly. Living as he did behind closed shutters as the sea spray battered the windows and he painted his pictures inside with frozen fingers.

moved away from Wakefield, a mile or two westwards across the valley of the Bronx river, to a small community called Woodlawn. These several streets intersecting a main street, and resembling a small midwestern town formed a place triangular in shape and cut off from New York on all three sides by two extensive parks, and a large cemetery. It was here in the front hall of our house on 236th Street that a telegram was delivered to my father informing him of his own father's death at the age of ninety three. As my father stood there, there were tears which I had never before seen in his eyes. And even as the event remained strange and unfamiliar, I was somehow conscious of something and somewhere which existed untouchable and unknown, far away out of my own world.

My father was one of the middle youngest boys in a family of fourteen. He and several sisters and most of his brothers had emigrated to America. Leaving land the Donleavys had occupied and still do, near Granard Co. Longford, as far back in the centuries as anyone can trace or remember. And my next consciousness of Ireland came when one of my father's brother's wives had died and I spent a late afternoon in a funeral parlour somewhere deep down town in this poorer part of New York City. I played or at least conferred with two cousins who were at their mother's wake. Who were trying to explain to me in the funeral parlour's lavatory that they were circumcised. Although I did not know it at the time, there must have been the Erse haunting ghosts within the tinted lit rooms and a banshee outside the window wailing under the thundering passing wheels of the elevated train. The world of sombre Ireland, where the memory of the dead is forever living, was hovering here. Amid the dark whispers within the words of fond recall. For someone, lips to lips, kissed the corpse of this still beautiful young woman in her coffin. And I sensed, in that curious stretch of the Irish imagination.

That death
Is God
And living
Is unholy

II

In the ethnically mixed community of Woodlawn where I was
growing up, one or two of my earliest playing friends' names were
Irish, like Hennessy and Farrell, but more of my pals were Italian,
German and even Dutch. With names like Briggi, Gerosa, Kuntze
and Rotterhan. The friend Hennessy never mentioned Ireland.
Indeed his first foreign reference was when he spoke his newly
learned words of French to me. Vous êtes stupide. Italian was the
other alien sound one heard in which one early learned to curse and
profane. And as one grew up, conscious of being in one of the most
fabled and talked about capitals in the world, not an Irish word or
sentiment did I ever hear said. And even St Patrick's Day was
everybody's day and many a Jew and Muslim sported a shamrock
and wore a green tie.

But in the early years of the nineteen forties on a summer Saturday
night on a windswept peninsula sticking out from the eastern shore
of Long Island, my first full revelation of Ireland and the Irish
unfolded. Reached by train across a long bridge of marsh and bay
with islands and channels and names like Canarsie, Pumpkin Patch,
Big Egg, Little Egg and Winhole Hassock, Rockaway as it was called,
was a bereft long strip of sand dune on the shores of the Atlantic
Ocean. It was here on a street full of bars, that I first heard a live Ceili
band, saw Irish dancing and rubbed shoulders with the pure and
simple Irish like myself. Two or three of my friends, champion
swimmers, spent their summers here, working as lifeguards on these
crowded sands which lay along the ocean front. The peninsula's
length was cross sectioned by streets of summer boarding houses and
a boardwalk along a mile or two of beach which could be jammed by
New York's lower middle class poor in their thousands on New
York's oven hot sultry days. Through open windows at night one
could hear the crowded life packed in these wooden framed and
porched houses. On a street, 103rd Street, saloons and bars were next

American childhood friends, the Kuntze family. From the left, Donald, Carol and Alan, in Woodlawn. Their mother was of Irish extraction and their father German. Donald, a Collegiate Champion, was first to indoctrinate me into boxing and wrestling which one pursued with Alan, my closest childhood friend and both brothers would gently threaten me for any maltreatment of Carol, their sister who was an early girlfriend.

to one another, and I had, on this, one of my first overnight unchaperoned trips, got drunk for the first time. And later, lurching in the dark on the boardwalk was nearly arrested by a benign Irish policeman voicing his concern that 'A kid drunk at your age is a disgrace'. And a young friend Richard Gallagher, upon his pale Irish skin got the worst sunburn of his life.

But I remember the fiddle playing and the strange dancing and jigs taking place in the centre of the large roomed saloon. The long bar, and the beer frothing as the glasses landed thump on the mahogany and upended down the throats. I found no pain in drinking as did everyone else, one glass after another. I met and danced with a handsome girl of raven black hair and blue eyes and a splendid smile. And was mystified by her presence here instead of at one of my more polite afternoon tea dances at Fordham Preparatory School where no girl had ever been as beautiful. Back in the city I saw her again. And went to a party down in the Irish ghetto where she lived. Finding it

Photographed here with two cousins, my father standing with his constant cigar to hand behind me, his brother Jim to his right. At this time I had just completed my first naval training and was later to get a fleet appointment to the Naval Academy and to prior attend the Naval Academy Preparatory School easily one of the world's strangest institutions of learning and where I first heard the name of James Joyce and wrote my first writing which ever received critically appreciative notice.

strange to be, as the saying was, among me own. And yet feel singularly alien.

My next awareness and the first awakening of an interest in Ireland came in the strangest of places. A unique school in the Navy. Throughout my relatively short service career I had become obsessed with not dying as an ordinary seaman swabbing decks. If I were to sacrifice my life for my country I wanted to do it as someone of some rank as high as possible and preferably as an admiral. I had risen to the low heights of second class seaman with a qualification of radar man. And had been assigned to an amphibious landing ship. I forget the reason now why I did not sail with her to the Pacific but my next ship to which I was assigned was a much more lethal weapon feared by both those at whom it was aimed and equally by all those aboard her. Such ship taking up its station off the beach at sea and armed with launchers and 100 tons of rockets, the vessel for three hours had the firepower of a battleship. The Japanese chose them as the first items to blast by any means out of the water, which was simplicity itself once they were hit. Although I always heartily lent my voice to the corps' song which graphically embodied its purpose and intentions, 'Off To The Beach Fighting Amphibians, We Sail At Break Of Day', I nevertheless preferred to command a flotilla of these ships, rather than have my life disrupted forever while merely sitting and watching a radar screen. When I heard about a chance to go to the Naval Academy, I rather think I jumped at it.

Although I had succeeded in the Navy in passing exams, both mental and physical, my academic record was otherwise unimpressive, not to say mildly appalling. In fact an officer interviewing prospective candidates to sit the Naval Academy appointment exam, point blank refused me permission, saying I had no chance against the records of other candidates he'd seen. It was a rare and perhaps the only occasion in my life I had ever verged upon pleading with someone. And was benefitted by having chosen a moment that this officer was in a desperate hurry to go out and play golf, and simply to get rid of me from the room, ended up giving me permission. Out of the many who took the exam on this base of 10,000 men, I ended up being the only one who got an appointment to the Naval Academy. Still to this day, I do not know what became of the two amphibious crews I left behind and who sailed southwest without me.

But there was before this, one other early factor of Irish influence in my life. Unlike all my other young friends growing up in America, I had an enlightened and wise mother who forbade soda pop, chocolate, fats and all American junk food and insisted they be avoided with the expression, 'You must eat something which will stick to your ribs'. So along with brown bread and other wholesome pure foods many of which were home grown and bottled by my parents, I was also fed upon oats out of a shamrock adorned, green tin imported from Ireland. My mother extolling to me that such oats came from the most fertile of ground, rained upon by the cleanest heavens and sprouted up in the purest of air. All of which distinctions the word Irish now became associated with.

However, the Naval Academy Preparatory School was where I first heard the name James Joyce. The school, formerly the Tome School for boys and taken over by the Navy, stood luxuriously in its parkland splendour in Maryland, precipitously overlooking the Susquehanna River and the tiny town Port Deposit which was

hidden with its single long main street pressed between the river and the steep rising hill behind, upon which the school stood. Having received an appointment to the Naval Academy, it entitled the appointee to attend an academic year to prepare for the final entrance exams to the Naval Academy. A Professor of English now a Chief Petty Officer in the Navy and recruited from the fleet, was our English instructor. This erudite droll gentleman who was widely acquainted not only with literature, but with a splendid variety of jokes, managed, in the context of war and the military, to enthrall an extremely intelligent but nearly deliberately illiterate class. For the most illiterate of whom I ghost wrote their required themes. As these were read aloud to the class our instructor remarked concerning touches of James Joyce he perceived in the writing. Shattered to know someone had already imitated me I repaired to the mostly deserted school library, and immediately searched out and read the little I could find mentioned of this gentleman. Who seemed described as a combination of renegade Catholic and former medical student who, as a blaspheming anti christ, profane and pagan, drank and caroused his way through Dublin with his cronies, and who had in a stream of consciousness written somewhat obscenely about his native city. I lost no time in looking up Dublin in the encyclopedia. From which I gleaned three principal superlatives. That Dublin was possessed of the world's biggest brewery, that Phoenix Park was one of the largest municipal parks in the world, and that O'Connell Street was one of the widest thoroughfares in Europe. None of these facts may have been true then or are true now but they, all three, remained fixed indelibly in my imagination and became the first adult things I knew about Ireland.

The war suddenly over, and on a spring afternoon amid the gentle rolling hills of Maryland, discharged from the Navy, I exited the gates of this naval base for the last time. But remained pleasantly haunted by the widest street in Europe. Imagining it as I did, lined with trees. A spacious boulevard upon which one could contentedly stroll or

(Opposite) *My mother in the United States. Although taken as she said, barefoot from an Irish field she was brought to America by a rich Australian uncle and her indoctrination there took place in the company of an elegant lady in private railway cars and the suites of famed hotels across America. My mother was never impressed by America's modern way of life or its wonder foods and I was always forbidden white bread and soda pop and fed on our own compost grown garden produce.*

stride, arms stretched out to the world. Wander in its biggest park or drink a brew from its vast brewery. I still vividly recalled the abdication radio broadcast of a King of England. And prior to this monarch's speech, the nine o'clock tolling of the bell, Big Ben. And the strange profundity it proclaimed. Aware that Europe was a more ancient place than America. And with a heavier accent on the living of life. Where, although one might not be encouraged to, a fart might be called a fart.

Towards the end of the war a few old friends were turning up. Some of whom, in military service, had been to Europe. And one with whom I'd been at prep school and who lived in the nearby community of Yonkers. While stationed in England he went on a weekend leave to Ireland. With some relish and amusement he described a Dublin pub. The closeted privacy of little cubby holes into which you might go to drink a strange black beer called Guinness. And that you could order things like cheese, sausages or a pickled onion. The mystery of the word stout which was lifted up to the lips and which I'd seen mentioned in Joyce's *Ulysses*, was solved. Somehow this brief description of a public house in Ireland made a memorable impression on me. I imagined somewhere safe, timeless, cosy and insulated from the world.

Except for my hearing of James Joyce and knowing that John Barry, Wexford born in Ireland, had distinguished himself enough to be called the father of the American navy, nothing else Irish crossed my sights during my brief naval career. But now having left the service it was time to try to go to college. With my poor academic record not much improved at the Naval Academy Preparatory School, I applied to various East Coast Ivy League American higher institutions of learning. And then to more obscure institutions further west as far away as Wisconsin, before I could get anyone to even consider to take me. As I was now nearly having to search across 3,000 miles and with the vision still vivid of my friend eating cheese in a pub in a stray beam of Dublin sunlight, and the widest street in Europe, I, out of the blue, asked my Irish Galway born mother, were there any colleges in Ireland. Her instant singular reply was Trinity College Dublin. Again I rushed to my tiny and local library for the address, which I discovered was simply that. University of Dublin, Trinity College, Dublin.

I wrote off immediately. Luck, combined with their unavoidable ignorance of American academic qualifications, which I must have attempted vaguely to glorify, had W. B. Stanford, my duly appointed tutor, writing back acknowledging receiving a testimonial from a former principal, and without further ado said that classes would begin on 21 October 1946 and that it would be advisable to arrive some days beforehand as it might be necessary to find accommodation in the city at first. And for the first time I saw the use of the word Esquire after one's name.

Ireland began to become a strange almost unIrish destination. Almost as if one might think one was going to the legendary gaiety and boulevards of Paris. At first I booked to go by ship. The word spreading fast of my departure among friends. Who thought the whole idea more humorous than anything else. In the boxing room of the New York Athletic Club, Commodore Manning, captain of the S.S. *America*, wrote me a note to take when booking my passage on that ship. Then, all set for Europe, suddenly a port strike occurred. And I found myself arriving at Idlewild airport, as it was then known, to go much more expensively by plane.

My departure presented what must have been two of the most enjoyable days for my father. As we gained speed down the runway for take off, the plane suddenly slowed, stopped, turned around and taxied back to the terminal. At some mechanical fault afoot, we disembarked. No one in those days left an airport until a plane had disappeared safely into the sky. So passengers were again greeted by their friends. Both travellers and all their guests were conducted into a lounge for drinks and to the restaurant for lunch and the rest of the morning, afternoon and day went by while they were lavishly unstintingly entertained by the airline. Until the flight that day was finally cancelled, and I returned home with my parents. Next morning there was again the day long drive across the Bronx and Brooklyn and the same thing happened half way down the runway and a similar day unfolded of celebration and meals. I stayed that night in the New Yorker Hotel. And an airline limousine this time brought me back to the airport where my parents again awaited.

For two whole days of the aircraft's delay I was conscious of my father's big hands wrapped around his complimentary drinks, his fingernails garden darkened with soil in contrast to the sleekness of the airport lounge. As stories were swapped in this predominantly Irish group, I could hear my father's spontaneous and uninhibited roars of laughter. And I should have realized that growing up in the vicinity of my father's brogue, Ireland was being inculcated into me without my ever knowing. For throughout his life in America, my father, except for his constant smoking of cigars, remained as Irish as Ireland. Even to the taking up of the writing of poetry. And in the way he walked and looked at life. Like a poor farmer surveying his cattle in the field. Just as we would both go on an evening stroll during our family summer trips while growing up, which took us through the mid west. And my father, his hands folded behind his back, his interest keen in all around him and his insatiable asking of questions of anyone friendly enough to answer as we walked the main street of a prairie town surrounded to the horizon by fields of corn and the lonesome wail of freight trains.

As the ice tinkled in the glasses of whiskey during that forty eight hour delay, my parents befriended several of the passengers among whom was an ebullient gentleman called O'Callaghan. This silver haired handsome man, known to his friends as the silver fox of Wall Street, was full of laughter and hand rubbing optimisms on this his impending return to Ireland after many years away. Underlying his rakish elegant American patina was a thoroughly Irish soul. One of those people to whose coat tails one can attach and fly behind. And as he had met my parents and from their many hours of airport reverie together, I was in a manner entrusted to him to be looked after on this bleak trip out into the sky of the Atlantic Ocean.

The flight took something like fourteen hours. Flying first north to land for refuelling as it was growing dark on a cold bereft airport at Gander, Newfoundland. Disembarking and walking across a chill windswept ground to what seemed a barren grey building, there hardly appeared any human life save for a man standing warming his hands at the glow of an open fire in a barrel at the edge of the airfield. Runway lights again lit, the four propellors on the wings of this great long hawk beaked fuselage, roared. To take off over such strange dark cold names and places as Loon Bay, Fogo and Joe Batts Arm. And fly bumping up into the heavens again. Ireland beyond assumed a dark bewitchment on the other side of the world. In the black October sky, droning on towards dawn across the deeps of the Labrador Current and the Gulf Stream Drift far below. Coifed, tailored, starlet attractive hostesses patiently dancing attendance upon every journeyer's whim. Up and down the narrow aisle of the smoky aircraft, the constant interchange of passengers calling upon each other in their seats. The growing exhilaration in the anticipation of Ireland. As if arrival there were the answer to all eternal problems and prayers. The clinking of drinks being lofted into mouths. Every hour or two O'Callaghan would come conspiratorially to my elbow to inquire if I were having as good a time as he was and encouragingly pat me upon the back. And then descending through the thick cloud with daylight flooding east, suddenly below, a broad estuary, tiny islands and then low hills, nestling lakes and ponds gleaming black and then flashing silver. The first browny green sight of those small meandering fields clustered about some white tiny cottage with turf smoke rising from its chimney on this windswept land that reached to the edge of the great heaving Atlantic Ocean.

There were cheers as we landed at Shannon. And there was at least one passenger who made as if to kneel and kiss the wet ground. As all Americans do they regard foreign officialdom as being some toy game the natives play. But one of the returned exiles who had not yet achieved the sophistication of this patronising attitude, was carrying a large bundle of Irish currency he had bought at a discount in New York and when asked if he had any currency to declare, confessed. Fetching up the massive wad of bills out of his pocket in a fit of honesty to have the lot promptly confiscated by bemused customs officials eager to oblige. Tears now in the exile's eyes as he announced that he could not find it in himself to lie to his countrymen. A much more worldly gentleman, O'Callaghan, commenting on this imprudent act of candour, that foolish though it was, he nevertheless understood the overwhelmed feelings of this fellow Irishman. Although he thought he might have better kept the money in his pocket and dispose of it celebrating and be sure that illegal currency or not, every customs man able to bend his elbow would join him in the nearest pub.

While awaiting another plane to take me on to Dublin, I noticed the big crystal grains of sugar in the bowls of the restaurant where the tables were covered in neat white table cloths. The thick slabs of bacon and gleaming, deep orange yolked fried eggs on a plate. The butter a golden yellow white. The soda bread brown with bran. Following breakfast, a sliver of sun suddenly shafted down between the sweeping clouds. Out in the intoxicatingly clean, cool, moist fresh air, I walked a short distance away from the cluster of single storied white frame buildings and along a road into surrounding open countryside. On my feet were a pair of black and white saddle shoes. Perhaps the first ever seen in Europe. The lane wound gently between iridescent velvet green pastures. To where I suddenly came upon a pond with three swans. In the lonely silence, their stunning eloquent whiteness on the gentle black water was miraculous and a moment of unforgettable beauty. Ireland in one of her graces, leaving for me to discover yet, her sins.

And the grey
Rains
Not yet sprinkling
In one's heart

III

There was the choice of an all day train or less than an hour plane to Dublin. And in my first of many Irish extravagances I chose to fly, joining the ebullient O'Callaghan who was exerting his delight in all directions and who was in a marvellous hurry to get there. It was on that flight that I first encountered what other American college friends I was soon to meet, referred to as the Irish 'hook' and 'crut'. Both chronic conditions interrelated as they caused and perpetuated each other.

On board the two engined propellor plane, sitting next to me, was a youngish man who had business at Shannon and was returning to Dublin. In telling him that I had come to Ireland to attend Trinity College, he immediately launched into a painstakingly offhand explanation as to how I had made an awful mistake in not choosing University College, Dublin's other and Catholic higher institution of learning, instead. His vague reasons did sound suspicious to me, but as we were bouncing around in the clouds and I had a moderate disposition towards getting airsick, one may have had other discomforting things to worry about. And I don't know how deep my heart sank or if it did, but I did wonder how my usually extremely wise Galway mother could have let me down.

In Dublin, O'Callaghan had a hectic social round to attend to, meeting old cronies, friends and visiting with his elderly father who lived with his sister, and he kept a taxi on tap as he sped hither and thither in and about Dublin and its environs. In a nearby suburb called Monkstown, I had found someone, recommended on the Irish grapevine to America, with whom to stay, a policeman, a massive gentleman, as they nearly all were in those days, and his attractive wife. A small house near where a church stood dividing the road on which roared the double decker green upholstered trams. In a cold, clean, neat, unadorned room, waking up to my second sample of tastily delicious tea, bacon and eggs for breakfast. Encountering, without yet knowing it, my first taste of Irish bemused curiosity which provoked a shy smile on the beholders' lips as they listened to the naturally optimistic American accent and had their attentions caught by the appreciably brighter clothes from the New World.

Still in an unrelenting blaze of enthusiasm, O'Callaghan was ecstatically continuing his round of visiting. One or two of his former associates in his younger days were now ministers in the government. And he took a delight in visiting them at their offices exchanging presents and getting an export licence for a side of bacon from the very heads of government. He was amused to recall their less resplendent days as patriots, but remembered the glamour of his own and his friends' rank in the War of Independence, as being that equivalent to generals. And now they had their own nice little nation, and had he stayed he nostalgically reminded himself that he too would probably now be a minister of state.

It was with O'Callaghan that I went to my first Irish country house. Speeding the dark roads on a Sunday night in a noisy taxi between high granite walls, the canopy of tree branches closing like the entrance to a dark cave ahead of us as the dim headlights faintly peered into the blackness. Till finally we reached a pair of gates, wheels crunching the gravel, swept past a small gate lodge to motor up a long drive through spacious parklands. An array of ancient cars parked on this great pebbled apron before this ochre yellow mansion. And inside surprised by its warmth and grandeur. The elegance of its circular black and white tiled front hall. The soft carpets, fires blazing in the grate. Guests in black tie. The flowing abundance of food and drink. And my own unconscious bemusement at the luxury one had not expected and the easy pleasant welcome of one's presence. As I voiced my concern to my hostess over my choice of university, it was unequivocally pointed out to me that not only was I to attend the most important and revered of all Irish institutions but even being so much as a student at Trinity conferred upon one a social entitlement second to none in the city of Dublin. And with relief and pleasure, one departed this beautiful lady in her long white satin gown, reassured that I could cheerfully look forward to my years at Trinity College Dublin.

In a Georgian mansion off Fitzwilliam Square, I was introduced to O'Callaghan's sister, a marvellous cook and hostess. O'Callaghan's father, a charming and still handsome man in his nineties, lay abed where he managed to read a novel a day and only laughed to say that occasionally it took him a day and a half. It was here in this Dublin townhouse where I first encountered sherry prior to Sunday lunch. And the sacred ritual of such things as roast beef and Yorkshire pudding with black uniformed maids scurrying back and forth to keep the chill from superlative gravies, roast potatoes and Brussels sprouts. And following the spongy sweet delight of trifle, to withdraw upstairs to the drawing room, where a black stove nestled in the white marble chimney piece blazed out heat while one lay back on the soft upholstered sofas to listen to Mozart on a gramophone. And where it might not be found impolite if at four before tea, one had nodded on a chaise longue, sound asleep.

From my temporary lodging in Monkstown I stepped out in a moist mild breeze on this my first official day as a student at Trinity. And walked past the small front gardens in a moment of morning sunshine, the smell of the sea in the air blowing in over Dublin Bay. Near the church at the fork in the road, I boarded the wood panelled and green upholstered tram. Climbing up its narrow stairs to the top of its two tiers. Able to look from the windows down into the passing walled green suburban gardens. Their monkey puzzle trees, laurels, rhododendrons and subtropical greenery verdantly proclaiming the respectability of the inhabitants. This utterly beautiful vehicle's bell clanging as it roared and swayed on its iron wheels along its shiny tracks, destined to come to a final halt at a tall pillar of granite on which stood a statue of Nelson on that widest of European boulevards in the city of Dublin.

I was not to know this first day that this road and route were to play such a significant role in one's Irish life. The tram turning right into Newtownpark Avenue, and abruptly left again parallel with the coast of the sea. Roaring past the town hall and a tiny house standing but a few feet beyond the weathered ancient stone cross which marked the pale. This house with one door and window opening on the pavement and a single window above on the upstairs floor, was to become an historic location in one's college days. The tram now dipped down into the village of Blackrock past O'Rourke's public house and up a hill again along the higher Rock Road where one could see down into a small bereft park and out across the grey waters of Dublin Bay to North Bull Island and the mount of Howth the other side. I never tired of this marvellous journey. And the sight of the funerals with their black plumed gleaming horses pulling the coffins which rested in peace behind the polished glass of the hearse. Either on their way to or returning from the Grange Cemetery, the horse cabs would be seen pulled up waiting outside a pub, the bereaved inside being refreshed. From the tram, too, one could peer into the odd uncurtained window of the row of substantial suburban houses along Merrion Road. Perhaps see an electric fire's glow on some fitted purple Wilton carpet which gave one hope that one's own feet, now grown so cold, could somehow hope to be thawed again. Or at least such interiors gave the assurance that there were more than a few in this land who had more than a pot to piss in.

High and mighty elegant hopes could be inflamed, too, passing through the great Georgian square of Merrion, enclosed by its soft red brick elevations and fenestrations showing over the tips of its central park tree tops. An American flag fluttering in the breeze in front of that Consulate. And mention on a plaque of Oscar Wilde's name on a house on the northwest corner. Dublin all in a cultural handful. For that so oft, ad nauseam quoted piece of information that Handel's *Messiah* was first performed in Dublin, happened just fifty paces away. Nearby I alighted at an intersection in Clare Street. Just beyond the glass canopy over the open stalls in front of Greene's book shop. Stepping for the first time on the great grey granite paving stones worn smooth with a hundred years of feet. A chemist's window full of a rainbow of bottled salts. A feeling that the morning was being born. More shop front windows, decorated with loaves of bread, a café, Johnson Mooney & O'Brien's, serving cakes, tea and coffee inside and where, together with students of medicine and natural science, I was to occasionally sit in the pale daylight from its ceiling skylights.

Directly across from the back gates of Trinity College stood a middle eastern architectural extravagance, an eastern mosque with pinnacles, which once upon a Dublin time, housed Turkish baths. Which should tell all that ever need be known about this Dublin city of bizarre dreams. The remnants of which dot every street, dispossessed monuments to fervently possessed hopes. Yet on a building's door nearly opposite the mosque is an oft shined brass plaque. One of the rare few things of high intentioned endeavour that remains comfortingly unerased and still gleaming to the day of this writing.

THE MISSION TO LEPERS

Outside number 38 Trinity College and wearing the clothes I wore on my first arrival in Ireland, including black and white saddle shoes and holding onto the slung chains over which myself and other occasional undergraduates would, with belly bent, drape when returning from Dublin's pubs.

This brief stretch of street at the back Trinity gates also possessed an emporium for the treatment of teeth, the dental hospital. From whence I did, in all my time passing, always await a scream of anguished pain to emit from the darkened red brick building. But nary a sound ever emerged as I went in and out between the tall grey granite piers holding open these massive college gates. Through which, on this my first day, I stepped to confront a porter in his dark tail coated uniform, fox hunting cap on his head and who directed me forward to my tutor's office in Front Square, the other end of the college. Past these shadowy grey science buildings, wherein I would spend woefully few hours of my university years and those, all daydreamingly academically wasteful.

But I seemed more attentive in one building on a little rise on the left. Gold letters over the entrance proclaiming Pathology. Wide granite steps up to its oak doors. In there one did more than occasionally redden a spatula in the flame of a bunsen burner and bend over the oil immersion lens of a microscope to drop gentian violet stain upon some of these tiny organisms. Opposite on this back road into Trinity is the Chemistry building. And here amid the bottles

and bubbling, my hours were at their most bereft. I could never filtrate, titrate or make my experiments go pop like the rest of you. Certain was I that if I did mix together what I thought they said I should, there would be, if not a violently lethal, then at least one god awfully embarrassing explosion.

Standing a low squat building surveying the cricket pitch was the sports pavilion. Somehow always reminding me of a river steamer boat, which might, afloat, flags fluttering, take one on a picnic. Its tiers facing south and overlooking the splendidly mown grass. Many a time students collected there when spring mercifully came, to bathe in the warming sun. Within its clammy ground floor confines were the great tubs that cleansed mud from the rugby players. It had two showers which became the only place, that memorably cold first winter in Ireland, where myself and an American with whom I shared cold rooms could thaw in a sprinkle of hot water. My room mate, from Southern California, especially requiring hours standing in the steamy downpour. Indeed in his bedroom he lay abed every morning, eight hot water bottles from the night still packed about him and an electric fire perched on a chair faintly shining red rays on his damp blankets as he sipped restorative tea warming his long fingered hands around the green bowl.

Making my way that first day through the oasis of College Park enclosed by massive rhododendrons growing high up against the walls and iron fence along Nassau Street. Shutting out all but the roof and chimney pot tops and tram sounds of the city. To pass through into New Square. Its stark grey buildings to the south, east and north, and the mellow red of the rubrics to the west with its grey green slate roof from which chimneys reared against the sky. Suspended over the cobblestone gutter, the necklace of chain link fence strung round the square from pointed iron palings. Shadows cast by the branches of these ancient plane trees, the gnarled bark of their trunks twisting up from these lawns so flat, green and velvet. My whole life seemed to start here gazing out of my window at number 38. The street aglisten with rain. An occasional early morning fusty academic going

(Opposite) A winter view of New Square Trinity College Dublin from the sitting room window of number 38. This glistening wet view of an empty college was the most frequent one seen out of my college windows. And it was always possible to identify a visitor long before he or she approached to knock on my door.

to and fro, slippers shuffling in the wet, kimono held wrapped about him as he scurried from one granite open doorway into another. Not then nor during the many after years could I have ever thought that the pure Irish would ever get their hands on Trinity. To banish its elegance and traditions. Uproot its rhododendrons. Park cars in its sacred confines. And they have. But the ancient fabric of its beauty for the most part has stayed even that destructive hand.

With these black gowned students threading crisscross in Front Square this Monday, 21 October of Michaelmas term, undergraduate lectures in arts and science began. It was, too, according to the College Calendar, the last day for payment of half yearly fees without fines. As I made my way on the cobbles asking directions to my tutor's office, an autumnal sun brightening the grey stone and making the grass gleam emerald. Tall, weather whitened pillars in front of the chapel. And past an entrance in which was located the students' cooperative where, tucked in under the stairs, bread and simple provisions could be bought. My tutor's name so neatly writ white on black at another entrance. My feet thumping up wooden stairs to gently knock on a door on the first landing. Come in please. In the morning rays of sun a handsome wavy haired man stood in a grey pinstripe suit, waistcoat, white shirt and solemn tie, his quietly elegant manners bespeaking the civilized splendours of this university. To whose politely formal but friendly words I tried so hard to show I listened and believed devoutly all that he was saying. Welcome to Trinity. Thank you. He was the great classicist Regius Professor of Greek, William Bedell Stanford. Who had, despite his many charges and much more serious pursuits, marvellously managed to get me rooms in college. And a nice unAmerican touch, that I, a student of science should have as my tutor this scholar of ancient languages.

In the northeast corner of New Square and up a flight of stairs past a landing and behind four large neo Georgian windows were my college chambers. Set in the city like a semi precious jewel of peace and silence. With their giraffe tall ceilings they consisted of an entrance hall, two bedrooms, sitting room and skippery. Although with its own large front window, the latter was but a glorified kitchen with a gas burner, a counter, and a turf box. On a chair was perched a bucket of water. Which each morning was filled by a college servant from a tap alongside the slung chain in the college square. And then lugged up the stairs. I often watched this little ritual of my skip as he was called. His hand arest on the small iron spire of the paling post waiting as his bucket filled. Bicycle clips on his trousers. The brim of his hat down around the edges. Whose bald head one would only see when a lady called when he would, with pleasant military overtones, bow and click his heels to receive her.

My first and nearly last furnishing purchases were a mattress and blue blanket, a bedroom water pitcher, a wash basin, and providing one exception at least to my father's dictum, a pot to piss in. With no indoor plumbing in my rooms at 38 Trinity, one had to travel 200 yards to a semi open latrine. Constipation became an unpleasant condition if one wanted to avoid the chill wind and rain. Although in some rougher college circles there was evidence of urine stains down the college stone work. And the dawn hours might find a crunched up lump of one of the better English newspapers parachuting certain contents as distantly as possible away from the window out of which they came. And that first 1946 cold snowy winter in Dublin, a near warm place civilized with plumbing became of paramount importance. Towards which one set one's sights upon the moment of morning's first eye opening. And the nearest being Jury's Hotel just beyond the great pillars and curvatures of the old parliament building, out the front gates in a straight line a short way down Dame Street. In a side entrance down Anglesea Street one stepped up four steps to this narrow door of stained glass. To the left one of the most exquisite bars in all of Europe with its tiled walls and sombre cloistered interior, and ahead, from a turning in a cosy lobby, was the palm court with its wicker furniture and palms. And welcome warmth.

But there were a few marvellous comfortable compensations in college itself. Especially within the austere dignified walls of the dining hall. To which, engowned, one would set off evenings at seven o'clock for Commons. Convening in the vestibule with its two coal fires glowing against the brass bands of its grate. An eagle eye of a college porter noting each student by face who'd paid his quarterly Commons' Fund of three pounds thirteen shillings and sixpence. The dining doors opening. And the invariably hungry rushing in. Professors descending from the common room above where they had taken their pre dinner sherry, now assembled at the high table. A college scholar, whose free meal this was, rushing to mount the steps

1946 seated in my sitting room at Trinity, which except for odd elegances embellishing, which overflowed from James Leathers' personal bedroom, was generally kept like a military barracks. And because of its high ceilings and large windows was always uncomfortably cold through the winter. But it did occasionally heat up with antics normally forbidden in the college.

of the lectern to recite out across these heads, Latin grace with as much speed and immaculate pronunciation of which he was capable. A ritual closely listened to by other scholars for its every nuance of perfection. Beseatment with a loud shuffle of chairs. The sweating faces and darting eyes of young servant girls fetching great barons of beef up from the dungeon kitchens. Pushing the massive platters through the hatchway into this great room. They stood there catching their breath and surveying this assembly from which rose this loud throb of voices. These massive roasts placed on tables for the carvers to slice off the slabs of meat. The hustle and bustle of other college porters doubling as waiters flying with their laden plates between the tables. Steaming Brussels sprouts, turnip, cabbage and potatoes. A jug served of specially brewed beer made by Guinness, one to each table. Which led to heavy drinkers seeking to sit with as many teetotallers as possible.

There were musty dusty if not warm places to go in college. Two of the most conspicuous were The Historical Society and The Philosophical Society, located one on top of the other in the Graduates Memorial Building. I joined 'The Hist.' as it was called for the reason that I was told it was where newspapers and letter writing paper were available, plus a library, a silence room and a billiard room. But alas I only entered the Reading and Writing room once, feeling immeasurably ill at ease to go sit in view of others while reading a periodical. Then passing one cold gloomy winter evening I saw lights and heard voices in a back room. And found myself attending one of the Society's debates at which one nearly always heard apropros of nothing at all, reference to America as being uncultured. As I sat listening to this again expressed opinion this night, I was suddenly pointed out as being a member of the Society not wearing a gown as required and that the speaker should expel me for academic nudity which he did.

Forever thereafter I was never again seen at a college society but did make one bereft further foray to the Dublin University Gramophone Club, which held three concerts every term on a Friday evening at eight o'clock in the Physics amphitheatre, there to listen in its cool silence and on the hard benches, to Mozart on the gramophone. Later I did work my nerve up enough to peer through the window near the front of college into the quiet room of the Student Christian Movement during one of their every Thursday evening eight p.m. assemblies. Invited in, one did find solace among these kindly compassionate faces, knowing that these who tried so sincerely to discover the Christian attitude to every question which confronts man in his daily life, would never point a finger to the door to say get out.

But my rooms, then barren as they were, save for college issue of a sitting room table and few chairs, soon became a meeting place establishing its own society. Members pouring in each morning for cups of tea, and before, between and after classes convening. Parking their books and gowns while encouraging me to get up out of my cold bed and pour cold water into my wash bowl, pull on damp clothes and stagger off with them to have coffee.

The terms at Trinity extending to a brief total of eighteen weeks out of the year, presented to those living within these walls and behind these rhododendron shrouded fences, thirty four weeks of semi solitary peace to be pursued amid these quiet cloistered squares. To sit and stare hours of an afternoon away, from the sitting room window, out over the perspectives of the wet shiny pavement. With only an occasional figure passing in the college and a constant seagull or two squawking from roof gutters. The bell tower of the Campanile rearing above the slates of the Rubrics as if it were one of its chimneys. The evening glow of the gas lamps in the lonely enfolding comforting darkness. Here within this granite enclave, protected in body if not in mind and spirit. Many a morn, late afternoon and evening went by, kicking around life's imponderables. Conscious of this academic sovereignty holding one aloof and safe from the struggling troubles of the outer world.

Where among the shamrocks
One must find
One's own Irish pot
To piss in

IV

Unused as I was to religion being an identity, it took me some time to realize Trinity College was a British redoubt of the Protestant Anglo Irish. In this city full of Catholics. More than a few of whom aped and admired the English. And some of whom defied their Bishop's ban on Catholics attending within this verdured piece of central Dublin where British Protestants proclaimed their occupation. A not infrequent phenomenon of the strains of 'God Save The King' blaring out over the college walls as the West Brit students, turning up the volume of their radios, opened their windows when the BBC closed down their night's broadcasting. Collecting at the College front gates, politically aggrieved Dublin street shouters, who would batter at the big closed front portals to gain admittance as college porters within held them shut. And upon occasion when the pubs had emptied their inmates for the night, such person attempting fist and foot hammering admission was the likes of Brendan Behan, poet, playwright and patriot.

It was in this English, Anglo Irish atmosphere that my earliest point of view was formed of Ireland. But seeing it also through the American eyes of the handful, who like myself had arrived for the first time at Trinity. And hearing my first whispers from a Catholic professor at College revealing to me that he was a Catholic, here in this forbidden world for Catholics. But hastening, too, to tell that such a declaration of one's religion would not be held against one. Even so, that if I were in need of knowing who a Catholic friend might be to let him know. But amid Muslims, Hindus, Buddhists, both black and white, Quakers and Unitarians, rarely can I remember the issue of religion being raised within Trinity's walls. And certainly never outside at the idolatrous pagan parties which raged in their various venues throughout the twenty six counties and especially fulminated in this city of 300,000 mostly devout souls.

But the early concern of many of these arrived Americans from whom I heard initial opinions expressed about Ireland was not about religion, politics or sanitation but about money and food. As the foremost thing to befall many of them was slow starvation. U.S. government documents in triplicate in the hands of the Irish could be treated with the wry sceptical humour such complicated forms deserved, but as they slowly made their way across the Atlantic Ocean and through American bureaucracy, subsistence cheques on the G.I. Bill of Rights failed to arrive. And a few of these ex servicemen now found themselves entering restaurants and announcing to the manager at the end of their meals, that they couldn't pay the bill. And were told, sure sir, that's no problem come back and pay it when you can. Just as they could be infernal in efficiency, and provided it wasn't a matter of religion or politics, the Irish could be sympathetic to an otherwise respectable gentleman temporarily caught in adversity. And one early learned that a strange unwritten law of generosity pervaded this land. And the biggest sin to be committed was that of meanness.

My first college invitation was to go and have a cup of coffee. Thus one embarked upon this sacred rite in Dublin. To be indulged either by morning, noon, afternoon or all three. Each café with its adherents. In my case it became Bewley's Oriental Café in Grafton Street which involved turning left out the front gates, past the Provost's House and traversing the city's cultural spine of Grafton Street. Paved with its wooden blocks aswarm with bicycles and off which variously extended Suffolk, Duke, Ann, Harry and Lemon Streets. Although there were cafés in these side street nooks and crannies, the élite coffee scented emporiums were all on the socially desired thoroughfare of Grafton Street. Where early morning gossip could be meteorically spread between the cheerful chattering of briefly pausing pedestrians. And where the wives of bank managers with light hearted things to think and do could flaunt their better than thou high heeled utter respectability.

Starting at the bottom of Grafton Street on the left, in a grey stone neo Georgian building, was Mitchell's. Definitely for the lady of society who'd been at a play the evening before, and carrying a catalogue from an exhibition of paintings, had just been to a fitting for a frock. Then further up, the glass table tops of Bewley's, its butter balls piled on plates, its stacks of fragrant fresh buns, its creamy glasses of Jersey milk and its roasted coffee smells perfuming the

Front Square Trinity College. The author his beard growing sparsely during his earliest days at Trinity and dressed in corduroys but having taken care to blacken the white of his saddle shoes which had caused many an unwary Dubliner to walk smack into posts and walls while staring at them and which once required the author to give medical attention to a girl knocked unconcious thereby.

street. This sacredly oriental interior was especially favoured by mothers whose sons had become priests. And by young ladies who were thinking of becoming nuns. Occasionally the tranquillity would be broken by a hungover poet rustling his paper who would sit examining the day's racing form at the courses while nursing in his celibacy his agonizing impure thoughts. Tucked away on other crimson banquettes were solitary men of the minor merchant class who secretly read recently banned novels and were experts at crossword puzzles. But I had repaired for my first Dublin coffee to Switzer's, down iron balustraded stairs to the warm and cosy basement of this, for Dublin, large department store. There, frequented by hockey playing lady students from Trinity and tweedy Anglo Irish matrons from the country, one luxuriated in the optimism pleasantly floating on the din of these animated voices.

But there were other fashionable cafés full of other more curious kettles of fish. And nearly next to Fannin & Co. suppliers of surgical instruments, was Robert Robert's at the top of Grafton Street. Where in the door past its cake counters and ground floor tables, it had a back section elevated up some stairs. This was the habitat of local accountants, managers of the better nearby haberdasheries, and a plethora of non practising physicians from out of the respectably prosperous middle class. But it was uniquely and especially full of aficionados of the Royal College of Surgeons in Ireland. These were a strange breed of medical student who despite growing grey, and many balding, remained anciently in attendance at this revered institution of medicine. Always affirming over their morning coffee that they could pass 2nd, 3rd years, 4th and even their final exams if only they could succeed in passing their 1st year, which, in view of their enormously accumulated sophisticated knowledge, now presented subjects which were so rudimentary, that they were now beneath them to retain as learning. Such gentlemen of surgeons invariably originated from modestly comfortable farming families out in the provinces who had one son a priest, one a dentist and a daughter a nun, and the whole family together mumbled the Rosary on their knees at night.

In a Dublin so full of charming chancers, these medically dedicated con men survived on their wits and the adoring women they attracted who had no option in their loneliness but to be gullible and sew back buttons on their seducers' shirts. But as perpetual apprentice physicians they were always ready with a smile to greet you, sporting their Aran Islands tweed ties and with their vast medical knowledge at their fingertips and never without a stethoscope in their pocket, would in their best bedside manner, slip upon a chair beside you, and order a black coffee as they borrowed their desperately needed early morning cigarettes. After their first deep inhalation, asking after your health and supplying an instant diagnosis and a suitably illegally scrawled prescription on the back of your bill which included his two coffees and plate of rashers and eggs. Ah, but the bedside manner would soon smoothly change to a more matter of fact and confidential comportment and in a quick shuffle of blandishing words, an attempt would be made to relieve you of legal tender. Preferably in the form of a big white British five pound note. Which in those days was majestically unscrawled in its own elegant flowing script. But if not that high a financial dimension you deign to loan on an immediately repayable basis following a certainty in the afternoon races, there came a rapidly diminishing politely mild pleading for a pound, a ten shilling note, and if no sign of paper money looked to be soon soothing their palms, anything at all, all the way down to a six pence would do. The latter at least being the price of one bottle of Mountjoy Nourishing Stout from that lesser known brewery situated in the north of Dublin near the banks of the Royal Canal. And seven bottles of whose brew you could drink, while saving a theoretical penny on each, in order to have an eighth bottle of Guinness costing seven pence. A routine religiously followed by the better poets stretching their imaginations and pockets of an evening.

But these strange perennial forever unqualified medical students did get involved in a final commencement of sorts, albeit non academic. Which would generally take place when a gentle moist breeze was blowing over Dublin. They would upon such a clement sudden bright and cheery morning, commence without warning to borrow at the drop of a hat as much as they could smilingly blandish in the space of one day from every friend and acquaintance met as they stretched their legs throughout the metropolis. Repayment due in the usual way of a promised counting out of notes over a bucket of champagne from the massive stack that was to be won on a guaranteed absolute certainty running in the fifth race at Leopardstown, a filly kept under top secret wraps the whole season who would explode from behind in the last furlong to overtake and fly past the winning post at one hundred to one. However these particular accumulated funds instead of being placed on this filly, went instantly to make a down payment purchase on credit of every vacuum cleaner available from every unsuspecting shop. These modern deposers of dust, marvels so recently new to the country, were either resold or pawned within the hour. The sale usually consummated by the perennial medical student providing his stethoscope to the victim to listen close up to the magical whirr of the impeccably reliable vacuum's motor. And this anciently apprenticing sawbones with his brand new tweed pockets stuffed with Lady

Laverys as the Irish Punt was then called, would be gone that night in a cloud of cigarette smoke and blaze of brandy on the mail boat to England to be ne'er heard of again. But sheepishly remembered enough by his ruefully admiring victims.

The epicentre of art and literature in its smoking, drinking, betting and talking attitudes, was also in Grafton Street. Forming as it did, the main hallway between the narrower corridors to the left and right into the cafés and pubs which in turn were like the rooms of a sprawling country house. It was the first thoroughfare in the world where nude streaking on two running legs was to become known. But at that censorious time in Ireland it required the perpetrator to sport the bottom part of a pair of pyjamas over the head and from this facial disguise peek through the fly while side stepping pedestrians, cyclists and vehicular traffic. Starting at Fannin's the medical supply depot near the top of Grafton Street, the streaker emerged from this revered black doorway flanked with windows full of bed pans, spatulas, forceps and microscopes, and giving the war whoop of the Seminole Indian, the naked speeder launched himself flying down past the Monument Creamery Café. Grabbing up a pre paid for fish from the grey marble slab of the fishmonger's and followed by suitable protesting shouts from an assistant would, waving the fish by the tail, streak by the jewellers' shops and the high quality furnishing emporium of Cavendish's. On that famed corner of Duke Street, it was incumbent upon the streaker to pause and hold aloft his fish and say aloud the whole of the Roman Catholic Act of Contrition. Such latter pause only forgiven if a member of the Garda Síochána was visible within thirty yards. The streaker then making for Davy Byrnes pub forty strides to the east where clothes and further disguises awaited in the gents. A fiver being duly peeled off as the award for this excursion. It was, of course, the first symbolic attempt of the intelligentsia to break the hold of sexual repression upon the country. But as always it was significant that no one present in the pub took the least notice of the event except to wrap their hands around the drink it was customary for the achiever of 'the deed of the nude velocity' to buy.

If Grafton Street were the main hallway in the cultural mansion of Dublin then Duke Street to the east was a breezeway to its preferred salons of the Bailey and Davy Byrnes as well as a highly frequented betting shop located mid way along its short length. There was also

Myself in front of Davy Byrnes pub which became a frequent place to visit in the early days of one's undergraduate life. Later, with the noise and the people, one did shift to the quieter privacy of Jammet's back bar and the cool beauty of the Shelbourne Rooms. Bicycles at the time were a major form of transport and the sound of draught horses pounding with their rumbling carts through the streets, was a daily sound of the city.

nearer Dawson Street a small Georgian edifice in the top floors of which few discouraging words were ever said against amusement and where many an astonishing post pub closing party raged. Davy Byrnes pub was what one might imagine to be a Victorianised twentieth century interior. With its curving pink marble counter decorated underneath with the sediment end of dark wine bottles. Along its walls were exotic Bacchanalian murals by Cecil Salkeld which seemed to glow in the subdued lighting and under which the habitués sat on soft crimson banquettes. But at the rear of the pub was one of the strangest of all strange places in Dublin called the Gilded Cage. Reserved for drinkers of spirits and champagne, access to which was through a trellis door in an iron lattice work. This exalted enclosure was furnished in burnished beige velvet covered stools and cushioned settees. Its polo coated cavalry twill trousered inmates with their silk and satin frocked ladies hesitated not, to assume the elevated status and essence of superiority which this revered inner sanctum conferred upon its habitués. As puff puff went the cigar smoke and pop pop went the champagne bottles like guns at the grouse shoot as all within here convincingly demonstrated their assets. And where by raising their vowels and laughing loudly, they assumed safety from any perennial medical student propositioning for a loan or selling a vacuum cleaner. And where to be sure such hapless gent with his stethoscope plugged in his ears would find all backs turned in his face as he hoovered between these indifferent legs.

The Gilded Cage was further insulated from questionable accostings or any temporary rubbing of elbows with beer imbibers, by being separately entered from a side lane off Duke Street, thereby keeping discreet these élite comings and goings. Eager social climbers eavesdropped on the whispered confidential revelations concerning Hollywood legends. And many an awesome snub was perpetrated here and ignominy delivered with the aplomb of a sledge hammer by these privileged inmates many of whom were current plaintiffs and defendants in large libel actions. Here, too, could be found drinking blond haired and nattily suited silk tied stockbrokers from the stock exchange who traded financially advantageous secrets with the owners of famed stallions and winning fillies. The only hazard being for these grabbers at life's banquet, that sometimes upon a late night exiting into a deserted narrow Duke's Lane, they might be set upon by gurriers lurking with pickaxe handles who would not necessarily take your money but would enjoy to the utmost as underprivileged Irishmen, if not militant socialists, to beat the living bejesus out of you and blind and choke you with the dust raised out of your own belted polo coat. And it was no use shouting out that you were a friend of the working classes.

Around each and every corner of Grafton Street environs there were other pubs and places and spaces to be sure. Within this kingdom westwards from the Shelbourne Hotel to Great George's Street, and south from King to Dame Street, the whole of the fashionable world then extended. Boisterous saloons of post rugby matches where spouting a sonnet or giving a favourable opinion of James Joyce would get you a fist in the gob. The Dawson Lounge with its narrow stairs down to its basement tiny bar and its upstairs squeezed full of not a few resigned poets and painters, convicted and sentenced to Ireland for the rest of their lives. On the outskirts of this milieu were the more peaceful neutral houses of refreshment to which folk repaired taking time out to avoid familiar faces or more often rehearse revenges while licking their wounds from the life and death contests of conversation. There were the confidential taverns, too, especially in the vicinity west of Grafton Street. Where the likes of certain of your Trinity College porters collected of an evening and where you might venture to discreetly straighten out a college indiscretion. But only a few paces further afield were the secret dens and snugs where conspiracies could brew. To fight for Ireland and drive the British invader out,except for the richer tourists among them. To loft and flutter the tricolour across the northern border. But to drink outside these boundaries other than being forced to by pub closing hours or in the emergency of your mother's death or funeral was a self imposed form of banishment which could shrivel up the soul and blow you away. Unless of course you were writing a novel.

And ah, too, in those days, the premier pubs were jammed tight, not only with native customers squeezing in the doors but with an invasion of curious foreigners not seen before nor known since. From Spitzbergen, from Ohio and Khartoum, from East Jesus California and even from Alcatraz. And many of whom were gentlemen who preferred gentlemen. Assembling with their wrists adorned and cigarettes held at lofty dainty angles. They were actors and organists. They were party givers and goers. Who merrily pranced and pleasantly preyed upon each other. With their homemade instant night clubs to which admission was granted for a bon mot or an armful of stout. Some of them held court in castles and country houses chock full of butlers and maids where one in utter centrally heated comfort could ooh and aah at the Meissen and Tiepolos. And the rare females mingling among them were lulus indeed. Much given to painting the male nude or exercising impromptu recitals on musical saws or clothed in nothing at all, with bosoms bouncing, entertain as they weaved hips flashing through an assembly, belligerently clacking their castanets. Highly welcome behaviour in this land full of suspicious ice cold virgins where hot women were hard to find.

The most serious part of Dublin drinking life was the timing. Especially of your degree of inebriation. Ten or eleven of a morn, stone cold sober, you would not want to set your own still faintly bleary eyes on many of these pub habitués in their depressions deeply hungover a marble or mahogany counter. But as noon passed and early afternoon progressed over a lunch during 'holy hour' when the pubs were shut, and the evening approached and the mind had grown rosy with tipple, these same faces avoided earlier, were by the verge of pub closing time more than made pleasantly palatable by the alcoholic confidences now being disclosed. And it was throughout the day a matter of musical chairs. Repairing first to a safe quiet pub where the initial tanking up with a more intimate friend could take place. To insulate from what would come later, and was in every Irish pub where a group of cronies were drinking, always a condition of your arriving presence. That those grouped there already long engrossed in the chosen subject of dispute, were in control of what was known as 'the snub'. A rebuff so lethal that nothing resembling it is known in the sadder annals of mankind. Each man present jealously guarding his small preserve already established by his opinions expressed on the urgent questions of the day. Usually imponderables chosen at random for their limitless scope of dispute. 'Does wood float' or 'Is the sky without clouds blue'. Entrance to such company was a very ticklish manoeuvre indeed, carefully taken step by step. And often easiest and quickest achieved by quietly pretending to be laggards drunk. For in this part of Dublin city there were few donkeys and pet horses upon whose back you might drape inebriated and be trotted home, and every accommodating understanding and sympathy was offered the man incompletely in control of himself. It helped, too, to spout a few quotes made by esteemed deceased figures from the world of science, literature and art, slurring your speech in the process in case of inaccuracies which would be pounced upon like a cobra striking a mouse. But if too embarrassed not to be in possession of your sober senses, you had but to lonely patiently wait. Till the buyer of a round of drinks, who would for that purpose among his cronies be the moderator of proceedings and would out of the corner of his eye assess the ripe time to finally invite you with the words, 'what are you having'.

If a snub remained chronic, the simmering victim was bound to finally boil over with epithets instead of epigrams renting the air. And as fists followed, it led to another condition arising, that of being banned and disbarred. Such edict being bestowed for obstreperousness beyond the call of erudite argument and the barman in all cases acting as judge and meting out sentence. Which could last a week to a month or six months to a year, depending upon the number of doors ripped off, bottles or windows broken. And could be indefinitely extended if prominent front teeth or eyes were knocked out or if enough stitches were sewn in the various injured faces to leave scars as reminders of the original mayhem. A general lack of heinousness in such battle could also mitigate in the length of disbarment but it helped too, if you were otherwise a published poet or race horse trainer. There were those, too, who were barred for life, and who usually declared such distinction as warning to anyone in their present pub who might be foolhardy enough to accuse them of splitting an infinitive. Alone exempt as a class of person from barring were gas meter readers being always regarded as innocent parties, well known to be the most benign of all peace loving citizens.

Most disbarment was usually finally purged following restitutions, contrite apologies and if necessary, intercessions by other pub habitués. But it was only ever certain that it was lifted when you found yourself served alone as a customer. For if you arrived with a group it was accepted that in the full glare of bonhomie to be asked to leave was too gross an embarrassment and at such times you'd be served with one drink till the discreet message was got to you that it was to be your last. Many protracted disbarments resulted in reimposition due to the over zealous celebration of its lifting. When the blamed again might resort to fisticuffs over the meaning of the word 'clarity', giving as one pub philologist did his own definition with a war cry turned into a physical sample, 'Clarity is that force without witticism given to this fist sent in the direction of your face, that when hit will have no trouble seeing stars.'

But let us out of the better bars, pubs and snugs and even out of the Gilded Cage, pop up a social notch or two to where disbarments were rare indeed. To just around the corner of Duke into Dawson Street and forty paces north along that boulevard. To take a sharp turn right up these steps under a glass canopy. Through swingdoors and enter upon the black and white tiled vestibule always pink tinted aglow by winter with a blazing coal fire. The smiling greetings of an ever attentive concierge to pause you pleasantly in your tracks. A porter or two to take and safely keep your parcel. And always a comely pair of girls at the reception desk to witness your passing and purring deeper into the interior. Strolling by the friendly splendour of the grand stairs arising under a crystal chandelier and Georgian ceiling to the cosy accommodations above. Bless yourself here, to now thankfully enter this, sanctum of all Dublin sanctums. An arena in spite of its access to the public, so exalted and spiritually enclosing in its private intimacy that to merely go there and sit was a loneliness so pleasant it put one aseat among the gods. This was the lounge of the Royal Hibernian Hotel. The most austerely and beautifully elegant meeting place in all the world. And long lain now a dismantled treasure entombed with the other ghosts of Dublin.

And go there I did to sit over many many a year. Where only spectres go now like do the sorrows that have passed in that place. But where once any paupered impostor merely by crossing his legs, sniffing his snuff and shooting a cuff, could assume the pretentions of a solvent prince. As so many of that charming chancer ilk chose to do then. And bask the day away under the smoked green stained glass ceiling dome from which gently the pale light descended upon the habitués of this room. Their love of it making them members of a private club. Its waiters and waitresses famed figures long endeared to its clientele who patiently tolerated even the most delayed attention from these ministers of refreshment. To whom a request was addressed, 'whenever you're ready'. And the response 'I'll be with you any minute now'.

The Royal Hibernian Lounge, although an atmosphere not to awe an American, would even to the most uncomprehending of that breed, finally make him find quaintly singular the eye of observation of gentlemen here found who surveyed all from behind their flashing monocles. And who spouted Anglo Irish vowels so echoingly haughty that they made the tables' glasses shiver and tinkle where they touched. Even I once, sitting innocently entweeded and perusing a sonnet on vellum, through a not so innocent temporarily phoney monocle sporting in my eye, had my reverie most appropriately disturbed. By a lady. She was a tall lady. Physically long of neck. From which six strings of natural pearls were displayed. She originated diagonally from the extreme opposite of the room expiring her breath as she approached. Her chiffons flying behind her in her own breeze. I was in fact obscurely just around the corner of an alcove utterly minding my own unbloody business. As she silkily swept in to loud breathing proximity with her long black tresses falling forward. She stood towering suddenly over me. As I in my chair sought to decide if I should politely arise, when she announced in some of the spiritually loudest words I may have ever heard.

'Sir, you are, as I am sure you may be utterly unaware, as indeed I dare to hope to God you are, wearing represented in the three stripes upon your tie, my family's anciently established and royally bestowed racing colours.'

Ever so gently closing my book of poetry, the contents of which in significance were quite beyond me anyway, I stood instantly. Bowed deeply. Fortunately without breaking wind as one is so wont to do on such occasions. Or indeed wanting to ask how much her pearls were worth. Then further without demur, I swept the offending neck wear instantly from around my throat and out of my collar and tried to rip it up but the damn silken thing was so indestructibly strong I crumpled it away in my pocket. And in yet a deeper bow apologized to the lady for being now tieless in her presence. To which she immediately trumpeted her comment for everyone not stone deaf in the lounge to hear. 'Better that, sir, than for you to continue to be an arrant impostor.'

I was for some next several minutes making the most ironclad of resolutions never to set foot in this pompously pretentious place again. With ladies loose who ought to be back inside their own iron barred stables. But even that vision did little to cheer me and I was descending rapidly into the deep despair that such incidents invariably devolved upon one, when suddenly there came the waiter to my table with an ice bucket containing a vintage bottle of Charles Heidsieck champagne with a scribbled name and legend on Royal Hibernian Hotel notepaper. 'Mocking Laughter in the last today at Fairyhouse'. As I knew what strange words such as these meant in Dublin, I instantly sent this short advice on a card with a suitable tip and a fiver to the concierge who popped with it the few paces to the turf accountant in Duke Street around the corner and such proverbial fiver was placed on 'Mocking Laughter' to win at twenty to one. And I found myself not only that day but on many a day thereafter.

Many the pounds
Pleasantly
The richer

V

The 1946 year of my arrival in Ireland coincided with one of the harshest winters on record. Past Christmas the snows were piled high and even the odd days above freezing point were chillingly damp and cold. The largest municipal park which had so first caught my imagination had massive long high ricks of turf upon which it rained and snowed. These sodden chunks of fuel with which to heat our chambers could rarely be lit due to their wet condition, and if ever lit would only coldly smoulder. In the tall ceilinged and large windowed college rooms, lying long abed mornings, one's frozen feet of the night before not ever thawing before dawn. The dry warmth of Bewley's Oriental Café in Grafton Street becoming the day's first destination. So, too, for the survival of chilled limbs, did I have the early, middle and the latter part of one's evening planned.

In the inner core of Dublin city and within a half mile radius of the centre of O'Connell Street Bridge, you never at any point were more than one hundred and thirty nine and one half paces from a pint of porter or ball of whiskey. Or your trusty bottle of stout standing in their hundreds on shelves ready for their corks to be levered out with a hand puller and a suitable pop. In the better bars were clarets and burgundies, pickled onions, sausages, boiled eggs and sandwiches of ham, cheese and roast beef. But always on the very edges of these blessings lurked the cold desperate reality of the city and its stark gloomy poverty only a stone's throw away. Begging for a penny or selling a newspaper, shoeless urchins, faces streaming phlegm, scattering across the grey glisteningly wet streets. Steeling one to the necessity of food and shelter. For which there was still yet another place of a different and albeit less haughty kind of bliss than the lounge of the Royal Hibernian Hotel.

Following my first few days at Trinity, it was a rare occasion that my social life ever permitted me to dine at evening commons with regularity. Being abroad in Dublin in a city where it quickly became

Two serious geologists, Frank Tuffy and Anthony Byrne, in College Park. These two gentlemen were always faithful callers to number 38. Frank Tuffy having been a prisoner of war, who in order to avoid typhus and death, daily had taken outdoor ice cold showers in the camp and was therefore able to tolerate my winterish rooms.

apparent that appointments were rarely made, and if made, rarely kept. One seemed to become involved in social occasions without beginning or end, time disappearing without warning, and I never seemed able to manage, in spite of the short walk and having already quarterly paid for the meal, to get back to college to dine. Out gallivanting in Dublin, one was invariably pacing oneself to abide one's inevitable and hopefully unsnubbed appearance later in a pub. For me, as evening approached, this often took the form of a long wandering walk through Dublin's by ways. And alone as night fell I would venture back to Grafton Street. Emerging gently around the corner and peeking north and south to spy the way was clear of any hungry, thirsty, qualified idle habitué of the College of Surgeons. Then taking a few bounding leaps across the street to number 72, a marvellous small mock Elizabethan building which housed in a floor above its cinema, a wondrous café.

This eating emporium was not a precinct where one was likely to deliberately or innocently infringe anyone's racing colours. Nor was such place licensed to sell alcoholic beverages. Its mullioned windows looking down from an elevation of brick and faded bruised strawberry hued stone. Inside its vestibule a stray customer or two buying tickets to a cowboy film set on a sunny prairie. And the second feature always a travelogue on venturing to the steamy jungles of Central America or somewhere bereft up in the mountain ranges of the Andes. Tearing myself away from the temptation of such entertainment one would go up the carpeted staircase variegated to prepare one above for this sombrely illumined room. Its tall ceilinged interior, like a galleried hall of a great country house. Its bill of fare hallowed in one's memory. Consisting totally as it did of variations under a theme of different names, all nearly amounting to exactly the same thing. Combinations of bread, butter, bacon rashers, sausages and eggs, fried, grilled, poached or boiled. Each described as either a 'Tasty Tea', 'Evening Tea', 'Tempting Tea', 'Afternoon Tea', 'Dainty Tea', 'Savoury Tea', 'Snack Tea', and one latter tea described awesomely in italics as 'The Gourmet's Tea' to which an anchovy on a piece of toast was added. Be that menu as it may, I agonized each evening over my decision, even at times calling after the waitress to change my order yet again. But with a scalding pot of tea, always devouring with gusto my generous stack of buttered bread, rashers, sausages and eggs.

In the faint light of its shaded little table lamps, more often than not one found the Grafton Picture House Café empty with no other customer there but myself. A screen in a darkened corner behind which an elevator brought food up from kitchens below. Upholstered chairs and banquettes upon which to sit under the lofted imitation beamed ceiling. The recessed wide sills of the fake Tudor windows and mock mahogany furnishings. All giving an atmosphere, albeit ersatz, of utter comforting permanence. Always whispers of the country girl waitresses upon my arrival. Their urgent reminders down the serving hatch to hurry up down there as that poor man's stomach is shouting that his throat is cut. Such was the solemnity of this place's marvellous strange peace that I never once but dined there alone. Nor even said to another soul where I was going or where I'd been. And I suppose if ever a place on this earth or throughout my entire life ever gave one solace it could not be greater than that given me on any one of the gloomy wet Dublin wintry duskingtides that I dined on a 'Tasty Tea' in the Grafton Picture

House Café, and read as I did in the evening newspaper the In Memoriams to those of Dublin's departed dead.

Just as the raindrops were breaking one's back the winter did end and the buds came out on the trees. At such time St Stephen's Green North became the other great fashionable boulevard upon which your better class of Dubliner might be met sprinkling threepenny bits to begging tinkers. Or eyes askance, stroll head high betwixt and between the more sheepish and ingratiating chancers who also hopefully tread here. The southwestern sun shone upon these elevations, lifting the spirits of those who passed on these granite squares of stone, pleasantly in sight of the park. And just to the left out of Grafton Street, one found Smyth's of the Green, an emporium of many exotic groceries to incite your dreams. In the next nearby door of number 7, you might attend to have your portrait painted by the society portrait painter of the day. A tall ample handsome gentleman well known for his silk cravats and who would conspicuously correct a grammatical error heard in French, Irish or English. In this same building, yours truly gave three exhibitions of paintings in the Dublin Painter's Gallery, a large skylit studio deep in the interior up a flight of stairs and echoing many an artist's aspirations. Here I had the nerve not only to outrage and make one's first artistic enemies but to also painfully embarrass friends. Some of whom were asked to lug my still wet canvasses of the female nude from my rooms in Trinity, and watched by many a celibate eye, to transport such work up the entire length of Grafton Street.

Anybody who was anybody, and this was always anybody in Dublin, was to be seen on north St Stephen's Green. Popping in and out of its clubs located in this terrace of massive Edwardian, Victorian and Georgian houses. Down the basement of one was the Country Shop selling Aran Islands' sweaters, and serving teas of home baked scones and home made jams where the waitresses were all from the better families. If not heading towards Adams the auctioneers to bid for an antique, then one was usually on one's way to the glass canopy extending its awning out over the pavement under which clients were protected from inclemency when entering the Shelbourne Hotel. Admitting the ladies but keeping the rabble out was always a great tradition of all doormen in Dublin and letting the right sort in, their golden duty. And such traditions were in no better place enforced than in these precincts. If the Royal Hibernian was where

Anthony Cronin, Gainor Crist and Tony McInerney at one of my exhibitions which frequently became the subject of much discussion due to my forewords in the catalogue. These gentlemen would delight to await and be present at the gallery when a violent member of the Legion of Decency would attack a picture with her umbrella. As, at one time of an attack all of these three were behind my reception desk, they each in turn got a swat over the noggin. While I was out having a drink at a pub.

One of my oil paintings exhibited in Dublin. These executed in a technique resembling that used for water colours and such paintings as this one may have ended up patching a fence in order that Ernie Gebler could keep a neighbouring farmer's sheep from breaking into his lush acres surrounding Lake Park. Gebler's motto being, in this case at least, farming should always come before Art. Especially his farming and somebody else's art.

you might while reading a sonnet be accosted for infringing someone's racing colours, then the Shelbourne was the hotel where you might be whipped unceremoniously with a riding crop for calling a hound a dog. For here you encountered the worshippers of the pursuit of the fox, attenders at point to points, lovers of eventing, race horse breeders, and last and not the least smelling of horse piss, Masters of Foxhounds.

Entering the lobby with its pillars, a lift straight ahead waiting in its wire cage to ascend you up the well of the mahogany balustraded staircase to wide crimson carpeted halls from which doors opened into tall ceilinged rooms that looked out over the tree tops of the park of St Stephen's Green to the purple heathered Dublin Mountains. Attached to a discreet wall of an inside hall downstairs were the current season's fox hunting fixtures. And you would never be noticed if you suddenly decided to neigh and raise your front hooves churning in the air to gallop around the hotel. As indeed a patron or two did when the doors of this élite hostelry were locked to outsiders for the night. And ghosts walk here too. Tiptoeing so as not to disturb the tourists. And so lonely now, for another world has come. From all over the world. In pursuit of speculation and seeking industrial exploitative opportunity. And those who haunted these environs with the passion of their lives. All of them are gone. Dirndl skirts aswirl. Silk kerchiefs flying from their sporty cars. Their pearls nestled on the cashmere of their twinsets and their long gentle fingers alive on the keys that made music on their harpsichords. They've walked with their shooting sticks and their country tweeds. Right out the door. Standing one last time sighing at the Green across the street. Before they step into oblivion. Washed away by the more plebeian waves breaking with Philistine inelegance upon this island nation.

Also in the vicinity of the Shelbourne's venerable location and within a stone's throw of each other were to be found two of the best and most ancient gentlemen's hairdressers in the western reaches of Europe. Where an appointment was akin to a knighthood. And where the intellectual flavour of conversation could range from architecture to agriculture or from ballet to greasepaint, with any amount you might require of Jewish, Irish or Scottish jokes thrown in between. But the funnier of these witticisms were always avoided in case hysterical laughter made one shake while one's neck was being close shaved. And for the same reason nary a contrary word was mentioned on politics or religion. From the ceiling of one coiffeur's, pulley operated rotating brushes were lowered to the head and hair and there spun to brush, massage and altogether invigorate the scalp. Under such treatment one emerged back into Dublin life a new and entirely refreshed man. Solicitors, Protestant bishops, barristers, physicians and wine merchants flocked here to be barbered and shampooed. Rested in bowls of scented waters, their hands awaited to be beautified by the lady manicurist. And I'm sure if I at the time only knew what they looked like, there were also to be seen ministers of the government who had only to make a hop, skip and stumble to reach here from the nearby Dail Eireann. Such gentlemen taking time out from this God fearing nation's business, could lean back, eyes closed in peace. And let us hope, their spirits as mine always did, purred in bliss.

Following a haircut and a shampoo and in particular a good wiping, drying and powdering deep in the collar and neck interstices to rid of the niggling irritation of minutiae of hair, nothing was better than at this five thirty crucial time than to return across Kildare Street to this redbrick grand palace of an hotel where by its side entrance one could discreetly enter. And tread hushed upon a carpeted narrow corridor and up a stair, across a foyer, down again, and through the residents' lounge of flowered soft sofas and out a door into the shadows to climb another stair, walk through another small hall, descend yet another stair and then from a stately vestibule enter the most beautiful and serene of all of Dublin bars, the Shelbourne Rooms.

Fabled for its airy ambience and white friezes on its pale blue walls, this was where your pretending and unpretending better variety of folk spaciously sequestered themselves within two large interconnecting rooms. Its wicker furniture and glass topped tables allowing for the easy crossing of knees. Savoury sticks, cashew and Brazil nuts in bowls. Its curved bar at which never more than three or four would deign to congregate, thus allowing for vowels to effervesce and the bon mot to echo. Its habitués, for fear it would seem frightfully forward, did not look you up and down till your back was well and truly turned. Then, by God beware of who your dressmaker, boot-maker or tailor was. Because this was, too, the winter launching pad of gentry for the provinces. Where came hawkeyed English and

American visiting masters of foxhounds to acclimatize their servants and themselves before subjection to the rigours and foibles of the Irish country house. And where they might, for a few days, kneeling nightly by their bedsides, say their prayers in some comfort before their necks were risked in some severe discomfort, braving walls, hedgerows, bogs and ditches out to the north, south and west.

In autumn when a chill descended or in June with summer suddenly warming an evening, one would go there to sit. Wrapped up in one's own loneliness and taking one's own comfort from the comfort of champagne. Viewing the ladies and gents in black tie and gowns as they appeared prior to dinner or a ball to stoke up their allégresse. Or as happened once when my fellow college lassies and lads suddenly sauntering in to drink before a dance, found me there. On this long mild evening in June. After the college races. On a Wednesday night. When all so hoped to make this sacred undergraduate occasion a social success. And one is somewhat sad now. To admit that although present in the Shelbourne Rooms lurking in my contented loneliness and albeit happy to cheer such fellow senior freshmen on over their drinks, not then, nor once did I, in all my university years, with the single exception of one cold rainy night at the Dublin University Gramophone Club, ever attend a college social occasion. Having been swept away invariably as I was, by the inexhaustibly teeming endless embroilment of life in Dublin by day and especially by night.

In Ireland in the immediate years after World War II, one was comparatively rich, and certainly richer than I'd ever been before and, alas, have been since. An allowance from my wise Galway mother was sent regularly without strings attached from New York, which was in frequent addition to my monthly bonanza cheque from the G.I. Bill of Rights. In the midst of my fellow starving Americans, my own way of life was led in some splendour. My stipend even being several times greater than my college servant's wage with which he respectably supported a small house, wife and clothed and fed four children. Under the banner of 'Incidentals Account with Trinity College' my bill for the quarter ending 1 March 1947, while incurring no debits for Baths, Repairs and Dilapidations or Punishments, amount to £18.8s.11d. For which total one was supplied with college servant, daily bottle of milk, quarterly rent of chambers and 'Commons Fund' of £3.13s.6d which provided one daily reasonably

From the Incidentals Account it will be seen that I took no baths, and incurred a tardy payment fine of seven and six pence. 'Commons Fund' each evening provided one with being served in the dining hall by acrobatically skilled porters who placed in front of one soup, a plate of meat, two vegetables and a sweet. A special beer brewed by Guinness was also available for the occasion. And it helped to find a seat between two of the better-mannered students.

sumptuous evening meal with its glass or two of beer.

In those days an orange coloured ten shilling note bought an evening's drinking of seventeen bottles of Guinness, or it could also provide nine pints of porter, or eleven balls of malt. And last and most of all, twenty bottles of Mountjoy Nourishing Stout. But prior to arrival at these party outposts where the drink flowed freely and without additional charge, there remained the custom at these counters of these pubs, of a strange ritual somewhat alien to me as an American. Of buying round after round. And voices heard, as one voice would say, what are you having. And another voice answering, no no, what are you having, it's my round now. There would then invariably ensue a mild insistence as to whose privilege the buying of the next round would be. Before I knew it, one's turn to buy a round inevitably came. Yet as I would offer, and make the attempt again and again, there came protests too numerous and apparently vehement, to subdue. And it was a long time before anyone even hinted that you were occasionally expected to threaten, shout and even shove and punch the opposition down. But one cannot imagine that even from the poorer among the group, that it would ever be severely held against one for not buying your round. Although it would surely be noticed and remembered till the end of time. For even with your wife and tiny numerous children at home starving as many were, not to be generous was the unforgettably unforgivable. Which would earn you the invariably resentful eternal sobriquet, 'He's nothing but a dirty no good mean bastard.'

Pub life almost entirely regulated one's own. At morning opening these meeting places would start to slowly fill with their habitués drifting in until reaching a peak of activity when holy hour arrived closing the pub between two thirty and three thirty. In the case of Davy Byrnes much of the company would retire across Duke Street to the Bailey Restaurant where the drinking could endure accompanied by food thought the least harmful to the thirst. By four thirty all were ready to decamp again back over the road. In a nation moving at the slower pace of Ireland, the only thing that was ever fast were the clocks in every pub. The bartender always ten to fifteen minutes prior to closing time noisily collecting glasses and bottles as he announced in ever more insistent and mock angry tones, 'Now please. Time now gentlemen please. Way past the time. Gentleman please. If you will.' This was the one moment of a bartender's and publican's day when he could indulge speaking in a voice hinting of a slight lack in diplomacy. Or even to take the liberty if not pleasure of leavening his voice with a tinge of severity. As everyone within sight and sound stood their ground assured in the knowledge that the remaining contents of their glasses was a sacred right to consume. I never once saw a member of the Garda Síochána in uniform enter to see that closing time was being observed. But I did encounter those in mufti quietly drinking away with the other dilatory customers, and sometimes silently deliberating into the foam of their Guinness as whether to take action or, as was invariably done, resignedly down-ing the contents of their glass and ordering up another one to further breech the licensing laws.

But as was with the likes of the Shelbourne Rooms, or even after the pub, if there was not the ball, there was always the shindy. The plans for which got whispered urgently from ear to ear as closing time approached. The succinct words being. 'There's a bash on.' Whiskey, in measures of twenty six and two thirds fluid ounces, gin in other volumes and even odd exotics in liquid quarts were ordered together with grey parcels packed with dozens of bottles of stout, and handed up and over the bar. And with such recently confided invitations one emerged with such groups ferrying such armfuls out pub doors. In the case of my acquaintances frequenting the thronged confines of Davy Byrnes, there was not far to go to pull further corks out of further bottles of stout. In fact not many yards as the crow flies or legs might wobble to a terraced redbrick discreetly anonymous Georgian building. With rooms on top of one another, a couple to each floor where the indiscretion increased as one ascended and where, under the motto, Bash On Regardless, the parties throbbed the night away. The more serious fights and arguments being engaged on the top floors from whence the losers could conveniently be fenestrated through an oft demolished window and land four storeys below in a rubbish heap mound of discarded rotting felt and disintegrating burlap. While much intermediary peeing might follow upon their heads if the revellers upstairs weren't more discreetly urinating down the balustrades to give just arriving visitors a taste of what they might expect should they ascend.

But let us not forget the slightly more serene post pub closing ritual of the Bonafide. In those days a term used to refer to public houses open after your normal licensing hours and permitted to give refreshment to the weary thirsty traveller. The rule being that such wayfarer had come some great distance on a dusty or more likely wet road and in passing on his way elsewhere and suitably parched, was craving liquid sustenance. Although there were your occasional two footed uphill and down dale pedestrian Bonafiders, more usually used a beast of burden, bicycle or automobile for such migrations. And with the customary plethora of people desperate to continue a night's drinking, this nightly nomadic pursuit was often a party in itself. Arms and legs along with the empty bottles from the previous pub, flailing and flying out windows. The boozing occupants hell bent countrywards in a din of epithets, the vehicle on its suspension rolling and pitching like a ship in a hurricane. Bumps and potholes on the road blinking headlights on and off as sane citizens out late on foot, hid behind thick walls and stout trees till such vehicles had safely careered past. And death, sadly, was not unknown.

Bonafides ranged around the outer vicinities and environs of Dublin. And south of the River Liffey this usually meant village pubs in the foothills of the Dublin Mountains. The beneficial aspect of such places and locations often being that verbal battles originating earlier in the inner city pub could blossom into full scale violence and take place in plenty of room. The aggrieved as it were, repairing outside to settle their differences in the late night peace and tranquillity of an untrafficked village street. Thereby permitting a large circle to gather around the antagonists either as spectators or as many invariably became, participants, engaging themselves in the battle when the circumstances incited. Usually this was when some poor unfortunate, ganged up on, bit the dust or mud, and prostrate was ripe to receive an additional battering of a boot in the ribcage.

It was an unwritten law that owners of vehicles used to transport to the Bonafide were to be left unharmed. Such persons usually were socially perched high as indeed only the financially better off members of the community in such post war days could afford to own a motor car. However such folk, as designated immune from bodily harm, were not estopped themselves from meting out punishment where they deemed it deserved. Their exemption from flying fists and feet being insured by several who would surround and protect such motorists without whom people could not get the ten or so miles back to populated civilization. There were, of course, occasionally present some of your gurrier folk without scruples who would attack anyone, and especially a more affluent automobilist. Such low types were fortunately not in abundance and usually were of a sort who

Tony Byrne and Val Hines taking time out during a geological expedition to Malahide, a lady student in the background. During such expeditions some romantically explosive situations were also explored.

ingratiated themselves in the company by spouting a verse or two of simple poetry purporting to be original from their own lips. And did then by their further pseudo intellectual blandishments inveigle to these Bonafide environs. However, once loose there in a general discord they could be depended upon to curse, swear and swing nail studded clubs and bring lead pipes down thudding on craniums. Thus adding a touch of true vulgarity, calculated viciousness and utter savagery to the mayhem.

But if in the night exterior, goings on went raging, the metacarpals splintering and the blood splashing in the puddles of water, there were always among such groups the peace lovers who continued their discussions and deliberations inside the pub. Reminding that this sovereign state was still a land of saints and scholars, who took no notice whatsoever of the sorrowful contusions being administered without. Indeed, so engrossed in their various schools of thought were they, that upon reappearance of the bloody faces of the maimed they might not even deign to examine the finer details of the carnage until the victors or the vanquished drew such attention by including them in an order for a round of drinks.

Ah but the open scope provided by the Bonafide was nothing in mayhem. Compared to the retirement for a bash in the venue of the country house. Many of such being houses perched precipitously on some edge or cliff over the sea. By the not curious coincidence that their owners were heavy drinkers of a sort who liked a marine atmosphere in their lives. Catching crabs or lobsters from the back garden or indeed availing of the convenience of a cold morning plunge in the ocean to sober up for the serious day's drinking ahead. But such architecturally spectacular places were usually the exclusive province of the hereditarily well heeled élite of the élite. In whose company there was never any need to travel far to risk your neck fox hunting. Often, too, such host would be a large yacht owner who would suicidally seek the life threatening hospitality of the Irish Sea and while frequently away in such a pursuit would leave his wife at home on the edges of the cliff. Who, as such ladies would, heading to town for cocktails and dinners, convene a few friends to return to her empty house. There to puff on hemp, foxtrot and drink in the spacious grandeur. And such battles as did there take place always began typically and innocently enough, invariably being merely an expression of opinion on an artistic matter.

One such famed evening erupting in this sumptuous drawing room when a dark blue suited gentleman in a bright red yellow spotted bow tie took exception to the slow pulsation of the music being played on the gramophone. And while the needle merrily passed over the record, he feathered his neck wear, shot his gold linked cuffs, ceremoniously opened his fly, and then in the pure, albeit faint, electric light of this evening, took out his appendage member, through which he commenced to pee upon the rotating plastic platter of fine grooves. The change in tempo from largo to a very watery andante instantly called attention to his act of disapproval from every quarter of the room. In which were present three members of the Royal Dublin Society and four members of the Royal Irish Automobile Club, the latter indubitably one of the most exclusive private clubs on the face of the earth. With suitable words of shock and dismay followed by those of chastisement, the seven encroached upon the perpetrator of the peeing to drag him away from the committing of this disrespectful nuisance which, as the pee percolated down into the gears of the turntable, stopped it spinning and caused the music to groan to a halt. However, as the culprit was dragged away he grabbed and pulled a priceless Gobelin tapestry down from the wall and as he and the ornamented fabric were tugged across the room he peed further upon the latter which incited an art-loving lady to beat him with her handbag wounding him in the head. Thus was first blood drawn.

The culprit of the peeing was otherwise than in his present behaviour, a jolly and agreeable person. And of all surprising things, was a young ship's captain and opera lover guilty of only censoring another's musical taste. But as came the increased volume of imploring screams from the other engowned friends of the quite beautiful hostess, these members present of the Royal referred to Clubs laid into your man goodo. The hostess herself, however, cared not a hoot about her tapestry nor music nor gramophone, and was equally casual as to whom she let tamper with her body, enjoying as she did men in any and all variety. Thus, she vehemently cried out to the disciplinarians to desist. Whereupon the ship's captain being unhanded, the hostess promptly took him by the hand and by a secret door to the back servants' stairs, up which both disappeared to bed. While meanwhile his spilt blood required that sides be taken, consisting of those who approved the urinary censorship and those who abhorred such musical interruption. However a disagreement concerning the period in which an Italian master had painted a hall painting was already providing a violent battle of unbelievable proportions among the rest of the guests in the front hall. Where sides were also drawn up. From persons, many of whom at the time, were innocently dancing and enjoying to look as they waltzed by these works of art. However, the folk who having been long enough in Ireland to know what raised voices meant, and hearing the loud commotion, tried to escape to the drawing room. From which latter, however, now came an equally forceful commotion. Signalling all that it was distinctly time to have one's fists, if not a cudgel, at the ready. But too late, as the warring factions from the drawing room now confronted the warring factions from the hall. And as the battle now gave rise to two sources of contention, no side knew what side they might safely be on. All present realizing it was every man for himself. With each taking a doubtful look at the other and in lieu of continued doubt, commencing to fight for their lives. Indeed if someone's back was turned and such person not previously having indicated which triangular side he was on, he was for the sake of prudency instantly chosen as an opponent. Usually a bottle of stout being wielded to baptize him as he stood. And if he continued to stand and the bottle did not break, he was duly hammered without blessing to the black and white tiled floor without so much as a murmur of apology for such unsporting unfair play.

Having Celticly hard skulls most victims of attack from behind were able to withstand at least the first onslaught. The bottle often breaking and such hardy gents licking the stout from their lips, enabling them to turn to identify the sneak attacker. And woe be unto him. For such assailant could be assured of receiving one of the most unholy of woolings. This famed Dublin chastisement consisting of the aggrieved gent knocking the treacherous chap to the ground and grabbing him by both his port and starboard ears and engripped also with a goodly handful of hair, then pounding his skull repeatedly on the tiles, while removing the hirsute plumage about his hearing appendage and shaking the living daylights out of his neurons.

With the resulting jungle drum cacophony of many heads now being thumped and banged the length and breadth of this once dignified hall, those still upstanding gave a good account of themselves as the battle raged totally without rhyme and most certainly totally without reason. But always in the midst of such melée where the fists, boots and bottles were flying, one could catch the unforgettably calm sight of a philosophic gent perched somewhere above it all, safe from all harm. In this case one had but to look atop the main staircase and there he was. Smiling gently, sitting high, a bottle of champagne at his side, and sipping a glass as he quietly peered through the balustrade at the carnage below. The beguiling contentment upon this particular face clearly felt as a ravishingly attractive lady put her fingers gently through locks of his dark hair. Such folk as this philosopher might be thought to be, was not a barrister, solicitor or man in some context of the law. But in this case was a gentleman who dabbled in poetry and had in his earlier days carefully attempted to be only on the receiving end of handouts, but instead had received many a wooling for his opinions and had learned the lesson how to precisely remain a comfortable and uninjured spectator albeit a sheepishly guilty one.

The time was past midnight on this November night of the new moon. A sea wind shaking doors and windows. And a surf booming in the caves at the foot of the cliffs. The front hall marble tiles of this house like the opinions expressed upon them, were black and white only. Entry here was dramatically through great doors from an outer vestibule, a tier above. Indeed usually to get to such houses at all from the road you penetrated great dark portals in great granite walls and dramatically ascended or descended as one might to a sacrificial altar. In this case more than one hundred dark stone steps between mountainous rhododendrons, a sombre vista appropriate to the carnage now in full swing. Pilasters being chipped and smashed. Marble busts being toppled and cracking the tiles. Hepplewhite furniture flying. And everywhere transporting through the air were other and not much less valuable divers objets d'art. These missiles airborne with such abandon made it clear to even the members of the better Royally designated clubs and societies that no amount of their admonitions and civilized cautions had even a vague chance of according priority to the safety of the priceless antiques.

As windows smashed and drapes ripped, the wind blew a gale. Even wall niches were disfigured, and their marble busts toppled from their recesses. And now the sound of feet were heard pounding, running riot on the upper floors of the house. Ladies screaming as frocks were torn. Such mayhem always being a time to settle old scores, slanders and long sworn revenges. One well known eccentric beauty suddenly openly declaring as she exhibited her bosoms that the husband of every wife present had been at them and that she had the biggest nipples in Co. Dublin and was about to prove it. This increased the screaming as she made to rip open every other lady's bodice within fingernail grasp. But it did, as the many breasts present were revealed, have the effect of stopping the carnage and the blood splashing briefly. Allowing a dignified member of the Kildare Street Club to remind the combatants to come to their Anglo Irish, if not Irish, senses. And for someone to telephone for medical assistance. Duly the doctor did arrive. Qualified as it appropriately happened at the Royal College of Surgeons in Ireland. A gold watch chain suspended across his waistcoat, his elegant black case at his side as he stepped from the front door into the vestibule. From whence he could survey further and down upon this blood bespattered carnage strewn front hall. But before he could cut any gauze or get his stethoscope out, he dropped to the deck like a brick, felled with a heart attack.

The only place of partially untrammelled and seeming safety was a water closet adjoining the vestibule, the door of which was flanked by large potted palms. The good doctor was gently carried therein to be propped aseat upon the toilet bowl in order to keep at least his upper torso out of the wet. For a length of lead pipe had, as a weapon, been recently ripped from the lavatory wall and water was pouring out over the hall floors which were now aflood from this fractured pipe. Meanwhile, another sensible member of the Kildare Street Club summoned a second doctor. Who in turn arrived. Again with a gold watch chain and in an elegant blue pinstriped suit and sporting the subtle light blue, red, green and broad black stripes of a Trinity College graduate's tie. The doctor took one look at the carnage amid the strewn furnishings covering the length and breadth of the vast hall and then spied his colleague slumped unconscious on the toilet seat nearby. Whom, god help this poor latter physician and the fine cloth on the back of his trousers, which were residing upon such seat and to which he now adhered, being that it had only that very afternoon been freshly painted. And in an emerald bright green.

Trinity College graduates are among the most sophisticated of people and have long since gone out to distinguish themselves and triumph in all corners of the world. Especially those who have succeeded in the faculty of medicine. But this gentleman doctor so taken unawares, could not have imagined what was in store at this otherwise stately elegant home, and he stood rigidly in total shock. At least for the moment. For he too then did promptly become hors de combat, fainting backwards into a potted palm.

But who shall in this world ever say that such imbroglios do not befall even the most well and benignly intentioned of men in the best of country houses. For despite the unfortunate developments therein, to all these stately venues did proceed, in general, your usually better category of invited people. The semi pleasured class you might say. Who in the bliss of these mostly mixed husbandless and wifeless gatherings, convened to fight off the glooms of life. Albeit which frequently only deepened further in the close proximity of loose women and randy gentlemen. Requiring more bottles of stout and glasses of whiskey often accompanied by other alcoholic exotics whose headache making constituents were those derived of potato brewing. But which in the imbiber produced more arias, lullabys and cradlesongs. Which in turn somehow incited more insults and verbal lashings. For hours on end. Leading to these thrashings. When both battling and loving hugs merged into one another. And more times became tears and sobs. But at any stage it remained always unforgivable to go home. Commendable to wake in a heap somewhere. Bleary eyed in some strange cold room and lucky that your feet weren't soaking freezing in some mountain stream. Or in some thatched cottage or at the end of the anonymous hall of some great ancient house. Shivering under somebody else's coat. Dreaming a nightmare on somebody else's floor or sofa with the prong of a broken spring up a backside. Or looking for warmth in somebody else's arms. Wrapped around someone else's body or someone else's body wrapped around yours. And you knew you were well and truly arrived. In the free state sovereignty of boozers, spendthrifts, wife beaters, onanists and would be philanderers. And this indeed was, in the land of saints and scholars, an utter revelation of Irish life. Leaving this American so recently a newcomer.

Bewildered
In a complete state
Of moral shock

VI

The first of the doctors to arrive at the battle scene, who was a renowned fly fisherman, fortunately proved not to be dead but had only a minor heart attack, but did however have a shoulder dislocated as it required several party goers present to rip him off the toilet to whence the major part of the seat of his trousers was affixed in wet green paint. Of course, good Samaritan automobiles did ferry people back to be medically attended at the better hospitals in the city of Dublin. And indeed this coastal area, haunted with the legend of this battle that had taken place there, although it was never quite the same again, did eventually return to its normal every day exterior of peace and quiet.

But one had just cause to remember that night for in the very beginning of the melée I had been clubbed by a damn sneaky assailant with a stout bottle on the back of the head. Weathering the blow I turned to swear revenge, announcing loudly as I did so several of the bloodier battles of the then recently ended war. I'm sure my attacker had never been more than ten miles from Donnybrook in his life but I pretended such assumption to his having been present at Anzio, Bataan, Corregidor, Normandy and Stalingrad. And loudly inferred that none of these battles he'd been through, would, in the annals of violence, hold a candle to the battle that was now about to unfold about and upon him in reprisal for his diabolically dastard attack. But lo and behold, a distinct Dublin friend was already beating the bejesus out of him with fists, sending lefts, rights, and uppercuts to his jaw and bolos deep into his solar plexus.

It was my first lesson in Irish combat. That you did not sportingly present yourself in a frontal forthright manner declaiming to challenge your would be opponent and thus give him a gentlemanly chance of protecting himself. Nor did you stand anywhere mid scene with your back unprotected, gesticulating or uttering war cries or hysterically calling down the wrath of God upon one's foe. For unseen attack from the rear or an unguarded flank was the practised Celtic approach. Plenty of time to spout about comeuppance and fair play when you had your foot across your supine man's throat while he attempted to squeak out apologies between his gasps for mercy.

But there were other places. One resembling no pub, resembling no country house. Which if you couldn't find a venue by the sea suitable for late night social relations, you could, if you knew persons who knew the whereabouts of this locale, repair there for entertainment which was as various as it could be violent. Now over the years in Dublin there were many attempts to open up and run improvised gambling casinos and the like. Especially in the basements and cellars of the great Georgian townhouses. And indeed some were run. Roulette being played with a large ball bearing found somewhere, which was spun within the rim of an old discarded automobile wheel. The unreliable nature of the contraption often leading to disputes settled occasionally by someone found dead under such tables with a knife in the back. But never in the modern or ancient history of the Irish State was there anywhere at any time anything like Charnelchambers.

Perfectly describing the place, this name was uttered in awe from my own lips upon my first innocent visit there. Charnelchambers as it did, consisting of a series of cellar rooms located central in a once elegant Georgian Dublin square north of the Liffey. It was first where a charming cherubically rotund gentleman lived whose luxurious previous life had been reduced in circumstances and he was enduring an impecuniousness which had now prolonged beyond the temporary. While in his more undressed states, he was fond of reminding people that his Christian name was Basil, and from the Greek, meant kingly and royal. Afternoons he would be seen in the gilded cage of Davy Byrnes, the Dawson Lounge, or holding court in the public rooms of the Shelbourne and Royal Hibernian Hotels where he was devastatingly quick with both merry and unmerry quips.

Basil smoked cigarettes with a long ivory holder and spoke in what was then referred to as the King's English. To pay his own rent he initially took in carefully selected paying guests, many of whom were listed in The Almanach De Gotha if not Debrett. And who had, when their luck was down, repaired there as a temporary resort. Which frequently became their final one. Thus these chambers came to house princes, counts, moguls, black sheep, white sheep, and ultimately even members of the Irish Republican Army. Such was the irreligiously pagan nature of the place that it even with the latter, lodged the odd Orangeman and Unionist Presbyterian. And as Basil himself was a man who preferred other gentlemen, they too of this persuasion were frequently domiciled within. Ireland having become post war a fabled mecca for the more sincere elegantly cultured homosexualist. In fact every condition of mankind including sodomites, necrophiliacs, coprophiliacs, and especially erotomaniacs were to be in these dungeons finally found. It was overflowing too with the failed and bankrupt, the criminal as well as the contented insane. Even the odd honest to God gee whizz American from the midst of Minnesota could end up here. Although singularly short of hermaphrodites, it did in the course of its existence become the most astonishing place of festivity and mayhem ever invented. And did sadly leave many who wished it never had been.

It was upon a rainy wintry Thursday afternoon when I was having visitors to tea in my Trinity rooms, when an enormously tall eccentric gentleman with whom I occasionally played and lost one sided tennis matches, mostly due to the fact that he could serve a tennis ball at 200 miles an hour, arrived amidst the company with a breathtakingly beautiful blonde lady in tow. I was painting pictures at the time which, although she was too polite to condemn as appalling, she did at least admire my nerve. I thanked her for at least noticing them and expressed despair that it was the only way I had of spending my Sundays in a bereft, empty, closed up Dublin. And was then promptly upon the Sunday invited to call upon her. My enormously tall tennis serving friend had apoplexy on the spot. And nearly ripped her address out of my fingers. I was a little surprised to find reaching her residence in this highly dilapidated street, that one had also to descend down steep narrow stairs deep into a basement area where one had to rap one's knuckles on a rather shabby green door. I was agreeably reassured but not a little nonplussed when a corpulent, marvellously elegant gentleman appeared, answering the door with an ivory cigarette holder held high, scissored between the extreme tips of his first two index fingers. He was attired in what seemed some form of butler's regalia but with a gold chain hanging across his crimson waistcoat. I was not to know at that moment that after ten in the evenings following pub emptying time, he always greeted would be guests at the door, totally in the nude. With not only his cigarette holder stiffly horizontal but his private appendage as well.

Nor did I realize that by daytime Charnelchambers' seemingly open doors of these various rented crypts had to be padlocked and barred at night. But upon this swiftly darkening late afternoon these cellar rooms and former kitchens so vast, damp, dark and endless, and which extended into alcoves, wine vaults and coal bunkers, seemed anything but the setting for some of the most memorably exquisite social occasions I have ever attended. Housing as it then did this highborn lusciously curvaceous beautiful lady with such abundant radiant blond hair. Who having escaped Germans, Poles, Russians, and other middle European warring ethnics during the war, had now recently escaped a dangerously violent, alcoholic and highly eccentric Anglo Irish husband and was now in her straitened circumstances, secretly seeking solace there.

On this Sunday I followed the cherubically bubbling blond Basil clothed in his black jacket, crumpled white shirt and black tie, as he proceeded backwards through this dank dungeon to its very last rearmost room, while dropping the Princess' title every few steps. Basil, who astonishingly resembled a portly Hollywood matinée idol, had been an ace Spitfire pilot shot down over Germany who with one leg broken made his way back to England to fly again. But during the last weeks of the war further injury caused by a flying bomb repaired him to convalesce in Ireland. Now as the door opened he bowed and clicked his heels, as if one were being conducted into a sovereign's presence. And there awaiting me, seated within upon a chaise squeezed in her narrow damp cramped room, was this gracious Saxon skyblue eyed Princess. Her possessions stacked everywhere within and on top of everything up to the ceiling.

I was, of course, immensely anxious to enter upon the more socially less dangerous and preferably cultural side of activities in the Irish capital. Having now nearly every night at party or pub, had to fight for my life. And as a hostess at home to one on a damp, cold, winter Sunday evening for late afternoon tea followed by drinks at seven p.m., the Princess, albeit in her dank dungeon, was as much and more than I ever dared hope for. Basil, her landlord, continuing on my repeated visits to act as concièrge come butler rushing to fill a vase with water when I, desperately in love, also brought flowers.

These being an exotic bloom or two, by necessity lifted from the college botanical conservatory which housed such specimens. Upon these occasions the Princess baked the most exquisite scones which she served with whipped cream and her own home made strawberry jam. It was impossible to conceive of any husband ever battering or beating her. And my tall explosively serving tennis partner who had previously constantly turned up with dazzling foreign women at my rooms ceased suddenly to do so saying he was not about to introduce his love objects only to have various college roués run off with them as I had done with this cultured curvaceous aristocratic middle European beauty.

Of course I was merely lonely for the excitement of an intelligent female mind, and certainly no roué but I did most eagerly upon this particular and subsequent Sundays in my tweeds enter through the iron gate in the black fence which stood in front of this decaying Georgian mansion and proceed heart thumping down the steep iron stairs and trepidatiously knock on this basement door. Indeed even continuing to think Basil was the butler. As he would on subsequent occasions precede me through this first vast room, once the kitchen of the great mansion above, having already put a kettle to boil and arranged tea items at the ready to be delivered to the Princess at home beyond her door at the end of the long dark passage. Always enjoying to hear Basil's spiel declaimed in his exquisite vowels as he clicked heels and bowed.

'Ah how nice to see you again. And so soon. Her Royal Highness awaits. Ah and how good of you. Flowers. She'll be much pleased. I do wish more people were as thoughtful. And dear me. Shades of the African Congo. Dare I imagine. Orchids. How exotically surprising and pleasing. I think if someone were to bring me flowers, even a single tiny violet, I should swoon. Not on these damp stone floors, of course. But on the appropriate part of a chaise longue. And into desirably appropriate arms.'

Everyone, at least upon my first few occasions down in this dungeon, had damn decent vowels. The British accent then being used like a blow torch to cut a social swathe through all that was Irish. And even I, I must confess, undertook to subsequently overhaul and polish my own phonetics. As much from a sense of protective coloration as anything else. And it did undeniably ease one through the better places in town. But did little to impress the Princess who through her trials and tribulations had become somewhat socialistically minded. But not to the degree that this might have made her discourage capitalistic upper class men's attentions. Although sad as her countenance sometimes could be, the Princess would as soon as two or more gentlemen collected, rally her own aristocratic spirits, adoring as she did to be surrounded by her admirers. One of whom was already present on this initial occasion as I took a seat on the side of her bed. Coronets embroidered on her linen sheets, pillow cases and napkins. And just as I was discreetly examining such embossment between my thumb and a forefinger I felt my heel under the edge of her bed, knock against a nearly full porcelain vessel of urine. As it happened, a pot not begot in Ireland for it was a rare exquisite piece of Meissen emblazoned on its sides and cover with a coronet and her escutcheon. Which pot gave hint of chamber music to come. And in which, in view of my father's sentiments, I later took great pleasure to piss in.

The two orchids were placed on a Louis XV ormolu mounted marquetry poudreuse where the Princess kept a small altar and icon and where two candles flamed to illumine the room. We took China tea with lemon slices from her Dresden as she sat on a Louis XV giltwood chaise, reputed made for Madame du Barry. Sparkling were her one remaining pair of diamond and sapphire brooches being the most valuable of her few remaining unpawned possessions. Tea was always followed by a pure pot still Scotch whisky and fruit cake baked in the great stove out in the kitchen. Then my fellow guest Peter, maestro virtuoso, would arise. A gentleman who had long loved, worshipped and adored the very grimiest of Dublin pavements this Princess had been compelled to walk upon. And as you might know he was matriculating within that four foot thick granite walled bastion on St Stephen's Green, the Royal College of Surgeons. However, this brilliant student, unlike many of the balding perennial habitués there, had won exam prizes in midwifery and gynaecology and passed his first medical years with flying honours. He loved Ireland even as he abhorred the savage poverty and doom ridden slums where he delivered babies. An old Etonian as well as an ex Royal Air Force Spitfire pilot he was as exquisitely English as anyone could ever hope to be. Wearing his old school scarf, voluminously like a great boa constrictor around his neck, with the rest of its long length hanging down his back to his ankles. Flowing blond locks of hair framed a face so astonishing aquiline that women upon catching a glimpse of him were known to weep. And indeed Basil, fluent in Sanskrit, unleashed constant avouchments of love in this language which Peter embarrassingly understood. But these sentiments from both men and women were nothing. Nothing whatever. Compared to what happened to such ladies and gentlemen when Peter opened his violin case and brought forth his cherished fiddle built by Antonio Stradivari.

In her terribly tiny room, the Princess had strategically assembled us. Peter taking up the only unoccupied corner to carefully draw his bow back and forth in his rosin. And then tucking his fiddle lovingly between chin and shoulder, would with the faintest of frowns upon his brow, tune the strings. Beyond her heavily gauze curtained window which opened upon a tiny courtyard and outdoor privy, one could hear the rain splashing from broken gutters and gurgling in the outside drains. And if the gauze were parted one could see the rats scrabbling in the piles of debris. But here inside. Turf smoke from her small fireplace scenting the air. The whisky served. Peter began to play. All within and without becoming utterly still. In this hush now. As we listened. To the violin strains of Mozart, Brahms, Bruch, Dvořák. Played with all the warmth and exquisite tonalities alive in this gentleman's heart and skill.

Ah but inevitably. As such musical moment progressed there would finally find another Princess adoring member of this tiny audience appearing. Who out of one of the dark, dank, windowless wine cellar caves back along the hall, would now silently slip in the door. He was called Adolphus the Vicomte. And when whisky was poured at an intermission, Adolphus shuffling barefoot in slippers on the paving stone, would announce in his heavily accented but impeccable English.

'Your devoted servant madam. Brought forth from his abject hole by such wondrous music, apologizes to impose. And to you too, gentlemen, for my lack of sartorial elegance. But pyjamas somehow do, don't they, make one appear as if one were just arriving from South America, or in the case of their being silk, as mine happen to be, as if one were just departing to go there.'

Adolphus was a pale, thin, aristocratic titled black sheep from a family who forwarded a not unhandsome monthly emolument which would continue to arrive providing he physically stay forever and absolutely out of his native country. Although long a denizen of Charnelchambers, Adolphus preferred to live as much of his life as he could in the manner to which he had previously and sumptuously been accustomed. And did, upon arrival of his monthly cheque, have the Princess cash this for him and to summon a horse cab. Then in his slippers and a borrowed raincoat from Basil who sported it in his Foreign Office days, Adolphus thus covering his pyjamas would make his way up and out into Dublin life once more. Mounting the horse cab in which he would clip clop to the pawn shop to redeem his morning suit. Out of hock, too, would come his cufflinks, studs, shoes, shirts, tie and socks. Then taking off his pyjamas in a pawn shop cubby hole and folding them to rest in his repossessed attaché case, he would dress in his cutaway coat and striped trousers, stick in his pearl tie pin, and step out again to his waiting horse cab. The jarvey saluting as he held open the door.

'Ah yer honour, sure as the holy ghost himself never sneezed, youse is looking as great as the Protestant Bishop of Meath. 'Tis a treat to see and serve you. It is to the Shelbourne Hotel per as usual.'

Of course yours truly was, on a couple of late morning occasions, a passenger in such horse drawn brougham which took Adolphus directly to his suite already booked awaiting him at this renowned hotel. From whence each day the Vicomte would go racing and in the evenings dine within the comfortingly sprawling up and down rooms of the fabled French family's restaurant, Jammet's. Which had lace curtained windows and an entrance fronting on Nassau Street across from the Provost's back garden of Trinity College and the iron door for the use of College Fellows. But the restaurant could also be reached by a discreet dark alley just up and left off Grafton Street. If the Vicomte was not found here over pheasant and champagne he would be in attendance at dinner parties, balls and receptions, with as often as he could, the Princess in tow and might manage in this manner, depending upon his luck picking winners at races, for a week and at the absolute most a fortnight. But inevitably broke and penniless, paying his bill he would discharge from the Shelbourne, returning on foot to pawn his clothes and with the money buy sustenance to last until his emolument arrived once more and he was able again to emerge from his pyjamaed existence in his tiny, windowless wine cellar room in Charnelchambers.

But on musical evenings such as this, Adolphus would present himself, elaborately apologizing in his nightwear state. The Countess inviting him use of her giltwood chaise. Upon the edge of which he would contritely and solemnly sit. But from which he would inevitably rise in religious fervour, enthralled by the music of Peter's violin. The Vicomte's hand held over his heart as if it had been pierced and he was holding back the spurting blood. Which upon one occasion did come. When following a goodly amount of the Princess's Scotch whisky, and possessed by the beauty of Peter's playing, the Vicomte stood pressing and banging his forehead against the wall with such force that the skin on his brow was broken and the blood one thought would burst from his heart, cascaded instead out of his skull and down his face. As he would implore Peter.

'I beg of you don't stop. Play. Play.'

Except for a vision of the Blessed Virgin claimed seen by one of the more transient occupants, a devout member of both The Legion of Decency and Legion of Mary, little could be claimed of a religious nature in Charnelchambers. However, where the now departed member of The Legion of Decency had avowed witnessing his vision, indeed on the very site upon which the Virgin stood, miraculously a tiny spring was discovered flowing. But sceptics continuing to scoff until one night a Trinity College law student, short circuiting the lights, plunged the place into darkness and a life and death free for all. When suddenly a blue halo was seen glowing exactly in the niche where the original vision was witnessed. Sadly on this occasion disputes over who thought they saw the glow led to even greater mayhem. But other than this phenomenon such cultural and religious behaviour was rare indeed. For the later and now more historically associated activities down in these Charnelchambers of which I was not only soon to learn more, now dominated all. And yours truly was to be held accountable by many folk for their having ever started.

Nearly all the entrenched tenants of Charnelchambers were foreigners in this foreign dark land. And as adversity, inclemency and loneliness could do in Dublin, it wed many a man and woman together. In consolation if not in bliss. But meanwhile what one was more and more conscious of in Ireland was that most times in which a rare refined atmosphere created and prevailed, there would not be one Irish born earthling present. But plenty were there I'm telling you, one night as I lay dreaming in the Princess's arms and was suddenly awakened by a long agonizingly blood curdling scream. Like none ever heard from man, beast or woman which proved to be a herald of what was to come.

It was a Saturday. The Princess and I had been to the races and Jammet's. And I was a rather shaken man. For the night before, returning past midnight to my rooms and mounting the entrance steps of number 38 Trinity College, I had only gone a few steps into the dark hallway when I was grabbed from behind. I could feel my senses waning to unconsciousness in the process of being choked to death by an unbelievably strong pair of arms. I repeatedly slammed my elbows backwards into someone's ribs until, just as the voices of a celestial choir began to be heard, they finally let go and I fell gasping to the stone floor. In the dim light of a college lamp I saw the unmistakable figure of my tall explosively tennis serving friend running away along the cobbled gutter and by the slung chains of the quad. The Princess reassured me that only very few of her suitor boyfriends ever got that jealous enough to actually kill. But with the evening wearing on past pub closing time she thought it best I not for the meanwhile venture in the dark back to college. And, of course, I was glad to avail of the tranquil, blissful, peaceful hospitality of her bed for the night. And that I would be safe there, my head tucked in against her shoulder, an embroidered coronet pressing against my cheek and finally asleep. Till a different complexion altogether descended upon these subterranean premises.

Basil's impecuniousness had like many of his tenants now reached rock bottom due to his equal penchant for high and elegant if not riotous living in about the better Dublin social venues. Such pursuits requiring much more money than he managed to collect in his weekly rents. He had also recently taken up the expensive pastime of racing and with his blond locks newly rinsed, enjoyed to travel there by a rented chauffeured Bugatti Royale landau. On one such outing to the Curragh in this astonishingly long bonneted vehicle, Smyth's of the Green had provided a hamper crammed full of exotics previously unobtainable during the war. And with the Princess, the Vicomte and me invited along, Basil flicking his ash out the car window from his long ivory cigarette holder announced to his comfortable guests:

'But how good of you all to come with humble me to the races. Decent champagne, don't you think. And rather good smoked salmon. I must as landlord with such distinguished tenants, keep up appearances, don't you agree. Of course, darlings, tonight is the first of my "bring and drink" parties which I shall keep as brief and quiet as possible.'

The Vicomte in one of his dungeon incarcerated periods was, of course, shrouded in Basil's all covering military mackintosh, and a pair of Wellington boots. His pyjamas underneath with their strange light blue and vertically bright red striped colours catching many an eye as one cruised about the paddocks. On the mornings following these first shindigs Basil was able to collect together the empty stout bottles and with a barrow and a tiny barefoot boy pushing, would proceed to redeem them for cash at the pub. Admission to Charnelchambers being, for those not already living there, a minimum two dozen parcel of stout or a bottle of spirits. But you might even, as one notorious entrepreneur did whose current girlfriend working in a butcher's purloined such, gain entrance with a couple of pounds of steak. And upon entrance frequently sold and bartered his remaining sirloins. He would also have in reserve sausages, dozens of eggs and bacon. These latter often ending up in the stomach of a particularly starving lady sculptress who would after repairing to a vault to accommodate this gentleman's prodigious biological urges attempt to sneakily conduct herself a great fry up on the stove. And would loudly announce upon finishing her gargantuan greasy feed, that she was ready to select the biggest penis present for dessert.

As the fame of Charnelchambers spread, the number of bottles needed for entry increased. But not all paid admission however. For there were those who were welcomed without hindrance. These were folk of the titled or discernibly upper classes, having in their gowns and dinner jackets just taken leave of parties and balls and in search of fashionable low life, sought to confirm for themselves rumours heard north and south of the Liffey and the length and breadth of Dublin. Basil receiving them in his nightly naked and stiff appendaged condition at the door.

'Ah my dears and darling intending débauchees. By your vowels shall ye be known. Or indeed if you're not speaking, then by a peek, my dears, at your better and further particulars when the ladies' gowns are up and the gentlemen's trousers are down.'

Never was there ever a shortage of potential entrants to Charnelchambers. Ferocious battles often taking place at the door. Basil employing a docker or two from the Dublin quays to keep out some of the more objectionable types who would sometimes in a gang storm down the iron steep steps from the street, as even more would pile down the stairs behind them. But there were times too when some perspicacious people upon entering, took one brief look and were wisely instantly screaming to get out. As this reaction alone made them highly desirable to be made part of the profligacy within, such victims were often, utterly hysterical, actually pulled and dragged further over the threshold and the door locked behind them. Gurriers, aging newsboys, street walkers, amateur bookies, and others of poor reputations could only gain admittance in the company of someone known to Basil. And as many were known, Basil upon their flutes having played, few gurriers were ever refused admittance.

But as the nights wore on there was a variation on the theme of human beings that the Emerald Isle had not known before and may not have ever come to know since. In attendance, were hypnotists, carpet fitters, magicians, market gardeners, and upholsterers. These latter ready to cover anything in burlap which was all the rage of interior designers of the time. There were picture framers who would without hesitation perforate a canvas around your ears. Wrought iron craftsmen, and one who had actually made a cage to imprison virgins. Lady chiropodists, who would treat more than your long toe nails. Practitioners of acupuncture, one or two of whom, let me tell you, were up to their very own special kind of prodding. There were quislings from Sweden, Norway and Belgium. Safecrackers and spivs from England. Gas meter readers and earbitersoff. The latter so referred to as a group since in most battles there were those whose gnashing teeth would instantly go towards this hearing appendage. And many a chewed ear was found next morning on the Charnelchamber floor. And even a pure black African gentleman who adorned in his princely robes arrived with a retinue of servants carrying pots of cooked rice and a cauldron of boiled chickens. And with three drummers and their drums in tow, by god would he do an Irish jig.

Sadly, to an altogether previously benign habitat of Charnelchambers there finally arrived wholesale violence within the precincts. For which one pleads forgiveness for having albeit in self defence, first perpetrated. It was upon a misty depressingly damp evening when the Princess and I were huddling together in her narrow bed for warmth. The Princess's pot to piss in at the time was out of action having sprung a leak. And having had much stout to drink out in a pub I was putting off the evilly cold moment of heading out into the rat infested courtyard to the latrine. Although I could put her silk dressing gown on over my shoulders, my feet would not fit into the Princess's slippers. So in the sockless clammy discomfort of my own shoes, I unbolted and unlocked the door and stumbled out into the courtyard inclemency to the dreadfully inhospitable water closet there. Upon my return from an extremely long pee, there was a strange man inside the room. He was attempting to further pull back the covers from the Princess whose bosoms were already exposed as she clung with one hand to an edge of a coronet embroidered linen sheet. For some reason a British rather than an American expression seemed to leave one's lips, attesting to the bias of one's life within Trinity College.

'Damn it, sir, what do you think you're about.'

As I was in the Princess's kimono the obnoxious gent assumed he was facing a push over cream puff transvestite. Many of whom had been recently featuring as late late guests in Charnelchambers. His reply to my inquiries was, to say the least, not only rude but objectionably suggestive. And concerned the possible three of us there and then doing something together. I then repeatedly, firmly but politely requested him to pronto depart.

· 'Like bejesus fucking hell I will you English pansy.'

The next thing I knew I was having my face slapped. Which, considering previous mayhems, was innocuous enough. But one thing I had already learned in Ireland was not to, on such moments as this, stand on ceremony. For your man without declaiming his intentions, had already lowered his head and was about to butt me in the solar plexus. Stepping a pace back as he charged forward, I gathered every ounce of my weight behind my right clenched fist. Circling it past my knee upwards and letting it flower into what was clearly the most unmerciful uppercut ever unleashed. Catching your man on the left cheekbone and parting his feet from the stone floor which took him over, without touching, the seat of the Princess's Louis XV giltwood chaise. As one does at such times, you notice a lot of significant things and one happened to catch sight of a jewel encrusted dagger which the Princess had in her hand. Of course as the man reeled out the door holding his face pouring blood I was horrified. But at least he was still alive as he might not have been had he tangled with the Princess. His silhouette lurching side to side along the hall and upon reaching the front kitchen your man fainted face forward in the doorway. Appearing as an actor might in limelight. With a bone crashing sound as his skull hit the stone floor. A cacophony of voices rose with the cry.

'By God who hit him with a hatchet, who hit him. Let's get the dirty fucker who did that. Up the Republic.'

This was the more sporting side of Charnelchamber life. Those who were physically aggrieved did instantly attract their champions who immediately sought to wreak retribution. However this moment was, put in its historical context, merely the beginning of many ensuing nocturnal carnages to take place in these cellar crypts. For when your man disappeared off to the hospital, the most awful slaughter of the innocents took place that night. The Vicomte happily for him being ensconced spending his monthly emolument in his one week splurge at the Shelbourne Hotel. The Princess even thinking her room had better be turned into an infirmary. Which suggestion I vetoed vehemently, as the thumps and bangs boomed against the door. For this mob of your gentleman's avengers out on their spree were already marauding into the various tunnels and vaults. Descending upon the trusting guiltless occupants there even as they lay asleep. Then dragging them out into the hall and beating the living daylights out of them. Indeed women found entwined with men also became innocent victims. The Princess's door however remained securely bolted and locked and reinforced with two stout oak timbers slotted into place. While the Princess inside professed no knowledge of anything outside to the belligerently inquiring voices. And I anxiously shivered in her protectively enveloping arms. Terrified as much now by the dagger she obviously kept somewhere handy when she was abed.

Although the previously peaceful nature of Charnelchambers changed to one of acrimony and animal viciousness, nevertheless occasional moments of charm were still to be enjoyed. Including one unforgettable evening when a considerable number of members of a travelling circus arrived. Such folk spent long months slogging on tour across Ireland's countryside, performing in cold, windswept and rain leaking tents and shuttling about in trailers and caravans. And down in these cellars they seemed glad of a little change to the home like intimacy, as it were. Albeit in the company of a notorious tinker widely known and feared as Lead Pipe Daniel The Dangerous who had shepherded them to Charnelchambers, laden with booze of every description. And it wasn't long before the place was festivity itself and literally jumping. With three midget acrobats bouncing around like balls.

The Princess and I undid her barriers that night, and indeed dressed as for the opera where in fact we were headed but instead with Peter playing accompanying airs on his violin we formed a select audience right then and there in Charnelchambers as all these circus folk one after another performed on the kitchen table. All except the Iron Lady, a weight lifter, who had the whole lot of us sit on the table as she commenced to balance it while elevating it two handed over her head until our own heads were hitting the ceiling and doubt as to our safety was being expressed. Next was Madame Splitcrotch the contortionist with one leg straight up and the other straight down as she spun like a top and then turned herself into several sorts and shapes of pretzels. A lady sword swallower who had not a sword with her, did her act in the most obscene but none the less impressive manner possible. Lead Pipe Daniel The Dangerous providing a personal priapus which made the Princess gasp in disbelief and which the lady swallower engulfed to its hairy hilt. While a mortified outraged Peter refused to play. Indeed he stormed out. Which was as it happened just as well. For moments later his Stradivarius might have had a bath in jets of water.

The gathering otherwise was having such a good jolly peaceful if bawdy time. With another batch of uninvited revellers arriving. Until most perilous of all, but at least seemly, the fire eater while digesting his flames set the kitchen alight, igniting the Hessian wall hangings with their pornographic tableaux. The pompiers were called. And as you might expect meanwhile, someone threw on a bucket of piss. Stinking the place to high heaven. As people all at once tried to get out and up again to the street, the front door became jammed shut. And there was a god almighty surge to the rear. Which met head on with Lead Pipe Daniel mid corridor. returning as he was from having had his way with a lady temporarily residing within a vault, who was a distinguished professor of anthropology referred to as Molly Of The Apes. Not only was Lead Pipe Daniel, the ape, grunting and growling with satisfaction, but he was also emptying a whisky bottle down his throat which could shortly mean one of the most vicious and terrifying people in the length and breadth of Ireland was about to act up. All six foot five inches tall and seventeen stone of him. Announcing.

'Ah God, one good woman fucked gives me such an appetite for another. And as an illiterate untouchable humble tinker I don't mind telling you I prefer the lady intellectuals.'

In spite of the yells of fire, Lead Pipe Daniel The Dangerous thought the mob was rushing him, and was instantly grabbing around himself for a suitable length of his usual weapon after which he was named. But thank God he was not near plumbing. Instead merely fists and boots left, right and centre were being landed, until mercifully the fire fighters arrived. Not only dousing the conflagration but everyone in sight. The Princess and I only being saved from a soaking by managing to get back into the safety of her room. And dear me there we stood in our evening finery. The Princess near to tears. With another barbarian head bashing, testicle twisting affray substituting for opera that night. For that was the trouble with Charnelchambers. No matter what innocent pleasantry was in progress it inevitably ended up in some form of diabolical grief. Which you were always damn lucky wasn't terminal. And reflected in Lead Pipe Daniel's oft quoted poem.

Bad as I am
I am not for nothing
Daniel the Dangerous
The Lead Pipe Maniac
Searching for truth and justice
All over the fucking zodiac

Ah but enough of recounting the mayhem. It should not be forgot that it was in Dublin where soda water was first invented. And in the sphere of human ingenuity lay one other of the most astonishing aspects of Charnelchambers. For down in these dungeons also collected together some of the greatest thinkers, axiologists, scientists, philosophers and moral tacticians of this or any epoch. Although the tenets of such schools of thought as Bishop Berkeley's Immaterialism were long established by this Trinity College man, the bings, zings and nerts of nuclear fission and fusion had only then been a few years postulated. Indeed in Dublin lived one or two who had taken the first steps to disintegrate the nucleus of an atom which brought the dawn of the atomic age. And which has now led to folk spying upon the quarks, ziffs and piffs zinging tangential off their innocent electrons. In fairness to such eminent persons one does not suggest for one microsecond that they hatched their theories or even visited or were within a mile of these notorious crypts. But begrudging sceptics should remember that it was within the damp night time walls of Charnelchambers where the more eccentric and some of the most brilliant of these great minds collected who promulgated conceptual essences which have since pervaded the entire thinking and drinking world. And when one such metaphysician was accused of frequenting this barbarian basement in order that he be able to consort with loose women and to booze and fornicate the night away in the company of other layabout waster whoremongers, he announced loud and clear for all to hear.

'And how better to think and speculate upon the concealments of the universe than to dip one's wick in the depths of hell where the sexual and intellectual temperature is at melting point.'

So, as blows, curses and slander flew, and women screamed away, or clustered in safe corners whimpering, there were still those Guinness stout sippers who remained resolutely discoursing in quantum physics, electromagnetic theory, wave mechanics and the acceleration and focusing of charged particles. But, too, could be heard less rarefied discussion concerning the causes of the occasional abundance and scarcity of ladybird insects in the environs of St Stephen's Green. Nor was the trivial mundane ever eschewed. The cause and frequency of rain in Ireland and the effect it had on the psyches of the natives was a recurrent theme. Which sadly led to more heads being wooled and broken than nearly any other subject ever mentioned.

As well as the brilliance there were those who were of an immediate practical bent. Especially a trinity of gentlemen better known as The Awful Three. Who perhaps more than anyone helped to bring the days of Charnelchambers to a close. Composed of a geologist mining engineer, a musicologist part time undertaker and a philosopher of no fixed occupation or address, these eccentric persons were always one expedient jump ahead of everyone. In a pair of boots the geologist was often seen at midnight tramping through Dublin's most fashionable shopping venue, Grafton Street, pushing a wheelbarrow aglow with a lantern and full of instruments of exploration, pails, hammers and chemicals. A confirmed absolute atheist pagan, this gentleman, so scrupulously polite that no one ever could find cause to upbraid him, took one look at the Charnelchamber floor from whence now trickled the spring sprung at the time of the appearance of the Blessed Virgin to the devout member of The Legion of Decency. The geologist dipping his finger in the water, tasted it and in a thrice he and his cohorts were wielding pickaxes to take up the paving stones and with shovels digging where he said his Geiger counter nearly jumped out of its box registering readings. And they duly proceeded vertically down. At the time one certainly did not know if these gentlemen would find their precious and rare metals. But certainly there was no fear of fire when the geologist and his two assistants were finished. For by god the presence of water was everywhere, with the whole of Charnelchambers aflood a foot deep.

The Awful Three did compensate Basil and his other tenants handsomely and as fervent admirers of continental aristocracy, they cemented a waterproof bulkhead across the Princess's and Adolphus's doors to keep their rooms dry. In due course they also provided those inmates who did not immediately flee, with an elaborate network of stepping stones. But continue to explore they did. Erecting a caisson around where they dug. Till finally in muddy exasperation both the Princess and Adolphus moved out. The Princess taking up a post as housekeeper in a large Irish country house with Adolphus as butler. The understanding being that when the Vicomte's emolument arrived he was to revert to being a paying guest. An arrangement which after the Vicomte's first week as a guest proved fatally difficult even in the ultra eccentric atmosphere of your usual Anglo Irish country house. As Adolphus when he should have been butlering continued to smoke cigars and drink sherry all morning while lying in the bath.

But the nightly visitors still came to Charnelchambers. Some of whom were rumoured to be international secret agents and counter spies. And who mingled among those, whose only claim to notoriety was to have pawned and sold their worldly goods in order to drink the proceeds and now didn't mind risking standing or falling into water up to their knees. But there did remain, too, a few diehard thinkers who felt wet feet helped them delve into the obtuse infinities of the universe. Some drunkenly submerging even as they spouted facts and exactitudes of specific dimensions. But Charnelchambers without its previous elegant tenants who contributed at least some charm and grace to the atmosphere, was now, more than ever, a dangerous place. Groups of glowering malcontents collected who, along with their slandering, gossip, revilements, backbiting and character assassination which always led to fisticuffs, now resorted to the far more lethal chastisement of dunking.

With the Princess gone I returned but once more to Charnelchambers on a late Sunday afternoon to hopelessly fumble in the water now seeped in under the bulkhead of her room, to search for cufflinks I'd lost. Not trusting the stepping stones I came in a pair of trout fishing hip boots. Basil was asleep in his vault, snoring and gently floating in a dinghy. I found myself disbelievingly standing among a handful of professional scientists and a museum curator who invited by The Awful Three, watched the excavation and the mud being removed from some precious ancient gold Celtic artefacts. There were as well a sideline amateur or two who were equally enthralled not only with the treasure trove but also with the engineering brilliance of this mining shaft which had now penetrated down into the bowels of Dublin city. Admittedly no one at the time in all the stack of mud and depth of water, was tussling with the subjectively distant unknowns concerning the innards of the atom. Or waving a frustrated fist trying to get their theories heard. Everything seemed to be perfectly normal as one listened to the learned comments concerning the gold chalices and bracelets, and to the crunch of the digging far below. And why shouldn't someone without planning permission quite reasonably be engaged in mineral and archeological exploration in the basement of someone's innocent building. Ah, but there was a reason. Which came without warning. As disaster struck. And methane gas exploded. All of us were knocked backwards into the water. The spring poured forth with a vengeance once more. And screams erupted to get out, get out. But by god in the hand of one of The Awful Three there were not only the ancient gold artefacts but the confirming sample attesting to the presence of the metal for which they were originally searching.

Amazingly no one was injured. The Awful Three immediately taking credit that this was so. Even to the ridiculous point of suggesting the safety factor of there being water into which one was blasted flat. Suddenly one could understand this Ireland, and from whence came its strange intellectual dynamics. In other lands and places, similar professional gentlemen would be confined to institutions for the mentally unusual or at least restricted to traditional modes of experiment and scientific reasoning cooped up in their laboratories. But here down in Charnelchambers the great minds instead could commune with these variously doomed spirits and from their melancholy quibbling could even derive verities to formulate an equation which would explain time. Or even find a cube root of an infinity which would explain space. Here where the air vibrated hot with the intellectual wattage of the habitués and profound perceptions blossomed from the mathematical purity of the wit. Especially concerning the origin of the next drink. But where even among the most erudite of these minds, no conceit or pomposity was ever displayed.

But pure science and its triumphs were not the only reasons for Charnelchambers' claim to fame. For down here too came great artists from the world of the theatre, mime, ballet, puppeteering and even papier mâché. And practising the latter was a gentleman who was the first ever to make replicas of the head of the Blessed Oliver Plunkett, long before his sainthood. These being sold to tourists by the entrepreneur who used to gain admittance with his steaks and sausages. And became the last man to remain in possession of Charnelchambers, taking the entire place over and installing a plethora of native born Irish. And was heard to announce shortly thereafter.

'By god look at that now, the British pagan while they were here kept it as neat as a pin. And now since our own have taken over, the place is a disgraceful filthy disgusting pigsty. And it's a fact, that what the Englishman doth hold together in beauty, the Irishman by god in violence doth tear asunder.'

Charnelchambers did indeed become even more violent than ever. With racecourse touts, newsboys and the friends and enemies of Daniel The Dangerous, driving away the scientific minds and lyric thinkers. And especially those who latterly became one of the first serious architectural preservation groups in Ireland. And had convened under the auspices of The Awful Three, and established themselves under the name, The Society For The Prevention Of Cruelty And Disgrace To Dublin. But the worst came upon the occasion of Daniel The Dangerous impersonating a priest and inviting an innocent group of young nuns from a convent to attend at the grotto of The Blessed Virgin. And upon their descent into Charnel-chambers the nuns were invited by the ecclesiastically robed Daniel The Dangerous to commit a grossly indecent act.

Ah, but then to remember it was where once such was the eminent comings and goings to this refuge for temporarily distressed gentle-folk, that many a newsboy through a long cold night fought to station himself just at the top of the steps. There in snow and rain selling his newspapers and opening and closing doors of the arriving horse cabs out of which your gentry either stepped or flopped. Sadly whenever one climbed up those steps one always recalled Charnelchambers before it had ever become a scandalous bunker of the damned. Remembering it upon my first occasions there as a place of peace and spiritual refreshment. The night haunted by the agonizingly beauti-ful strains of Peter's Stradivarius as those vibrating strings sounded their strangely painfully sweet chords which just as strangely made one weep. But making one in the glooms of life glad to be alive again on this Gaelic trolley ride through the universe.

But to Charnelchambers, as the Irish poured in, there came too, one who made Daniel The Dangerous seem but as a celestial choir boy. Wives deserting husbands to throw themselves at his feet. And husbands deserting wives, their jobs and vocations merely to listen to him speak. Evicted by other landlords, he even appeared with a whole family of three children. The eyes of these tiny creatures could be seen hiding in the shadows and watching. Until finally came the departure of Basil himself. Dear old wonderful Basil who started it all. And was during his last days posing nude for an English lady painter who specialized in studies of gentlemen. Especially 'The Male Rampant' as many of her pictures were called. And not that long after his portrait in full length and stiffness was completed, he one dawn nearly got murdered in his dinghy bed. For a remark passed, concerning the face of this new Irish tenant's wife. This taken as an insult by the aggrieved husband, who after a late night out in the pubs and Bonafides working up his appetite for revenge, came creeping in his socks into the small wine cellar cave where Basil slept in the bottom of his boat which now rested on the damp paving stones. From the door your man took a tiger's flying leap. Landing with a great earthshaking thump on his knees on top of the sleeping Basil's chest. Who woke to find a powerful pair of hands around his throat squeezing it to the consistency of a bootlace. Only just still alive by morning, Basil decided he'd had enough. Of fights, battles and blood. Of people of every hue, cry and description ascending and descending his basement stairs. With motives mostly malign. His destination was as far away from Dublin as the Kashmir Mountains. To whence he said he would go and forever stay. As far as humanly possible away from Dublin. And speak only ever again in his beloved Sanskrit. And where sadly one has learned he how lies buried. A brief epitaph upon his tombstone.

I did my dears
At least have the courage
Of my desires

VII

Had he lived Basil would now never believe that in the years following his departure there existed a committee invoking his name which had approached the Tourist Board to have preserved those notorious crypts of Charnelchambers as a national shrine as the Lourdes of Ireland. For as you might know the vasectomized and pagan Awful Three made not only a fortune out of their previous archeological finds and metal deposits but also bottled holy water and manufactured religious artefacts, rosaries, scapulars, and holy pictures. Selling all these as having been blessed at the shrine dug so sincerely deep in that dungeon. But so that they would appeal locally to the natives such artefacts were imprinted as having come from Czechoslovakia.

Ah, but before entering upon another subject not entirely alien to the one just left, you may well wonder who on earth or in all that mud and pain was the freehold or leasehold owner of the land below and the building above, of which Charnelchambers formed the cellars and foundations. And I myself always marvelled that whoever he or she might be, they could never be accused, as every other landlord in Ireland could, of being nosey concerning their tenants' morals and standards of behaviour. But as many of the great old Georgian buildings of Dublin, if not being knocked down, were falling down anyway, many a landlord could afford and did take the attitude, live and let live. And bloody well get as much rent as you can while the walls still stand.

In a place as small as Dublin secrets were hard to keep. But the identity of the free or leasehold owner of Charnelchambers remained a mystery. Until Peter, during one of our last nights down in the crypts, pointed him out to me. And I was astonished to find he was one of the few people in Charnelchambers outside of Peter, Adolphus, Basil and the Princess, to whom I had ever spoken, and indeed did so at some length. For I immediately took to this strange gentleman's kindly, most benign and seemingly religious demeanour, who was such an entirely different kettle of fish to those swimming around him in his cellars. Admitting, of course, some little bias in this, as I recognized him as someone who had bought two or three of my amateurish paintings. Being as he was a generous patron and collector who worshipped art in all its forms. And upon the occasions this gent had incognito appeared down in his own very premises, he always arrived alone with a bottle of whisky, stood alone and departed alone. And regularly wearing a light tan trilby hat, a drab mackintosh buttoned conspicuously closed at the neck and his hands plunged deep into its pockets. Because of the constant trace of a smile he wore he was referred to as Your Man Mona Lisa. And indeed by this name was he designated when I was first introduced. Basil himself never knew nor did any of his tenantry ever learn who he was. When he was asked and answered that he was a patron of the arts, it was assumed he was on release from an institution and with such aspirations would remain harmless enough.

The rent for Charnelchambers was collected every Friday morning by ten by a solicitor's clerk who wore a light tan trilby hat and drab mackintosh buttoned tight at the neck almost identical to Your Man Mona Lisa upon whose behalf he acted. Peter said he was an ardent music lover, but would disclose no further concerning his identity. But I did at least learn who it was this strange landlord had as one close friend. None other than my tennis playing partner of the 200 mile an hour serve who attempted to strangle me to death. But I did not yet know this when Your Man Mona Lisa stood at my elbow down in Charnelchambers when he in his first strange shy whisper quietly informed me.

'I am not particularly devout but do perform my religious duties as a Catholic. I am not a paederast, bigamist nor I hope a bombast, nor indeed any kind of curious person. For which in this most refreshingly liberal minded company I apologize. I am instead a shy individual to whom God in his infinite kindness, if not wisdom, has given a certain financial substantiality. I write nothing, paint nothing, compose nothing, sculpt nothing, invent nothing. But I do so enjoy to be here merely to listen to and merely watch those of you who do all these things.'

Of course, not one of these habitués present, that Your Man Mona

Lisa referred to, had so much as written a word, painted an X, sculpted a lump or composed a note in a millennium. Including, too, yours truly who had merely latterly achieved notoriety by embarrassing everyone in Dublin by exhibiting a collection of still wet paintings. Which some wiseacre referred to as being work of my sticky period and guaranteed fresh in off the palette. But the true nature of Ireland was slowly unfolding. The art of living here was to be alive and listened to. Or as happened more often, to be told to shut up and be all ears before you had them bit off you altogether. And while you drank, talked, sang, disputed or gossiped, you might merely mildly worry as to who would buy the next round. But by God don't stop to think you're anybody special or anointed because you write, paint, sculpt or compose.

To some modest degree one had oneself adapted to Irish behaviour. Ignoring the rain, chill and discomfort, and even indeed occasionally enjoying it. But you did finally wonder, where did you go among the natives of this land, noted worldwide for its charm and friendliness to the stranger, to find more than a handful of decent, fair minded citizens. Men and women free of their thick coatings of repressive obtuse bigotry which held them imprisoned by their thwarted erotic desires. A condition known as suffering from the crut. And after a sample evening in Charnelchambers where some of this crut was nightly chipped off, you'd wonder sincerely and deeply where were all the saints and scholars, for whom this isle was famed. Or indeed for the matter of that where were all your actual writing writers, versifying poets and composing composers. The answer was, by God, they were everywhere. And in their myriad abundance. In every nook and cranny of the civil service. Even the gas company. And all the branches of the government. And mostly, by evening, sitting inert, facing their blank pieces of paper.

And now to fully enter upon the subject not entirely alien to Charnelchambers. Welcome then to the world of Irish art and literature. From whence an abundance of world celebrated writers has come. Who in each case performed an absolute and utter miracle of survival. For such men and women were on every side met by opposition both public and private to all their words and deeds. Such scheming hindrance in more than half, perpetrated by their contemporary would be writers and artists. And a more bitter, resentful and treacherous crew you'd spend a hard lifetime's work trying to find. Who did by their backbiting and venting envy attempt to still these lyric voices. Causing them to gather up their written sheets of paper, pack their bags and go down to the Dublin quays to board the mail boat for England.

But some with their penned words so few, did stay. Drinking and betting in the city. They were the word counters, adding up each one they managed to gruellingly scratch out on a page. As an encouragement to go on. And above all not stop if once you've started. To have at least at the end of each day a page, a paragraph or a sentence. And to least of all worry about what it said. And be better off than those without words at all to count. Who stared hours, days and weeks away, facing the blank sheet of paper. Pulled from their fresh stacks of more blank sheets. Their sharpened pencils ready to scribble and their typewriters oiled, ready to tap. Those few who had such typewriters and those, less than a few, who had such oil. As there they sat in their ill illumined quiet back rooms. A neat pile of turf awaiting to be put on the just lit smouldering fire. And in these romantically inclined gentlemen's minds, great literature was already alight and living. Tomes lying open to their favourite pages. Chapters unfolding as they saw themselves in the image of other famed past writers. Perhaps more in the Russian manner than in the French. An exiled Turgenev rather than a coffee drinking Balzac. And tomorrow when they really got down to work and wrote all over that blank page and filled those in wait, the publishers would be clamouring. The presses roaring. The masses buying, borrowing and grabbing and reading your every word. The royalties pouring in from every corner and language across the globe.

But back here now in Ireland, here in Dublin, down this rhododendron leafy street in Ranelagh or Rathgar. The kimonos remained draped at the ready. As the long night grows chilled. And never further than an elbow away sits a pack of twenty of your pink packed expensively priced 'Passing Clouds' cigarettes. Ready to be puffed, and the smoke sent overhead, and the ash tapped in the ashtray. The woman of the house to whom you were eight years betrothed before you got joined in the grimness of marriage, has fixed supper. Placed on your desk under a warmer. Two veg, chunk of ham and peeled boiled potatoes. Under a cosy is a pot of strong tea. The wife has gone to make a novena. And without her nagging complaint, silence reigns. Because in this beyond, here in the suburban edges of Dublin in these shrubbery environs, the general respectability is such that not one of your neighbours wants to be observed doing exactly what the other is doing. Writing a book.

But above all never let it be said or even suggested that such native born and reared men in their kimonos and puffing out their 'Passing Clouds' are of no consequence as writers. Or indeed were not already part of the great literature to which they aspired. For, modestly unbeknownst to themselves, they were. They'd read every trumpeted classic author. Or at least prepared damn well to pretend they had. Or were primed with the lore of these famed authors' lives. In the image of which they lived their own lives and they were if nothing else, discerning critics. Their collective atmosphere hung over Dublin. They awaited, even as they shunned and damned them, to read the work of the handful of writers in this land who wrote. And they, above all, remained open minded. Ready, before they condemned, to listen to the composers who composed. Or quote the poets who versified. And they would upon a Tuesday come from near and far to lurk in the pubs around the central city. Standing at the edges of gatherings. And were, some of them, the men about whom the writers wrote. And the latter were, because they did, quaking in fear of libel. Because having managed themselves to chip off their crut and put pen to paper and push, they found they hadn't a good or decent word to say about anybody. And the pursuit of such grievance resulting from such ridicule and contempt, was a much sought after opportunity eagerly availed of, there being no shortage of lawyers in Dublin. Such legal action often being easy to pursue, for there was nothing like using your man's real name for the sake of clarity. And making what he fictionally did as scurrilous as possible for the sake of reality. And, by God, meeting as one would do every day at court with the newspapers full of it, did your battle against obscurity a damn sight of good.

But to the origins of the literary stirrings. Let us go. In those days you could find them all happening within a donkey's roar of Grafton Street. A sound, too, you could hear coming out of some of the more prominent of the protagonists. As they went from pub to betting shop and back. Their noses in the racing sheets in the hope of winning, and roaring like scalded animals if they lost. But if fortune was smiling you can bet they were in haste to be a mile away in a different pub from their impecunious cronies, buying each round for themselves in their contented loneliness. But literary life was not all wagering on the horses. Occasionally you could find discreet, cultivated, non roaring gentlemen. Central among whom was a young man with the simple name of John Ryan. He had surplus to his needs what few people in Ireland had in those days. Namely and plainly money. His was a face I saw again and again at the various better and more respectable bashes. But to whom I had never spoken further than being introduced forty nine times. His behaviour never ostentatious nor even apparently rich. Then it was upon one Saturday autumn morning on the way to the races at Leopardstown that I, in the company of a friendly gentleman of another plain name, Pat O'Reilly, who, known to everyone, for he had been an Irish champion ballroom dancer, called at a large country house, Burton Hall. We were shown by a black uniformed, white aproned maid upstairs and along a corridor. As the door opened to a large comfortably furnished bedroom, faint sunlight streamed in the window after rain. In front of a white marble chimney piece stood an easel with a massive portrait of Wolfe Tone in the course of being painted. The picture was carefully marked off in squares to copy from a photograph similarly marked off. Ryan stood with his palette and brushes and for the fiftieth time I was introduced to this indisposed young gentleman recovering from a nasty bout of 'flu. It was to be my first serious, sober encounter with the Irish world of art. And I was memorably stunned to here find this gentleman so far away from the social turmoil of Dublin and content in his own solitude.

John Ryan seemed entirely different from your usual run of Irish folk. In his rakish tweed jacket and often a bright cheerful tweed tie loosely knotted at the collar of his silk shirt, his casual neat cleanliness alone, just following the war, bespoke of at least having some wherewithal. Quiet, unassuming, unfailingly polite, Ryan pleasantly listened as other people spoke. And only when they were finished their say would he then gently and equally pleasantly tell his own amusing story. Underlying every turn of which would always be an abundance of Irish irony. And I became one of his ardent listeners. But then, too, my ears would have pricked up at the mention of anything to do with writing, or indeed mention of that name James Joyce which had so much to do with my coming to this land in the first place. And suddenly in some astonishment after all the mad endless parties, I discovered through this gentleman, there was another

John Ryan in front of 38 Trinity College Dublin. Ryan was an early frequent visitor and would decorate with drawings the tiles of my fireplace as we would talk with James Leathers and others and sip Guinness late into the night. Ryan said there was nowhere else in Dublin he enjoyed to visit more than the monastic ancient enclosure of Trinity.

world in Ireland, an actual Irish world of culture. Albeit occasionally if vaguely connected with the sort of comings and goings one had encountered in the dungeons of Charnelchambers. But a world where fists weren't always flying and where you wouldn't, instead of listening to Mendelssohn, get a violin wrapped around your throat.

Before leaving Burton Hall that day we took Madeira in the music room and Ryan sat to the piano and played 'The Lark In The Clear Air', a piece inspired and composed in the vicinity of this very chamber. As the name of Joyce came up, Ryan appeared to have an astonishing knowledge of this man, his life and his work. He had all his books and a recording of Joyce reading from *Finnegans Wake*. And as nearly everywhere one ventured in the city of Dublin bespoke of him, Joyce was a frequent topic of conversation. Ryan knew the streets, the doorways, pubs and people Joyce wrote of. Some of them still alive and if not kicking at least ready to quaff a ball of malt or a pint as they would reminisce of this exiled author. Each scrap of information eagerly sought. Such places as we ourselves frequented as Davy Byrnes, the Bailey, conjured up stories and the ghosts of this man. Even places as anonymous as Clontarf and Sandymount reverberated with awe and atmosphere at the mention of his name. Of course Joyce knew Dublin in more tranquil times. When the like of Lead Pipe Daniel The Dangerous was not at large. Nor folk like The Awful Three. Nor indeed Brendan Behan or the American from Ohio, the saintly Gainor Stephen Crist.

Ryan too had a familiar knowledge of the one or two actually living and published working writers of the day such as Samuel Beckett, the scholarly, brilliant cricketer, product of Trinity College. Who had already transported himself from these shores. And of whose work 'More Pricks Than Kicks' I first heard mentioned down in the vaults of Charnelchambers. And which title in the context of the place, I associated more with penises and feet shod in hob nailed boots which were landing in your ribs, than with the sharp prods of misfortune. It was one of the first works I'd heard of produced by a living Irish writer, whose words in no way resembled a tourist brochure. Or sounded as if the author were covered all over in crut.

There were too, of their sort, what one might even refer to as salons in Dublin. These, not your legendary type where tea and sherry were taken aseat on your Louis XV chaise longues in elegant drawing rooms with your established notable men of letters in attendance. But your more rough and ready venue where someone's teeth might be pulling the cork out of a bottle of stout. Even so, these latter coarse textured parlours were more than occasionally frequented by scholarly gentlemen of astonishingly accumulated erudition. And one such salon was established right there smack in Grafton Street. Right in a building owned by Ryan's family business, the Monument Creameries. And in these premises, paying little or no rent, Ryan would allow the odd friend in pursuit of art to stay. In some comfort too, as there was a fitted green Wilton carpet, hot and cold running water, lamps, chairs, couches and other amenities. And some of these occupants were later to distinguish themselves in the fields of poetry, writing, painting and even sculpture. Making Dublin's most fashionable street the unlikely source of fine art.

But studded elsewhere over Dublin, were other ateliers in which thinkers, writers, composers and painters were lurking. And to these Ryan would periodically pay a visit. Occasionally, I went in his company. Always prepared for the no less than bizarre. Finding that such places would inevitably be crammed with the unbelievable. From venomous reptiles to birds of paradise. Or perhaps, safer less exotic amenities, but thought precious to these gentlemen in their fields of endeavour. And more than once involving the less than salubrious. Which in this case concerned an enormous pile of turf in the corner of the room in which was established a not inconsiderable compost heap. And into which went all this gentleman's bodily functions, plus left over potatoes, tea leaves and slops. In order to complete the life cycle therein, various vegetation and fungi sprouted on top. As calling time was usually prior to lunch, one tried as inconspicuously as possible to hold one's breath. For although our host claimed his manure pile to be without odour, and indeed would in proving this stand over it and deeply inhale several times while his fists beat on his chest, nevertheless one did nearly keel over from an utterly lethally disagreeable fume. The other tenant of the building being a wrecked car repairer who occupied the garage below and was usually wearing a mask as he sprayed vehicles. But then as our host served tea, burned incense and played on a small organ, music of his own composition, the stench miraculously and completely disappeared.

Ah, but back to the absolute eye of the hurricane, the address of 39 Grafton Street. Beneath which too emanated the smell of a renowned fish shop. This Victorian brick edifice stood across from the golden frieze of Woolworth's Five and Ten Cents Store. And Ryan's family business occupied it as it did several other Grafton Street buildings. Next to the fish shop on the ground floor was a large Monument Creamery café, which served meals and had both a bakery and grocery. Next to it, one entered a narrow hall and climbed up a flight of stairs. It was here at the top that one turned left to a suite of rooms Ryan had established for himself. The front room over the fish shop he used as a studio and back as a reception room and office. If a drink were needed in the pub as it invariably was following anyone's meeting one another for more than three minutes, folk would only have to descend the stairs, step out across the street and walk twenty yards to the corner, turn left by the exotic furs displayed in a window and proceed past Tom Nisbet's painting gallery and into John McDaid's pub. Which advertised 'Where the drink is efficacious and the conversation effervescent'. Slowly but surely this converted church at 3 Harry Street with its cold, barren, lofty interior, its grim downstairs lavatory and a back door out to a side lane, became an established meeting place for poets, painters, writers, and various

Interior McDaid's pub. Centred seated together and fourth from left Tony McInerney, Randall Hillis, Brendan Behan, Gainor Crist, and extreme right Desmond McNamara the puppeteer and sculptor and first frequenter of McDaid's. This astonishing photograph taken by one of Dublin's roving photographers was later obtained by Randall Hillis and may stand as the only photographic record of such intellectually sophisticated gentlemen all having an unrehearsed drink together.

chancers and con men, the latter who, poor souls, erroneously thought such people worth associating with. Although this public house had a bemused owner and an extremely pleasant and understanding bartender, the only one in Dublin to have ever bought yours truly a drink, nevertheless this big grim room to have become celebrated in any manner, was a mystery to all who went there. But it was certainly a place where many an insult and snub was delivered and fist thrown, and many a lady's tear was shed.

There was, all over Dublin plenty of space and time for the outspoken word. But by God to put it in print you had no shortage of troubles. And for a sincerely lyric word, the only possible outlet was the literary magazines. One such *The Bell*. The sound of which was then fading. And to which I submitted an early poetic effort. To finally have it rejected. But not ignored. Harry L. Craig who worked on the magazine and whom one later met in the pub Davy Byrnes, recalled my name and the poem. This handsome well built gentleman said he had not only read it but even thought of publishing it. Of course already having experienced in Ireland what was generally known as plamoss, one disbelieved him on the spot but appreciated his attempt at mitigating the first kick in my literary teeth. Which, of course, in my brash fulminating omniscience, had left me utterly stunned and horrified.

Yet I soon came to learn that I might have been lucky. For the gossipy stories in the world of belles lettres did spread and reach my ears. Concerning the kind of Dublin editor one might unfortunately encounter. Who, hung over from the night before in the company of the literati, was usually late to work of a morning or more likely afternoon or indeed didn't show up for days at a time. And meanwhile might have left the likes of an aspiring literary gent named Brendan Behan minding the office. And such folk suddenly blessed in their jacket pockets with a blood pudding and sausage or two ready to cook, would not hesitate to stuff the fireplace grate with manuscripts and putting a match to them, would boil a kettle for tea and when the fire was roaring hot, scald their sausages stuck on the end of any handy fountain pen. And when such culprits were tackled for such acts there would be a plausible reply.

'Ah, I'll grant you, it isn't the kind of encouraging rumour young hopeful writers are likely to take comfort from hearing. But as it was myself cooking me own sausages and someone else's manuscripts doing the conflagrating, sure I'd like you to tell me if you can think of a better way of advancing up the literary ladder.'

But one problem you never had in Dublin. Was advertising yourself as a writer. Which could be done on nerve alone and was achieved as fast as you could split an infinitive. For if you didn't declare yourself you could soon have someone else sarcastically doing it for you. The mere careless mention of owning a pencil and piece of blank paper could make you the day's if not a lifetime's victim of ridicule. As had happened on that encounter with Behan in my earliest Irish literary experience when we were first introduced, and were unaware of the gathering's efforts to make such occasion their first big uproarious laugh of the day. With neither Behan nor I thinking it at all funny. Indeed as I recall again, my fists were already tightening as I confronted this mildly belligerent unkempt individual with his great shock of black hair and a broken and twisted nose nearly snarling on his face. And over the years one was to know Behan, his chest was nearly always blazoning from a stained and soiled open jacket, his crumpled shirt open to the navel, and his belly thrust out over a belt barely holding up his baggy worn trousers. But it was his stumpy fists and fingers with which he gesticulated while stammering that gave Behan an almost benign and endearing comportment that bespoke of him as a writer. In contrast to his incidental companion Lead Pipe Daniel The Dangerous, another proclaimed man of letters, his bellowing voice spouting his poetry which Behan would sometimes write out for me in my notebooks. Taking a mischievous delight in the fact that this great violent monster feared everywhere could pen adoring lines to the Blessed Virgin Mary. Albeit Lead Pipe Daniel would in his poetic vision have her situated somewhere up a tree and would, while singing his paean of praises to her be unable to avert his eyes from looking up her holy robes which resulted in the poem's last lines being invariably sacrilegious.

But then Behan himself could be a violent man, having served time for the attempted murder of a policeman and always ready to break a pint glass on a pub table and shove the resulting jagged edges in your face. In spite of this, he was just as quick to make peace as happened in our first encounter previously mentioned, squaring off in the middle of the street in front of Davy Byrnes when Behan could see I meant business. At the same time, having already become much familiar with armed and unarmed combat in Ireland, I had already taken a quick glance behind me for any accomplices sneaking up to wield a bottle on the back of my head. And was also careful to stay out of range not only of his fists but also a flying kick in the balls. My usual precaution being to sense the first flicker of movement in one of my opponent's muscles. At which moment I would feint with a left and then unleash a straight right fist to concuss central on the nose of such pertinent face. But suspicious though I was I did shake Behan's hand when it was put forth.

'Ah, there's no need to fight. Why should the pair of us out here beat the bejesus out of one another to the satisfaction of the eegit likes of them inside. Sure I'm a writer. And I meant no harm in calling you a narrowback. But I can tell by the way you're ready to fight about it, that you're a writer too. And fuck the ignorant bunch back in there who wouldn't know a present participle from a hole in their buried mother's coffins. Come on, the two of us, we'll go somewhere and have a drink. And we'll tell the story around that the both of us were so fast at getting out of the way of each other's fists, neither of us could land a punch.'

This was literary Dublin. Without a sign of a book in anyone's hand and where the spoken word was your ready claim to fame. Where no one would ask, as they would in America, if you had anything published. And if you did, how rich did you get. Here, if you dared, you could stand up and declare yourself. And know that the ridicule would spread far and wide behind your back. But at least you could be in your own eyes what you said you were. As I dared to be in this city where there already existed a few published writers and poets. Patrick Kavanagh, conspicuous among them. This man, his powerful arms folding his big farmer's hands across his chest walked the streets like a battleship plunging through the waves. And with whom pedestrian encounters were quick and decisive. Mostly amounting to a few salvoes from his sixteen inch guns. Which blasted at you if you were not too timorous to acknowledge him with some kind of greeting, to which was his invariable reply.

'Have you got a pound to give me.'

'No.'

'Well fuck off then.'

My rooms at 38 Trinity College became a salon of sorts. Even Behan turning up. Not in search of conversation but to buy guns for the I.R.A. whose seller, unbeknownst to me had asked to store them on top of my clothes cupboard where they lay for some time in a great stack under thick wrapping paper. But in more peaceful pursuit, John Ryan would appear on many a cold winter evening. Sit content hunched in front of a pathetic fire and while talking, draw pictures on the tiles of the fireplace as one talked. Sharing these rooms and often in the company, was James H. Leathers who quite literally was held by all who came into contact with him as being the most charming man ever to set foot in Dublin. From Los Angeles, California, this six foot five inch tall unhurried American, who was not, by the way, my strangler, nor did Leathers ever play tennis or take any other strenuous exercise, but was instead a collector of exotic gems, Icelandic literature and lover of music, theatre and ballet. Daily he would prowl the auction rooms buying books and pictures. And he had commissioned a Celtic silversmith to put some of his jewels in settings. Leathers also took a keen interest in Irish folklore and its

James H. Leathers in his leather motoring coat descending the steps of Trinity College dining hall. This extremely tall and ultra shy gentleman with whom I shared rooms, and whose company was sought by hosts and hostesses alike all over Dublin and who turned one's Trinity rooms into a social mecca with his legendary charm, had no equal. For which one was indeed glad as this human insulation he attracted prevented both Leathers and I from freezing to death during one of Europe's coldest winters.

homespun industry. Even to outfitting himself in Aran Islands' sweaters and socks. And appearing one day in pampooties. The latter a slipper sandal of undressed cowskin sewn together and tied across the instep. Which raw and nearly still bloody was not suitable for dinner parties. As my painting career started dead centre of our college sitting room, Leathers, having unearthed himself from beneath his nightly covering of hot water bottles, would appear late in the day a cup of tea warming his hands, and striving to make as diplomatically kind as possible comments on my painting efforts. One of his more extreme statements being.

'Ah, I see you are rather more this afternoon than yesterday clearly painting with a rather fuller brush.'

However Leathers' presence attracted people from all walks and kinds of Dublin life. Both men and women, all of whom, struck by the strange magnetism of his company seemed content merely to be silently in his presence. Indeed many a friendship came asunder as some of these folk fought bitterly among themselves vying for the privilege. His bedroom mornings could be packed to overflowing with tea drinking and cigarette smoking visitors. Whom he would receive while he lay supine head and shoulders propped up on pillows, working up his fortitude to brave the cold in getting out of bed. It was indirectly Leathers who led to my coming across many a modern writer whose existence was then unknown in Ireland. For one of our visitors who sought out his company and who, liking the free and easy nature of life in our Trinity chambers at number 38, moved into Leathers' vacated room when the latter finally could no longer take the cold and damp and returned by slow boat to California. This next occupant of Leathers' room, a Michael Heron, not only brought his own charming company into the premises, but also his collection of books. Of such authors as Henry Miller and Albert Camus, whose work and names were acknowledged elsewhere in Europe and hardly heard of in Ireland.

Other callers at number 38 quickly made the influence of America evident. A. K. Donoghue, and Ray Guild, both from Boston and Harvard. Douglas Usher Wilson, James Hillman. All of these recently arrived on these shores. Each making his own not inconsiderable impression on the natives. Hillman on stage in a public college performance, gave a sample of jitterbugging never seen before. Wilson made his impression with his own brand of philosophy, cutting through Irish crut on every side. And to all forms of evasion and equivocation, including my own, he could be heard to thunder.

'You're talking through your paper Irish asshole.'

But perhaps most influential of all was A. K. Donoghue. This classically and politically minded gentleman introduced a strange behaviourism in the land. Resembling that of Wilson's who, also a Bostonian, came from the upper ends of society as Donoghue did the lower. And Donoghue's contribution was that of spoken honesty. First evidenced by his appearance in a pub when asked by the round buyer what he'd have to drink. Donoghue's blasphemous reply,

Kilcoole Village. The road up the hill led to Mr Poulton's pub. The road to the right was to Kilcoole station a mile away. And the lane between them to the right of the village shop led, as the crow would walk, another mile or so along to my cottage.

which had never been heard before in the land, stunned the entire public house and many a public house for miles around. When the immortal words were uttered.

'I'll have a sandwich.'

By now I had established for myself a tiny speck of notoriety in Dublin. More by one's fists than by one's paintbrushes. Meanwhile Ryan had begun a literary magazine called *Envoy* at 39 Grafton Street. And within this one publishing entity did much of Ireland's then literary world concentrate. Further in my own pursuit of painting survival I had bought a smallholding along the coast of Wicklow at Kilcoole beyond the pretty seaside village of Greystones. I would on occasion come up to Dublin. Usually calling on John Ryan at his studio which now also acted as an office for his literary enterprise *Envoy* magazine. For Dublin then these offices were luxurious indeed. Desks and fitted carpets. A gramophone and other comforts. And even the practically unknown personal instrument of a telephone. Kavanagh could often be found there by mornings read-

Surrounded by my chickens and scratching a living from the soil which Patrick Kavanagh rightly defined as entitling me to being called a phoney. Kavanagh, a small farmer knowing full well that any American could climb aboard an aeroplane and a few hours later, having stood under a hot shower could then sit down to bacon, eggs, sausages, pancakes and maple syrup back in the good old U.S.A. And God, there was many the odd moment when I wanted to do just that.

ing snippets from submitted manuscripts to which his invariable reply was.

'Rubbish. Utter drivel and the most appalling nonsense I have ever had the disinterest to read.'

Of course Kavanagh hadn't read more than four words of a single line but would fling the offending pages back where they came from. And upon this occasion and as the door opened a manuscript of my own hit me in the face. Kavanagh at least had the good manners to apologize. And knowing that Kavanagh had been a farmer or at least from a farming family I took the opportunity to avail of farming if not literary advice and asked him about growing potatoes. He looked at me with his most brilliant portrayal of sceptical disgust.

'Ah God, I suppose now you've got an acre or two.'

'Four acres.'

'Four acres have you. And I suppose you've got chickens.'

'Thirteen.'

'Thirteen have you. And I suppose too you've got cabbage, their leaves sparkling of a morning with dew.'

'Six rows.'

'And you're wading twice a day through the nettles and docks to fetch a bucket of water from the nearby stream.'

'Five times a day.'

'And I suppose it's a nice little three room cottage with a hedge around it and you've got a cow to milk and a patch of strawberries ripening for June.'

'I have.'

'Phoney, phoney, phoney. Utterly phoney. The whole thing is phoney. Nothing but phoniness.'

Kavanagh shook his fist as he shouted and lurched in his mock high dudgeon like a ship pitching in a storm. One saw the truth of his remarks knowing that this simple way of life had cost a fortune in education and existed upon a small private emolument arriving every week from an attentive mother and that I had come to this peasant land with my nice big American pot to piss in. And I laughed outright at his wisdom. But what he did not know was that I had taken my college mattress out of Trinity and placed it on a door torn off one of the cottage rooms and this stacked on bricks was my bed. And that I had found an old face of a rusted shovel in a hedgerow, cut down an ash sapling and shaped and fitted it as a handle. And with this same spade, dug a basin in the tiny nearby stream from where one fetched water. But as I left the office of *Envoy* that day. Still laughing. Kavanagh turned to talk behind my back.

'That man's no phoney. Sure if he were he couldn't laugh at what I said.'

I wasn't exactly

Guffawing

And Kavanagh left me

Feeling

Phoney enough

I can tell

You

VIII

Popular American tunes took three to five years to arrive in Ireland, making it altogether marvellously nostalgic to hear them again and be reminded that there was escape if escape were needed from this creature comfortless land. But before the world of art conspicuously reared its more than occasionally chastising head, and the desperate struggle for survival began to be fought, there were many other pleasant moments to be had in these early germinal days in the latter half of the nineteen forties. Which in this perennially poor land, once unforgettably havocked by a great famine, gave plausibility to the drawling nasal tones of an American accent which by itself spelt wondrous riches westwards across the seas. Such speech having long been the symbol of carefree wealth as bespoken by Hollywood movie sets, exterior and interior, and flashily elegant costumes both voluminous and scanty. Add shiny rooms, silk curtains, and steaming water pouring out of gold taps into big tubs bursting with bubbles and blondes, and you have an appropriate sample of what long queues lined up to see in the cold wintry rain on a Dublin Sunday afternoon.

But there did exist the occasional oasis from physical adversity. Attending upon the races, one would invariably repair to some nearby country house. And in the case of going to Leopardstown in south Co. Dublin it was cause to visit John Ryan's mother's house of Burton Hall. With Ryan's father dead, his mother single handedly ran the Monument Creameries. This for Ireland was a large business consisting of a string of more than twenty shops selling butter, cream and eggs throughout Dublin and environs and included two of the bigger cafés in the city. With John Ryan, a young painter with a strong interest in writing as well as politics, Burton Hall became unwittingly an accessory to these aspirations. Providing the antithesis to Dublin's desolate dens of iniquity. The most contrasting element being not only Burton Hall's sumptuous setting, interior grandeur and furnishings but also Ryan's stream of spectacularly beautiful sisters. Who could produce one highly pleasant shock after another as they appeared when least expected out of the various mahogany door frames and glided into the music room, drawing room or library. To beseat themselves in these splendid settings spreading flowing gowns on the vast Axminster rugs. Their charmingly attractive mother, chief of this dynasty, was an early collector of Jack Yeats's paintings. And these massive wistfully sad pictures with their figures aswirl in palette knife slashes of colour, of men in mists out on bog lands, at country fairs, and race meetings, always brought the wild cold mystery of the Irish countryside into the room. And beneath such a picture, I overheard Ryan's mother, as her children and their myriad friends unstintingly feasted in the lavish surrounds about her, laughingly rubbing her hands at her front hall blazing Christmas turf fire.

'I'll be glad when the festive season is over when instead of spending money I can get back to making it.'

Few Irish people have ever been far from hard times. Which always lurk in mind no matter how good present times are seeming. And in an Ireland where most were of less than modest means, Mrs Ryan was generously tolerant and indulgent especially of those who might reasonably be thought not to have a pot to piss in. And you might meet anyone at all at Burton Hall, from a university professor or Hollywood star to a gas meter reader, and of which latter there were plenty. Dublin, because of its intimate size, could find you knowing people much more quickly than you ever got the chance to forget them. And soon enough you'd find there was hardly an unfamiliar face in sight. I had made several of my earliest visits to Ryan's house before I realized a beautiful girl, Cora, who had become a girlfriend was also one of Ryan's sisters. Nor did I know that a silent gentleman of wry wit in the rare times he spoke, called Patrick and in whose company I spent many a long partying night when I would try to coax more from him than an amiable nod and smile, was also a Ryan brother. But this was the first I was to know in friendship of a world of the rich and prosperous and the purely Irish Irish. And to and from this large yellow ochre Georgian mansion one did more than occasionally go.

Surrounded by tree lined country lanes and set in its 200 acre park, Burton Hall in itself was a cornucopia. A hundred head of Guernsey cows grazed in gently rolling meadows. A champion pedigree bull tethered in a field by the drive awaiting to serve. Acres of walled vegetable and flower gardens. In long greenhouses glowingly golden peaches were ripening. Asparagus leaping from their beds to point their stalks at the sky. Artichokes splashing out their large thistle leaves around the fresh purple of their budding fruit. In the Hall's basements were vast, and even for Ireland, nearly inexhaustible wine cellars. A fleet of cars in the courtyard garages. And along with the family's cheese making, bakeries, chocolate factory, tobacconists, Burton Hall and its servants could supply your usual seven course feast without stress or strain or the morrow's impoverishment. Indeed, awake next morning under silk eiderdowns, your breakfast tray would groan with your sizzling sausages, rashers and eggs, toasted soda bread, marmalade, butter balls, coffee or tea. But prior to one Sunday evening when Leathers and I had been impromptu invited to stay to dinner I heard a mildly exasperated John Ryan saying to his sister.

'Cora, for god's sake see they don't serve us with the cured sides of a pig and the sunnyside up reproductive product of farmyard fowl.'

But there was plenty enough of your champagne in the library and your elaborate wine flowing dinners with *pâté de foie gras* on the Dresden. All put before you on the gleaming mahogany and with savouries before and after the entrée as you surfeited under these sparkling crystal chandeliers. And your vintage ports and special pale old brandies, followed by plans for late night excursions. With a wise Mrs Ryan insisting her trusted sober chauffeur drive us in her Daimler through this green sleeping kingdom of high granite walls and hedgerows to the ballroom dances, counties away. With rarely a light on the landscape to be seen. And you might be back again in a day or two. After another dinner in a different house. Another ball in another ballroom. Another hooley. More noise, more people.

To this place of comforts Ryan showed no favouritism in issuing his invitations to parties and the fearsome were invited along with the well behaved. Even though the former were definitely a bevy of them that doth drink from the finger bowls and doth wipe their knives between their teeth. But they would, like anyone else with a mouth on them, quaff barrels and bottles dispensed from the schoolroom under the servants' stairs. Brendan Behan came in his spectacular déshabillé. Even The Awful Three. But the latter were respectfully requested by the butler to leave their picks and shovels outside. And too there were aplenty, gatecrashers who would not take the hint that there was doubt about their welcome. I even recall seeing Lead Pipe Daniel The Dangerous, who normally would have had a romp wreaking havoc of endless and antique proportions, and who came in a suitably dark suit he'd stolen from an undertaker's, where he was temporarily employed dressing the corpses. But Ryan had a curiously sobering and calming effect even upon Daniel who did nothing more daring than to sing like an angel a song he'd composed.

> I may be
> In many quarters
> Known as Daniel The Dangerous
> And I don't want to be simplistic
> But believe me folks
> All I am is violently artistic

Ryan, although busy enough in his own life, was thoughtful and kindly in his patronage. And would in deserving cases even install the temporarily impecunious in Burton Hall. One such of whom being A. K. Donoghue, the introducer of blatant honesty to Ireland. Where lies had for so long reigned as being the truth told for the time being. Donoghue a first generation Irish American said he had come upon this personal philosophy when one of his young Catholic friends in Boston had said to him that if he told his mother the truth that he didn't believe in God, she would drop dead. Donoghue went immediately home where his mother was ironing in the kitchen and said, 'Hey ma I don't believe in God.' His mother without looking up from her ironing replied.

'Is that so, pass me that sprinkling bottle.'

Donoghue now in Dublin had awed all by his candour. With an encyclopedic knowledge ranging from plumbing to the classics he applied the telling of the truth to myriad subjects ranging from Irish politics to his own sex life. Whereas in a Boston bar he would have received a quick fist in the gob, here, among this bourgeoning group of intelligentsia, he was at worst greeted with encouraging amusement. And now when he continued to ask for something to eat when he was offered something to drink he often ended up with his requested ham sandwich with two pickles on the side. Even Brendan Behan, who usually took the stage and filled and shook it where e'er

A. K. Donoghue on the right and Tony McInerney on the left standing in Front Square Trinity College and en route to Bewley's Oriental Café for a morning coffee where no gap of silence ever occurred in the conversation.

he went, grew quiet and listened attentively in the presence of Donoghue. But as this crut crunching Harvard gentleman skewered many a sacredly held Irish pretension, his penchant for the truth did less than help him find continued food and shelter. And recently arrived in Ireland on the G.I. Bill, Donoghue had not brought a pot to piss in nor had he a recent cheque from the American government to buy one. And when an admirer was congratulating him on the observation that it was the ice age and not St Patrick that kept the snakes out of Ireland, Donoghue reflected that all his spoken truth had done for him was to bring him an agonizingly prolonged lack of women, sex and money.

Ryan, ever conscious of the survival difficulties of people he admired, and solicitous of Donoghue nearly starving and without somewhere to live, invited him to Burton Hall to sojourn at length. But advised that it would be best while doing so if he were to stay out of the way of the mother. Which in such commodious mansion seemed a minor problem, but Ryan said was best guaranteed avoided by accompanying him into Dublin every day and returning in the evening. But Donoghue disliking pubs in general and some of the more boisterous company Ryan occasionally kept with the likes of Brendan Behan, chose instead to stay the day in these lavish surroundings. Polishing off an early served breakfast tray. Late afternoons submerging in a bath he refilled to the brim twice with the heaps of endless hot water and drying in blanket sized fluffy clean white towels fresh off their heating rails. And throughout the day silently descending the deep carpeted grand staircase to choose from among the many books in the library and ensconce himself in a moss green upholstered George III mahogany armchair next to Mrs Ryan's Queen Anne writing desk. Just as he would prop his feet up on a foot cushion placed on a black and gold laquer centre table, Mrs Ryan would come walking in. Leading to the inevitable exchange of words two or three times a day as Donoghue would make to put down his feet and get up out of his chair.

'O sorry, do you want to come in here.'

'O no. Sorry, do please stay where you are. It's quite all right.'

Donoghue then repairing variously to the other reception rooms to which Mrs Ryan in search of privacy in her own house was now also fleeing, arriving only to find the ubiquitous Donoghue already there. Then in rapidly vacating such spots, Donoghue in a tiptoeing panic of avoidance seemed everywhere. In the hall, vestibule, schoolroom and conservatory, and still helplessly confronting this gracious lady. But as astute servants were in observance, suddenly Donoghue's breakfast did not arrive. Nor was his bed made, nor towels changed nor fresh flowers put on his various bedroom tables. And the message sank in. In a swift change of venue he became resident now in Ryan's studio and office at 39 Grafton Street. With another bigger and better drama about to unfold. At four in the morning. When after hours of a battle with a rat sheltering in under the bed taking place. And Donoghue finally trying to shine a torch upon this rodent in order to take aim with his shoe and hit it a fatal belt in the gob. Outside down in the street a patrolling guard saw the light of the torch flash across Ryan's front room studio ceiling. Immediately the alarm of a serious theft in progress was raised. With now more commotion outside and then inside. Donoghue in his nakedness peeked to look out the window. To see Grafton Street and the sidewalk in front of Woolworth's five and dime store aflood with police. Who, from the sound of another disturbance in a back lane to the rear of the building, were there, also staked out, hands at the ready for imaginary guns. Of course with its adversary otherwise occupied the rat's nerve increased and it now ventured to escape running along the wall skirting under the rear window, Donoghue now letting go with one of his shoes. Which overshot the target somewhat and with a loud shattering of silence in this wee hour of the morning, smashed through the window. From which the guards now expected to see at least the nose of a Luger project and spit bullets. When they announced by loud hailer that unless he came out with his hands up, they would open fire.

'Don't shoot. I'm a Harvard graduate.'

At four twenty three a.m. Donoghue, one shoe still raised in his hand, proceeded down the carpeted stairs and nakedly emerged from the literary portals of 39 Grafton Street. Repeating again and again in his best pronounced American, his academic qualifications as the best insurance against being gunned down. The guards levelling their Browning automatics as he stood on the pavement in front of the stacks of cakes displayed in the window of the Monument Creamery Café. From the top of Stephen's Green more guards advancing north in a phalanx down Grafton Street. As two more military units came around the corners of Chatham and Anne Streets advancing south. The fire brigade, bells in the distance clanging also on its way. It now began to rain. And one of the police upon snapping on handcuffs on Donoghue's wrists held behind his back, commented.

'Well you could sure use your cap and gown now.'

John Ryan, meanwhile, back at Burton Hall was woken in his sleep and motored into the rescue. Finding his barefoot guest shivering wrapped in a blanket in a police cell not that far from the scholarly granite walls and high iron fence of Trinity College Dublin. But it did not take long before Donoghue was back enjoying what he could in this ancient Danish city. Choosing his daily favourite spot at one of the cool, white grey marble tables in Bewley's Oriental Café in Westmoreland Street. Where he could have a delicious black coffee with two small jugs of cream, a butter ball and a spice bun. And read his admired columnist Myles na gCopaleen in *The Irish Times*, who frequently alluded in his daily pieces to classic matters wittily expressed in snippets of Greek and Latin.

In the strange micro macrocosm of Dublin I had found you could achieve all sorts of things, especially if you were a foreigner. And it infinitely provided scope for an amateur to dare enter into and embark upon a career in the world of art. My first step having come about one morning when I exited from my rooms at Trinity and strolled out into the city to take coffee, when I had also taken in an exhibition of Jack Yeats's paintings at the Victor Waddington Galleries in Anne Street. Impressed by the prices and delighted by these marvellous extravagant whorls of colour, and myself hardly capable of drawing an imitation of a triangle never mind a circle, I bought some paints, brushes and canvas. And in the centre of my sitting room at 38 Trinity College I set up an easel and commenced painting. As the rumour spread of my activity I was visited almost immediately by an English lady artist outraged that I had not spent the usual fifteen years in Florence at the feet of contemporary masters. She swept in. And in front of several visitors who although mystified, were at least up to that moment gently sympathetic to my efforts, the Bloomsbury lady stood floor centre in her tweeds and loudly declared.

'You are my dear, so obviously presently in your celluloid penis stage. And I fear will clearly remain there. How dare you presume to paint. I rushed here immediately I heard. How utterly dare you.

Private Showing . . .

OF

PAINTINGS AND WATERCOLORS

BY

DONLEAVY

AT

7 St. Stephen's Green Gallery,
MARCH 15th—3.30 TO 6.30 ···
EXHIBITION FROM MARCH 15th

(Above) *The author's then wife, Valerie with Michael Heron her brother and the author, at the author's third Dublin exhibition at 7 St Stephen's Green when more of the paintings were dry than they were at previous exhibitions, and when I was falsely being accused of hogging Dublin's cultural limelight.*

My drawings on my invitations were occasionally commented upon to zoology class by my Professor of Zoology and Comparative Anatomy, James Brontë Gatenby to whom such invitations were always sent. This world famed zoologist would always point out a dorsal or ventral liberty or two I might have taken with my morphological contours.

Private Showing . . .

OF

PAINTINGS AND WATERCOLORS

BY

DONLEAVY

AT

7, St. Stephen's Green Gallery, Dublin,
JUNE 8th — 3.30 TO 6.30 P.M.
EXHIBITION FROM JUNE 8th—22nd, 1950.

When five years of my life have been spent in the Prado painting reproductions before I took the liberty to put a brush stroke of my own upon a canvas.'

I, of course, out of humility broke one of my cheaper brushes in two. Trampled a nearly empty tube of flake white and was seizing my canvas off its easel when the English lady continued in a less accusatory voice.

'Well, since you've started to make such a fool of yourself my dear, don't for God's sake now stop. By being an even bigger fool and with the sort of nerve you've got you're simply bound to be some day not laughed at. Which, of course, if you don't mind I am about to do right now. Ha ha ha.'

John Ryan had now married as had I, both of us to tall, dark and beautiful women. Still keeping my rooms at Trinity, but fully combating what was to become country life in the raw in Ireland, I had now conceived my first story in an empty compartment on the train ride in from Kilcoole along the coast to Dublin. Where one looked out and down from the edge of the Killiney cliffs over the grey green of the Irish Sea. I wrote 'A Party on Saturday Afternoon' which was later published by John Ryan in his now established *Envoy* and over the objection of his other editors. But also with the enthusiastic encouragement of my other first fan, one of Ryan's beatifically beautiful sisters, Kathleen who had become a Hollywood film star in such films as *Odd Man Out*.

I had now also given my second exhibition of still wet paintings in the painters' gallery at 7 St Stephen's Green, writing introductions to the catalogues and availing of my own brand of Donoghue's blatant honesty as I did so. My foreword did not make people drop dead but they did sure as hell lead to a lot of begrudging and growling. My first foreword was concocted in part from my correspondence at the time and entitled 'From a Letter'.

In front of Dockrell's on Great George's Street they paused and his friend A. K. Donoghue said, 'Donleavy, shut your mouth and let me give you the entire truth in one sentence. The land is the basis of everything.' Donleavy was impressed, Donoghue being one of America's most monumental scholars and so Donleavy rushed back to Trinity College and made decisions. Firstly, he wanted to paint, secondly he would give up Trinity, thirdly, he would go to the land from whence all things came. He fled Dublin with a rolled mattress, a beautiful wife and a tin trunk containing an axe, blanket and frying pan. Then things began to happen. Peas were flung into the soil, followed by cabbage and potatoes. Donleavy searched the countryside for stones, lifting them he built a studio. Things were damp and cold and winter evenings long and lonely, but people like Doug Wilson would come out with his sleeping bag and have a chat. Month after month things were happening. Concrete floors were laid, furniture made, hedgerows torn down. Valerie made clothes, curtains, sowed flowers. Chickens arrived but the horrible things refused to lay and things looked desperate for a while, then Jim Hillman, a conscientious American, wired a chemical compound that made chickens make with eggs and sure enough, the American miracle drug began to work and prosperity settled, a great protective cloak. The spiritual warmth of the country, a morning birdwatch by the sea, the sound of salmon caught by the seal, the swallow's sexual song, and towards evening a read in the papers; an hour's tragedy during sunset; Horace Bones murders his illegitimate offspring in the Wicklow Mountains; Mrs Muldooneen, the landlady, serves arsenic in the spuds to several Anglo Irish Trinity students; Joe Ireland crosses the border, sabre between his teeth, baby Power in his pocket, shillelagh in one hand, the Sinn Fein Rebellion book in the other and establishes a stout-taster's post in the North; and A. K. Donoghue, having left Ireland because of lack of food, gets stones in his kidney because of too much food in America; and in all the pubs, across the expressionless face of Ireland, stand the still poised figures and a bottle of stout – the dictators, the poets, novelists, inventors, geniuses, gourmets, business tycoons, painters, politicians; a word in your ear and the cry of all Ireland, 'What will you have? A bottle?' And all the time Donleavy was painting.

As insults and complaints rained and a letter of mine appeared in *The Irish Times*, my exhibition did give me my first taste of fame. As I saw pouring into the gallery a stream of folk who in testing the wetness of my canvases were adding their finger prints. And amazingly some only came in to buy, for sixpence, one of my catalogues. In which I was serving up my own dish of what I hoped was the heartfelt truth. But Donoghue was already gone. However, upon his last ditch stand before he departed the shores of Ireland, he did at least establish The Irish Republican Publicity League at 39 Grafton Street and appoint himself as its secretary. Attesting further to the supreme tolerance of John Ryan whose address this was, albeit that he himself was sympathetic to Donoghue's espoused cause. Which was to fund a movement and purchase flags, and guns to make Ireland whole again. And Donoghue, searching out the best sounding Irish names in a Boston telephone book, sent off to America letter requests imploring aid to such cause. After hundreds of mailings and some few hungry weeks during which he got no replies, one finally came back with a modest donation. From an Italian gentleman who had just taken over the Irish pub to whom Donoghue had addressed his appeal. Evidence enough that not many of the sons of the ould sod gave a good god damn about the political plight of Ireland. Not to mention that of a totally destitute would be patriot.

Donoghue's dawning departure was the end of an era. And of the first bemusements with this land. In which very few could afford to remain. Finally one starving afternoon Donoghue presented himself across the street to the Woolworth's café. Which was up the stairs on a floor above that where they sold their wares and into which one could daily stare from John Ryan's studio. Donoghue, ordering a double pot of tea and a spread of your usual bacon, sausages, tomato and fried eggs and upon golfing these down, he called for the bill and put up his hands to tell the waitress.

'Shoot me, I can't pay.'

And sadly, just following by one week Donoghue's departure, there came a letter from a sympathetic friend in Paris in which was enough money to allow him to further survive and espouse his nationalism. And for such acts of kindness one to this day still remembers the man's name, a Stanley Carnow. And regrets that he never got a thank you reply, for Donoghue the non recipient had through the good offices of the American consul already secured free passage on a rusty cargo ship and was in a hurricane at the time, being tossed like a peanut all over the Atlantic waves.

Better funded people like James Hillman and Douglas Usher Wilson set off on their own grand tour of Africa and the Middle East. But ah. As well as myself, there was one other gent who remained. None other than the saintly calmly contented Gainor Stephen Crist. Who was nearly the counterpart of Donoghue. Raised in Ohio in the middle of the Middle West where his father was a prominent doctor. And where he was an indulged only child. Simply put, Crist revelled in Ireland. Attesting to certain abilities perhaps lacking in those who left. Salient among which was one, that of being able to obtain goods on account where e'er he went. Which was into grocery shops, pubs and department stores and even into the American Embassy. Crist in addition to being a refined American, had an astonishing resemblance to the Duke of Windsor and was also possessed of what could be described as an English accent. These added to his plethora of other social and moral advantages and being able to present himself in the at least sleeker and as yet untarnished garments of the new world, allowed him to effortlessly cut a swathe through Irish life. Except perhaps for one early unfortunate incident. When he had sent a grey herringbone tweed suit to be dry cleaned. Which duly returned, having been thoroughly washed and laundered. With the sleeves shrunken half way up to his elbows, the trouser legs half way up to his knees. And the garment nearly squeezing him to death.

Except that they left every customer pissing in debt, most Dublin pubs if they resembled anything at all, resembled banks. Stout mahogany doors, frosted glass windows etched with legends, 'Whiskey Bonders, Sherry Importers'. And constantly conducting transactions of handing over your pound note to have a Guinness or ball of malt deposited in your belly which in turn were guaranteed to give birth to dreams in your brain. Some pub owners were the nearest thing one could imagine to a priest presiding over his faithful flock. Listening to woes of the weather, racing, or the shocking price of petrol as they might listen to a confession of sins. Dispensing forgiveness as penance was paid in the price of a stout or ball of malt. Entering to take a pew. Kneel to adore this god and perform with these sacred liquids, the religious ceremony of quenching thirst. In this land where all of life had finally to become lived in the mind. And where there came no better man to do that than the eminently contemplative Gainor Stephen Crist. Who was able to do nearly the impossible, that of running up credit in an Irish public house.

Crist in sizing up Dublin and liking to have at his disposal liquid refreshment at all times and especially outside of pub closing hours, had to confront two problems, one of time and the other of money. In the first of these he paid a visit to a distinguished lawyer and man of letters, Terence de Vere White, to inquire concerning the establishing of a private drinking club in Dublin. Of which he would be the first founding member, Chairman, Grandmaster and President and who knows, even occasional bartender. One imagines that Mr de Vere White had cautioned upon the licensing difficulties and expense of such a venture for Crist failed to pursue the matter. However, he remained extremely concerned that he would ever be without a drink

(Right) *Gainor Stephen Crist with his first wife Constance in front of my rooms at number 38 Trinity College. My name just legible painted in white on the entrance behind us. Constance, being one of the few of the many like myself and Crist who braved the academic world of Trinity, but who succeeded in getting her degree.*

(Left) *Crist at the side gate of Trinity from which he is exiting to pawn an electric fire. This saintly expedient gentleman on this day had resolutely made the decision that money for a few pints and ball of malt in the pub would keep him as comfortably warm as any electric fire. And as he said, the steam from his piss could prove it.*

through the mere lack of money. And to this problem he paid his next attention. Elaborately biding his time in those strategically situated public houses that took his fancy, and wherein he prepared his carefully devised protocol. He would attend at the pub for two consecutive days and then arriving on the third, always shortly following morning opening, he would upon taking his first drink and paying for it, then present to a nonplussed barman, an extra ten shilling note. Explaining it was in repayment for the other night when without warning he had run short of cash while having a few drinks with friends. The barman, always a practised politician in facing any customer, but not recalling the incident, and facing this gent distinguished far beyond your usual calibre of your average American, and further faced with the dilemma of telling him he was mistaken, usually took the ten shillings. Which for any bartender could be a matter of relief that the principle of restitution was being observed in a city like Dublin where to incur a debt always meant you were leaving for somewhere and not returning soon. In any event bartenders had already found that this plausible gentleman's bon-homie was such that it often involved every customer in buying a substantially greater number of drinks, so that it became a profitable matter to nod back when Crist said put that round on my bill please. Thus did one of the greatest American drinkers ever to hit Ireland and pop back a ball of malt, prepare for his financially enforced dry days. And dear me, who is to say that such debts although they grew astronomically and unwieldy large, were not in their every penny always repaid in full. For Crist had not only enormous compassion for his fellow man but was an absolute stickler for fair play.

But even Gainor Crist was not without his difficulties in other areas of obtaining goods, particularly those of a rubber quality. For upon presenting himself in a chemist's shop for the first time to buy contraceptives, and making his condom request known, the chemist blessed himself, turned candy coloured purple and red and then knocking over his counter of laxatives and other highly in demand eliminating aids, not only retreated into the back of his apothecary but pushed his two young lady assistants before him. And as a nonplussed Crist persisted in his inquiry the white coated gentleman stood in the rear doorway of his premises shaking and speechless until his offending customer had left. Thinking this was a mere aberration of an overworked druggist Crist tried again, but with similar results, only this time the chemist became violent and threw a box of sanitary towels. It was not until the third attempt that the chemist, aware that he might have an errant tourist on his hands did at least, while firmly showing him the door, say that such unmentionable things were not for sale in Ireland. Crist being a man fond of family also had a further concern too for the consequences of the lack of contraceptives. For in the birth of a child in life threatening circumstances he heard that in Holy Catholic Ireland it would not be the mother who would be saved, but the new infant.

Crist ever fascinated by religion if not politics, was very largely instrumental in bringing to my notice aspects of Ireland I might never have come to know, due to my own absorbing fascination at the time with wine, women and song. Crist was an extremely politely precise gentleman. Indeed upon first ever confronting him in the Pearl Bar in Dublin he was already wearing a sweater belonging to me and was profusely apologizing for a small stain he'd got on it. Explaining he would only wear it till exactly five p.m. when he would take it off. The sweater, which Crist had on in some photographs posing as a male model had been borrowed for him by his brother in law Randall Hillis. It was from this connection to his first wife's father, stationed as a clergyman in the Irish north, that Crist first brought to my own attention the phenomenon of an Orangeman. Describing to me as he did these formidable men and boys who marched thumping great drums and who sang their songs with delight and fervour, of being up to their knees in Catholic blood and up to the knees in slaughter. Crist taking a nearly satanic delight and amusement that these two groups of Christian religionists could so oppose one another with such unChristian repugnance. His interest in this extending to Catholic martyrs as well as Cromwell who was responsible for slaughtering so many possible ones. Crist gloating to draw attention to the phenomenon of the strange similarity between the identically preserved ancient heads of both the Blessed Oliver Plunkett and that of Oliver Cromwell. And on this issue I would find Crist on many an occasion comfortably sitting in his sofa chair waging his own personal war against the crut. Which would take the form of writing a number of varying letters on the subject of the likeness of the heads, to the editors of the daily Dublin evening newspapers, *The Evening Herald* and *The Evening Mail*. Crist always remaining immune to the fact that such letters went unpublished.

Crist who was fond of saying, 'I taught Donleavy everything he knows', was essentially correct, especially concerning much of Ireland. But as I deliberately avoided storing knowledge, much of what Crist conveyed to me, did then, and has certainly since, vanished from mind. As an American, Crist spoke of wielding what amounted to a so called double edged sword in this land. Which by one's accent and tolerant outlook allowed one to assume alliances on nearly every religious and political side and enjoy a congenial fraternity right up and down the rungs of the jealously guarded Irish social ladder. An American could also identify when necessary, or pleasant, with the British ruling class, or the Anglo Irish or the Dublin suburban upper, or slum lower or working class. Leaving one totally free to associate among and even eagerly agree with either bigoted rabid Protestants, or crut encrusted Catholics or indeed with the odd mystified but invariably smiling Hindu or Mohammedan who had found his way to these shores, usually to medical school.

If anything, Crist himself was possessed with a triple edged sword. For, unlike any other American at Trinity, he could spend endless hours in the company of any Dubliner in a bar, and transform even the most lacklustre of these into electrifying company. Often by merely listening in concerned head shaking agreement to every word your man spoke. And in short order, and after a few pints of stout, these previously colourless repetitive pub stage Irishmen could even be moderately entertaining. But Crist out of Dublin and in the countryside, could wield even more astonishing transformations in some of these pub habitués. Which I discovered in an instance, when in the middle of a Trinity College summer afternoon, I was accosted by Crist as I exited along New Square from my rooms at number 38. And to which he immediately directed me urgently to return. To fetch my toothbrush. For he was inviting me to his country residence in Kerry. I was not to know then that it was to take us five days walking and hitch hiking in any and every direction to get there. And that I was appointed to buy all the drink on the way and spend nearly the total of three days and whole nights in various pubs. Each time, upon my suggestion that we should proceed, Crist's hand would come to stay me upon the arm. And as the man to whom he was talking would continue to ramble on as he had done for the three previous hours, Crist would also say, 'Mike, wait, this man knows something. Listen.'

On this same night, and finally dislodging Crist from his crony, who had sold his farm piecemeal to drink it, always prefacing the point by recounting how he would, cutting hay, go to the hedge and look down the road and lay down his scythe and then sell the field. And on his donkey cart would come and go to the pub till he'd drunk the proceeds. As Crist listened, this gentleman still had his donkey and cart outside into which he would fall unconscious that very night and the donkey would take him home. But Crist and I had nothing similar and I found myself with him utterly out in the middle of nowhere, finally coming across a fairground where Crist in a feat of strength rang the strong man's bell with a wooden hammer. Impressing a girl nearby whom he then insisted on escorting home because she said her father would beat her unconscious for returning so late. He set off with her cross country over the fields and I was left waiting half the night outside the fairground after it had closed. Crist duly returning. Armed with his usual stout bottles, having, by the dishevelled looks of him, either chastised the girl's cruel father or led his daughter further astray. But Crist's mood serene. We lay down on the side of the road to sleep. And as the sun came up breaking through the mists to wake me, there he was, sitting, shivering in the dawn chill in his shirt sleeves, his arms wrapped around his knees, and benignly content as he stared out into the green hushed silence. Both his sweater and jacket draped over me to keep me warm. I knew too, that anyone disparaging me behind my back, often justifiably, sad to admit, would find Crist giving them a 'wooling', pounding their heads on the floor until they made their apologies. Although he had other reputations frequently deserved, this man from Ohio was one of the most kindly, compassionate and saintly of men. And whose wearier sentiments in those days were occasionally voiced.

'Life in Ireland is a fight with the heavyweight champion of the world. But they don't let you lie there, knocked out, they throw water on you to get you up to knock you out again.'

At the end of our long journey, to a house overlooking Dingle Bay, we arrived to find Constance Crist, Gainor's first wife and their first baby daughter, Marianna. Petra, as Crist referred to his wife, was British and as directly outspoken as she was an extremely attractive sensual lady, and never averse to letting the Irish know what was on her mind. And I'm not sure that she wasn't even the originator of the word 'crut'. Were her anger to be aroused sufficiently, she was not afraid to publicly voice her critical opinion of Ireland or the Irish. As I heard her once not unreasonably do to the entire passenger population riding on the top of a Dublin tram. Who seemed actually to sympathize instead of attacking the pair of us. But equally she could be as charming and humorous as the Irish themselves when she chose. She it was who first introduced her husband to A. K. Donoghue when she met Donoghue sitting next to her in the American Embassy. And single among the three of us, at Trinity, as strong ladies can and do, she was the only one to attain a degree. She sang many an old song to us and as we all sat on the hillside of the mountain where we had climbed to picnic by a black lake, she would tell strange haunting tales of punishments, ghosts, tortures and murders in an ancient Yorkshire castle in which she grew up. Her voice so laughter rich in the rare June cool, clean sunshine. As we three lay there, the larks above ascending singing.

Into the same stunning
Blue
Under which Crist lies now
Alone
In an island grave elsewhere
So far
From this Ireland he had come
To love

IX

The small house on a hillside overlooking Dingle Bay to which Crist had invited me had actually been rented by a gentleman who was instrumental in Crist's first introducing me, a confirmed theatre hater, to the actual live world of Irish stage drama. Where again one encountered the presence of one of these foreign catalysts who made things happen in Ireland. It was my first ever evening at the Gaiety Theatre, a place which much later was to cause a more considerable incident for me. I attended in the company of Crist, who was there to see a friend of his perform. But as it turned out as it usually did on most of these occasions, Crist was early to attend and late to leave the theatre bar, resulting in nearly the whole of the play being heard in the distant background. But I did at least catch a brief stage sight of Crist's friend performing. In a scene where he rushed out of the wings to stamp his feet, and shout suitably impressively while flinging a paper on the stage. His name was George Roy Hill later to become the distinguished film director.

Hill, of partially Irish origins, was another Middle Western American. Having been at Yale, he was an ex Marine fighter pilot whom Crist, as a sailor in the U.S. Navy had first met when volunteering in a Florida bar one night to do Hill a favour. Hill was then taking his last steps in flight training and Crist was a naval yeoman who assigned the various pilots to their various examiners in flight tests. Crist overhearing Hill at a bar say he thought he might fail, introduced himself and informed Hill that it was possible he could assign him to a lenient examiner. All of which happily happened and Hill got his wings. Then more than 3,000 miles away and fully three years later, in the front square of Trinity College Dublin, Crist spotted again this familiar face and introduced himself.

Hill like Crist was from your distinctly better sort of American background, indeed of the Brahmin class. Tall, dignified and handsome, Hill wore a bowler and walked Dublin's streets accompanied by a properly rolled brolly. But he was not to be mistaken for someone unable to give a strong account of himself when called upon. As proved when he wasn't long first in Crist's company. When both their very capable fistic abilities were put to the test. To the point of attracting the attention of the Garda Síochána. If there was any certain thing these two men had in common it was that neither would suffer to witness insult to a lady. And it was such an instance, of a disparaging remark being made by someone as to the abilities of a distinguished lady of the theatre, Ria Mooney, that a battle of two against four ensued in a village street with Crist and Hill victors, having avenged Miss Mooney. But both then being apprehended by the Garda Síochána in the process.

If Crist was among the few who could succeed in running up credit in a pub, then Hill was the other astonishing phenomenon as one of the rare men who was not forced to finally flee Ireland with his tail unfirmly between his legs. For Hill was one of Dublin's few American success stories, not only acting in this play at the Gaiety but producing it as well, the play being a hit and making money and Hill able to go off and sojourn in Paris. But Hill had not been entirely without his difficult moments in Dublin. Indeed, as had other Americans, he reached the actual point of starvation. But having sworn a principle to himself not to rely upon his family or anyone else for support he attempted to subsist upon what was due him on the American government's G.I. Bill of Rights. But the non arrival of such emolument, as it had for Donoghue, driving him to Woolworth's for a plate of bacon and eggs, so too did it force Hill into the Red Bank Restaurant, one of Dublin's best and most expensive dining venues, and fully in keeping with Hill's own standards and background. Hill having there his first full meal for nearly a week. But with your usual half bottle of Chablis with the smoked salmon. A Bonne Mare with the filet mignon and a Bearnaise sauce. Creamed spinach, with your butter anointed boiled baby potatoes. And all followed by a whipped cream decorated chocolate mousse and an Irish coffee. Asking for the manager, Hill was quietly wiping his mouth with his linen napkin and sipping his drink when he arrived. Hill explaining he could not pay the bill but would do so upon the first opportunity. The manager benignly taking the whole matter in his stride and inviting Hill to another Irish coffee compliments of the house.

'And I quite understand your temporary impecuniousness, sir.

And certainly we remain appreciative of your continued esteemed patronage.'

One has the temerity and fondness now to recall Abraham Jacob Leventhal, or Con as he was mostly called, a Jewish gentleman, Dublin scholar, wit and man of letters who was also the patron saint of Americans on the G.I. Bill attending Trinity College and whose mouths he more than occasionally helped fill. Leventhal, bundled up in his tweeds, sat behind his desk in his ground floor office in Front Square, his window overlooking the cobblestones and the velvet grass. There was much sober bemusement on his face as chilled starving Americans entered his presence and took a moment's respite by a rosy coal fire in his grate. He was asked favours and approvals which sometimes were gently questioned but never refused. Although I knew then nothing of this gentleman's literary abilities or associations, I marvelled at his patience and his unhesitation to sign these endless bizarre in triplicate documents confronting him. And which he so often would do in the clear certainty of the applicant's unentitlement. His was a shy, unassuming way, and the reference to him as Con Leventhal was thought to have come about with his frequently prefacing his sentences with the phrase, 'When I was on the Continent'. But there is no question that when Con was on the job as registrar, many an American neck did he save including my own, by merely saying.

'I do think I sign here, don't I. O yes. And on these. In a trinity, of course.'

These were all matters happening in a country where one was wont to complain about many things, but you could never say you were constrained by documents. Over which rules were broken and exceptions made at the sound of a brogue, and where a gesture or a smile could get you a lot more than a writ. Although, by God, some of your smiles and gestures were not of the best and plenty of your writs wax stamped and emblazoned were served flying all over the place.

There were no documents and not much cash upon us on the impromptu toothbrush trip with Crist to the west. But it was my first extended stay in the Irish countryside. Kells Cove was no more than a house and cottage or two at the end of a path between boulder built walls and overlooking a tiny inlet on Dingle Bay. The nearest transport, a mile and a half away, was reached by a rutted dirt lane leading up to where the main road ran and at where a once daily train

Gainor Stephen Crist, David O'Leary and John Ryan on the Dingle peninsula. 'The West's Awake' was a frequent cry and when made in Dublin usually meant that all those in hearing distance would set off towards the Atlantic like lemmings and would often walk the entire way.

stopped in each direction at an isolated unmarked lonely spot at the foot of a dark rising mountain. On the main road there was a grocery tucked into the side of the hill, where Gainor Stephen Crist, Esq. already had opened an account for your best of bacon, eggs and tea to be supplied. And there was a pub. Two miles away across the fields as the crow flies and as Crist and I stumbled. Such forays necessitating a wet foot slog across treacherous bits of bog and upon an inebriated return it was a life risking venture. The nearest town was Cahirciveen another seven or so miles to the southwest along the coast. Crist, who was a ferocious walker, could transverse those miles in no time, twiddling his thumbs nervously in front of him as he did so. And waiting patiently as I would shout for him to let me catch up. But once he did stop dead in his tracks to call me up from behind and ask me to investigate something on the road ahead. It was a dead bird. Crist grew nervously white as the blood drained from his face. And I watched him detour down into a ditch, climb a wall and wade through nettles to circumvent this area of the road where the dead bird lay. I once asked him what would he do if a dead bird came to him in a box.

'Mike, I would kill the man who sent it.'

Cahirciveen itself on this sunshining day reminded me of a main street of Western cowboy territory. And as one entered it on foot, striding centre of the road, the curtains twitched at the windows.

News of your arrival would have already reached the other end of the town. Where Crist was heading as he always did to a post office. If not to send something then to see if something desperately sought had arrived. Cahirciveen, although a spooky town, was one of Crist's most favourite places. Not least for its reputation of having more pubs per population than any other half square mile area on earth. Except for the church and Garda Síochána, nearly every other building and shop, no matter what else it was for or sold, had a board supported between two barrels as a bar. Everywhere we entered the corks out of the Guinness bottles went pop. Thus producing an ambience much to Crist's liking. We set off to walk the seven miles back and for some of it got a ride standing up in the rear of a lurching donkey cart which a young monosyllabic boy was driving. Who was suspicious and shy of his strange passengers. But as Irish custom would have it, you could not pass without offering a lift to another on the road. And back we came. Down the winding, twisting, stony lane. Through the trees the sound of a brook in this glen. Back to the bliss of this little house. From which you had only feet to take you somewhere. Only a candle to light your night. A bucket to hold your water from a stream. A turf fire to cook your meals. Nothing to get up for tomorrow. And no need to do anything today. Cloaked in this protection. With the West awake. Like strange, unseen lightning and unsounding thunder. Premonitions shimmering, tingling in the air. The haunting deathly strangeness. Of the hush out across Dingle Bay.

Ah, but let us not forget there were full blooded born Irish Irishmen living in Ireland. Robust of spirit. Brave in adversity. Randy in appetite. Thirsty in drinking. Right fisted and left footed in fighting. Ready always as a sacred duty to do you a favour. Or be on your side when the chips were down. And one of the first of whom I met through John Ryan. And his name Tony McInerney. McInerney was about the closest you could get to your Irish country gentry of the time. From a farm on the banks of the Shannon where their fields sloped down to its edge. The house nestled in trees and approached by a drive through front gates. From such respectable, comfortable background McInerney and his brothers proceeded to the best schools and into various professions as did Tony into the field of accountancy. He was one of the first to appreciate Donoghue's imported honesty. Smilingly listening to that iconoclastic latter gent blow holes in the myths and disembowel long held Irish beliefs and spout his stream of insights and observations for hours at a time. McInerney finally maintaining that one of his cherished ambitions in life was that upon getting his inheritance he would take Donoghue to the West and sit him on the end of Slea Head. And with the next parish being America across the Atlantic and the great waves slamming the cliffs below, to listen to him for the rest of his days. But alas when McInerney did get his inheritance, Donoghue was gone to America and McInerney went instead to Paris. In the company of such always readily available universal tourists such as Crist, Behan, and Michael Heron, my Trinity room mate. But on the same occasion McInerney also saved my bacon on the very eve of my first marriage. Where in front of my prosperous in laws and under some scrutiny due to my artistic bent, I was standing without a bean to my name, unable even to buy a wedding ring. When that very morning an envelope arrived containing a sheaf of money and a cryptic note. 'You never expected to get this did you.' It was money I'd loaned him on a trip to the West an entire year previous. And such sums then usually being treated as a gift for life. With this manna from Ireland, Valerie, my wife to be, and I travelled into Bradford and there I bought a platinum wedding band.

For political reasons McInerney had been interned at The Curragh. And he still moved with that strange curious gait of a man who was following someone or being followed and which Behan was so fond of parodying in his characters on stage as the raincoated gunman, collar up, surreptitiously moving. McInerney, although capable of adding up a column of figures in the blink of an eye was also an insatiably scholarly man, as incurably curious as he could sometimes be unrelentingly stubborn over an opinion. Although accumulating cultural knowledge was not my forte, it was McInerney who exposed an Ireland of traditions and he who had secured the pampooties for James H. Leathers. But it was astonishing how well one could know someone like McInerney and yet know so little about him. As one day I thought I had the absolute well thought out brilliant solution to his life. One morning putting it to him upstairs in Bewley's Oriental Café in Grafton Street.

'Tony, why don't you get married and have a family.'

'Mike, I already am and have three children.'

And as well as having a talent for fatherhood, McInerney was full

(Right) *Tony McInerney on the banks of the Shannon near where his family's farm sloped down to the shores and where we spent much time whiling away many an afternoon. Someone like McInerney, either on the streets of the city of Limerick or the lanes of the countryside would, every short distance be stopped to pass the time of day with one acquaintance or another. Making for a powerful network of communication from coast to coast.*

(Left) *McInerney at Kells Cove, Co. Kerry, as a father. In our Dublin days together it was some years before I knew McInerney was married and had children and not until I suggested this as a solution to his life did I learn that he had already taken the step.*

of many others. When we first sat down to play chess and I who could already defeat the formidable likes of Gainor Crist found myself on this board being slowly but surely outpositioned and systematically routed. And McInerney finally putting me in checkmate, spoke up at my shattering dismay.

'Mike, you mustn't think you're still not a great chess player. Interned at the Curragh for three years, playing every day, I could beat everyone in the place. And against some of them, a Russian Grand Master wouldn't stand a chance.'

It was by happenstance with McInerney that I ended up living where I did when I fled to the land and struggled there for survival as his and my forefathers had done when there was nowhere else to go. McInerney, after his grand tour of the Continent with friends, still had a remainder of his inheritance left and was looking to purchase a little farm. And one day I accompanied him on his search. Out along the Wicklow coast. To a bereft, flat, strange, barren stretch of bogs between the land and the sea. McInerney upon reconnoitering this four acre plot with its corrugated iron bungalow shrouded by its overgrown hedges, its old slate roof cottage in disrepair and lean to shed and a small stone barn, decided it was not suitable for him. I already had, following my marriage, attacks of anxiety concerning one's survival. In spite of returning to Dublin after my wedding richer than I had left. But it was upon my then wife Valerie renting us a bed sitting room in which there was merely a bed, a stove and a sink and that the w.c. was on a landing out in a semi public corridor, that I panicked. Having been brought up in reasonably large houses in America, I had till that time little idea that people lived in such limited circumstances. The claustrophobia struck me with a sledgehammer profundity. And to such degree that I found myself returning that night back to my commodious if primitive rooms in Trinity.

By the time I was aseat in my sitting room in number 38, my heart was palpitating in what I thought was a serious heart attack. Struggling to the door, holding desperately to the bannister as I descended and hoping desperately that my 200 mile an hour tennis serving opponent wasn't lurking there ready to jump me. I emerged safely from the open hall and to the terra firma of New Square and summoned two students in the distance to assist me. They, of course, at first thought it part of a playful joke but my increasingly plaintive cries finally convinced them. Fortunately they were rugby players and each catching me under arm lugged me on my quavering legs to the front gate's porter's lodge where a taxi was got to take me to the nearest Trinity College affiliated hospital. On the way I remember recalling a similar taxi in New York when I'd cut my arm in a fight and the taxi driver refused payment for what he said he regarded an emergency. But there was on this occasion no hesitation on the part of the taxi driver to make sure he got his fare from a man clearly dying in his tracks. Searching in my wallet for the money I was nearly angered enough to stretch your man out flat on his back. Slight proof that I wasn't quite dead yet. I vaguely recognized the young doctor on duty from Trinity's medical school who put his stethoscope over my heart and announced in some surprise.

'There are few patients I've ever examined with a heart sounding anything near as healthy as yours.'

But such catastrophic event and the realization that kind parents and kind governments weren't going to support me for the rest of my life drove me to buy land. The source of all and where I at least could die standing on ground in which I could be buried cheaply. And it was my very rich father in law, who made it possible. His name was John MacMichael Heron. Whose custom it had been to give expensive canteens of silverware to all his friends' children upon their weddings. And my to be mother in law, who had discreetly discussed with me one morning as to my assets, concluded I had neither those nor prospects. And I seemed even poorer upon disclosing that I had a small allowance from my own mother. Suddenly invitations were rushed out all over Ilkley and beyond throughout Yorkshire. To an impromptu cocktail party to celebrate our wedding. John Mac-Michael Heron lay these days in his bed, ill. I had got him to take up painting and he overnight began to produce a series of talented attractive well crafted pictures. And with him I played chess and spent much time fascinatedly listening to him telling me stories of his struggles and triumphs in his business career. His advice about my staying to live in Ireland was simple. Buy Guinness shares. Ireland to my in laws being a distant place where perhaps the only acceptable respectable thing about it was its famed brewery, Trinity College Dublin, its wartime plenitude of beef, butter, bacon and eggs, and its race horses.

Upon the evening of the cocktail party I was summoned to my father in law's luxurious mirrored and rosewood panelled bedroom and was handed a cheque. Which at first I hadn't looked at and then later was entirely staggered to view in highly pleasant disbelief. And then as the cocktails were quaffed and the canapés downed, from nearly every guest came more cheques. And now just back from a brief paid for honeymoon at Kettlewell in the Yorkshire Dales and having at six thirty p.m. been destitute save for a pound or two left over from McInerney's returned loan with which I had bought the wedding ring, by eight thirty p.m. I was staring in my continued disbelief at the sum total of the astonishing cheques in my hand. Of course, everyone in this rich community of Ilkley thought it was a shotgun marriage to a ne'er do well claiming to be an artist on top of it. And certainly one felt the slight resentment since every mill owner's son for miles around had assiduously courted and tried to marry one of the stunningly beautiful Heron daughters. The last of whom was now to vanish to Ireland in the company of an American not only without a mill or factory but also conspicuously without a pot to piss in.

My first mother in law at my last Dublin exhibition. This brave lady with a sense of taste would always indulgently buy one or two of my pictures even in the blaze of adverse publicity and accusations of such efforts being not only still wet, but tasteless and obscene. Of course, in truth they were really not half bad at all.

Michael Heron in his gents' natty suiting. His father upon seeing how he lived in our rooms at Trinity sent him immediately to the tailor and haberdashery in order as he suggested, he maintain his dignity. Heron senior being a prominent Bradford wool merchant.

But having now enough money to buy at least a pot did nothing for the terror I felt for my future in Ireland. And upon that day with McInerney and looking around this bereft and forlorn gathering of buildings, I thought I had nothing to lose in making an offer for what appeared to be a basic necessity in life. No doubt thinking there was money in things like chickens and pigs. Plus around one, all was green with space to breathe and move. Instead of being abjectly incarcerated in a bed sitting room paying rent on somewhere to be you did not own. But this was back to Irish peasantry. And I recalled an earlier day when Michael Heron's father called to our Trinity rooms long before I was ever a prospect of marriage to one of his daughters. With this elegantly tall, professorial looking gentleman arriving, wearing a gaberdine raincoat of his own design and manufacture. His son Michael was out and as he waited there, looking about him, his suit lapels hand stitched, and trying to appear unconcerned at the sight and condition of the college sitting room which I was then using as a studio. Crusts of bread, open milk bottles on the table among my paints and brushes. As he kept repeating.

'Well, you're young, you're young.'

But a day or two later in the pedestrian joy of a Dublin morning I met Michael Heron walking up from the bottom of Grafton Street, a silk Trinity scarf flying from his neck. He'd been to the haberdasher's and was utterly transformed out of his previously baggy and unkempt clothes and was now sartorially resplendent in your best gent's natty suiting from the top of his trilby hat to the tips of his brand new shoes from a reputable bootmaker's. It appeared that his father, utterly shaken by his visit to his son's rooms had given him a large cheque with which to refurbish his appearance if not his college living conditions. The cheque being handed over with the words.

'Michael, I'd like you to keep up your dignity.'

Heron in those days, from an English public school and previously at Cambridge and a wartime serving British naval reserve officer, had been before the war sent by his father, in view of his expanding business, on a grand tour from Sweden to Corsica and from France to Russia. Heron ending up speaking many languages fluently but more than anything relishing strange cities and the writers and poets who lived in them. Although familiar with Paris, Rome, Stockholm and Berlin, the city he was coming most to adore, was Dublin. Patiently and even indulgently accepting its hardships and impecunious life. Haggling at length with the old ladies at their stalls over a pound of tomatoes. Heron, as well as his rooms in college, kept another place out in Dublin. And many an evening we walked up Great George's Street in its direction. Visiting pubs, one or two of which had literary connections but usually bore no trace or commemoration of these. And at a fork in the road of Camden and Charlotte Streets we would end up drinking the early night away in the pub then called The Bleeding Horse. And, albeit indirectly, it was through Heron and later meeting his sister and then his father, and followed by Gainor Crist's insistent counselling that I should marry that I ended up being driven to become an American imitation of an Irish peasant. And according to Patrick Kavanagh, a full blown rural phoney.

After long, stubborn haggling, when even the estate agent shook his head in disbelief at my refusal to budge from my offer, declaring finally that if the price were any lower the vendor would be out of his mind to sell. Terence de Vere White solicitously handling the sale. And even he thought £350 for three buildings and four acres had to be a reasonable bargain. And like happens at every country fair all over Ireland the estate agent uttered those words you hear at the verge of attempting to finally consummate a deal.

'Would you split the difference now that stands between you?'

Although the vendor was back in the village of Kilcoole I split the difference. The agent and I drank on it in the lounge of the Grand

Hotel in Greystones. I signed a caretaker's agreement and practically the next day, my college servant Noctor and I lugged my possessions out of my college rooms and out Trinity's side gate into Pearse Street to the bus whose last stop was Kilcoole. Without knowing it, I had come to one of the strangest places in all of Ireland. A patch of land just raised above the sea, a vacant landscape north and south with the Wicklow Mountains rising inland to the grey pointed peak of the Sugar Loaf. Waking in the morning to find myself listening to a donkey's bray and then half shattered out of my wits to see this animal's hoary head peering at dawn in our cottage window. It was the month of February. But a kinder one than usual. Although I still rose shivering from a wet mattress. My newly wed wife more mystified than complaining. Coping with cooking on an open fire and lugging water from a stream. Asking only to be able to own a cat and go take an occasional bath for a shilling at the Grand Hotel.

I was now in Ireland literally dug in, body and soul. And venturing to Dublin I would on return progress through St Stephen's Green and up Harcourt Street to its elegant granite station to come home by train. In order to stop at Kilcoole, one had to go up to the engine driver before leaving and make the request. Kilcoole surely being one

Valerie going to fetch the milk along the entrance lane to the cottage. It was along this muddy path that Behan went to the pub a mile away, carrying a suitcase full of my shoes and throwing a pair away into the field on the right as soon as they got wet and then putting on a dry pair. All easily done as Behan never wore or tied up shoelaces.

of the loneliest train stations in all of Europe. And where it was chosen to land guns in the time of the Troubles. It was a straight mile towards the sea from the village and four miles beyond Greystones. From where the sand and pebble beach went as a twin wavering ribbon with the white surf and a line of telegraph poles stood along the tracks like little pins stuck in a map. With hardly a habitation on this stretch of coast, farther south beyond Kilcoole station was yet another ten miles of watery bog called The Breeches. On windy, wintry days alighting on the station itself, half built on stacked great cast blocks of cement to hold back the sea, one was swept by the spray of the waves. The train tootling its whistle to abandon you there as it now made its way down the track to Wicklow town. Leaving a ghostly loneliness in its wake. I would then, jumping from stone to stone, have to negotiate a narrow path which led half submerged through a bog and past a tiny shrouded neighbour's cottage where lived a Mr and Mrs Smith. An astonishingly handsome couple both in their middle eighties and retired from Dublin. Behind their tiny gate they

Valerie, Patricia and John Ryan in the early days before improvements at Kilcoole. These two elegantly beautiful ladies in these primitive rural surroundings still seemed able to effect a garden party air of Henley and Ascot. Their host having abandoned his dinner jacket was now with rolled up tattered sleeves fighting the world with hammer, spade, brush and pen.

With Valerie in a field at Kilcoole, the Irish sea in the background and the leash of a visiting pedigree dog in my hand which might have symbolized my last contact with the respectable world. In those days one cannot imagine who might have owned a dog which might needlessly compete with the eating of food stuffs.

were enclosed in massive shrubberies. Their big blue grey cat Snooky, who was a marvellous ratter even with his balls cut off, sat like a sphinx on guard. The bog extended into their garden and came within yards of their front door and their chickens pecked and wet their claws in it. Their tiny three rooms were stuffed with their big pieces of mahogany Victorian furniture. And here is where they would stay to live out their lives. Sometimes walking four miles along the track to Greystones and back.

Strange stories, rumours and mystery surrounded this area. Grey Fort, a large mansion, stood empty just across the fields. Where Marconi was reputed to have once lived. As well as an AngloIrish family called the Hamiltons. To the north was a large estate in ruins with the remnants of fine brick barns and a massive walled garden. The builder of it said to have been shipwrecked on the shore and returned from America to build his home there. The area also seemed to have found other odd foreign folk like myself settling on this boggy coast. And my first lessons of the Irish countryside and being an imitation peasant farmer were learned here.

I had also come to Kilcoole with a steamer trunk full of fifteen suits and twenty pairs of shoes, two of which were for playing golf. I had a beaver collared polo coat as well as other extravagant and inappropri-

(Left) *Myself, Douglas Usher Wilson and Michael Heron at Kilcoole early 1950. The cottage behind, prior to any improvements but in which, over dinner and wine, many a late night discussion would take place in front of the fire. During which Douglas Wilson would invariably declare that I was talking through my paper asshole. Which I hope by now has at least hardened up to cardboard.*

(Right) *Michael Heron seated, Douglas Wilson, holding open a book in his hand and James Hillman looking on, a luggage case full of my books and documents is being perused. To the left lies my first efforts at a garden with my first mechanical farming implement, a wheelbarrow. And these visiting gentlemen are standing on the first lawn I ever mowed. Or pissed on.*

(Left) *Among my earliest visitors, Elspeth Bostock and James Hillman on the lawn at Kilcoole. Hillman an enthusiastic guest would usually rise at dawn and ask for the sledgehammer to knock down a building and invariably be found minutes later buried in its ruins and dust and needing to be nursed by Elspeth on my chaise longue throughout the rest of his stay.*

ate garments. The nearest my hand had got to holding a farm implement or tool had been in wielding a squash and tennis racquet. And above all other things there came something else new in life, my first country squabbles. And in this overnight I reverted to being as suspicious and paranoid as any peasant farmer. In my continued battle of survival, my reputation for a short temper and tough dealing soon spread. And was even used as an example as far as the village as an expression for people to say to others, 'Why don't you go down there and try that on the American.' Of course some did. To find me standing there with pitchfork, scythe and axe at the ready. But I was still painting my pictures which were now being exhibited a little less wet than they were previously. And at the same time I was still writing my forewords. Which were now far less optimistic. And under my heading, 'From Notes And Letters'.

We are not dead yet. Where there is life there is success. Two days until Christmas, the most vulgar and vicious time of the year – the time of the big kill, adultery and commerce when only the child has any purity or love. I have just come from a pub where they are drunk and fighting. In Ireland friendship is on the lips but not in the heart. The past six months I have been as bitter as acid and suddenly feel sad. When you're sad you don't want to fight the system and when you stop fighting the system it's time for the big sleep. When hatred turns to love, the will to kill is lost and that's bad in these hard times.

Recent reports from cosmologists have kept me on the philosophical jump. It looks as if the whole set up is tumescence and detumescence; bloom, blossom and seed. Is it any better to know. It prevents the blunders of giving to the poor or of having the fear of not giving. It teaches you the lesson that the integrity is in your own heart and in no one else's. Ireland has everything which is too much of nothing. It rots and kills the enlightened and corrupts that which is born original. Much better to dream of Ireland from 3,000 miles away. In the climb to disappointment, I feel a need of love and trust, but I have only met with calculation which is of money and faithlessness.

The animal wants its back protected and to eat. Man is that animal and when he has eaten, he deals in art and artifice, and it becomes lie and compromise; a soft, ingrate murmur of accents and incomes. They tell you to have Horace Ictericton, Bart. open your show, it will get a picture in the paper and give the opening 'class'; this is the universal feeling, the feeling to which all animals respond; the great aesthetic communion without body odour. Where do we go for love?

As outspokenness does in Ireland, it is first met by silence. Then the forces collect. Then the whispers. To see how they can shut you up. And then drive you out. But as a foreigner they always figure you're going to go soon sometime anyway.

As a matter of fact and publicity I did get a picture in the newspaper. Large and central and conspicuous on a page of *The Irish Times*. And coming into Greystones' train station as I did then to catch the train, parking my small red van across from the local garage of Watson and Johnson, there were awed gasps from various folk from whom one might buy a newspaper or apple. 'I didn't know it was your wife.' And clearly one secret was manifest right there, nearly on the spot where the Irish patriot Eamon de Valera was once arrested, that the whole of the neighbourhood for miles around assumed I was living in sin. Not least because of our young age for marriage. And that there were 'goings on' in the isolated 'down there' at Kilcoole.

Greystones was a small village with tiny fishing cottages still tucked in between some of the larger Victorian houses. It was with its tiny harbour cloistered and safe on an otherwise exposed windswept coast. It had what was unique in Southern Ireland, a large Protestant population and its most prominent social core was that of the modest-sized Grand Hotel. Its panelled comfortable interior of public rooms and a sun terrace overlooked a croquet lawn on its sea side where the morning sun arose out of the Irish Sea, and warmly, on such days, bathed this palace like place, flanked each side north and south by a collection of respectably commodious houses. Greystones was also possessed of a unique area known as The Burnaby. Crisscrossed by tree lined roads, with large houses within their lawns secluded behind high hedges and evergreen sub tropical shrubberies, this tranquil purlieu was as close to an English suburban elegance as one could get. And its inmates, if not Protestant, were then many of them of an ilk best described as Protestant Catholics. These highly respectable refined folk were prosperous professional and business owning people who made up the population of altogether one of the most attractive communities in the whole of Ireland. My own mother, sojourning at the Grand Hotel and one day having visited me at Kilcoole and then taking her afternoon stroll, came by a house being sold on the sea front. Taking tea with the lady owner who then removed the For Sale sign out of her window as my mother bought the house that very afternoon.

My mother's house in Greystones as it is today and lived in by my sister Rita. The two upstairs side windows stare directly down the bereft coast towards where one had settled near to Kilcoole. For five years alone behind its shutters closed against night and the sea sprays, my brother T. J. painted many of his hauntingly marvellous paintings.

Bathing in the chill waters at Greystones harbour. This idyllic setting was one to which one would frequently gravitate either to sit on the rocks in the sun or, late at night during a storm, to witness the mountainous seas crashing against the sea wall.

In my studio at Kilcoole with the early manuscript of The Ginger Man *and an early painting on the wall above my makeshift desk the top of which was a door torn off a cattle shed. It was upon this desk that Behan's manuscript of* Borstal Boy *lay next to that of* The Ginger Man *while Behan wrote his editorial comments in the margin of* The Ginger Man *manuscript. Although Behan thought that the book would shake the world, there is little evidence on the author's face that he so believed.*

Inland Greystones extended to merge with an equally attractive village situated further west near the Glen of the Downs, a hamlet on a hill called Delgany. Again with an attractive small hotel, marvellous Protestant old rectory as well as having an elegant Catholic curate who was also the distinguished painter, Jack Hanlon. And many a famed French artist's glowing picture hung in the shadowy gloom of his small reception rooms. As one went south from these two pleasant places there was along the coast, an area of Wicklow populated by a myriad variety of nationalities from all over Europe, from Dutch to Russian. Most finding their way here after the war. Just up the lane from me an Englishman from Leicester bought and cleared an acre and turned it into a market garden. Having that morning at four a.m. collected his vegetables from his holding, washed them in the stream and then rode with them on his bicycle twenty miles to Dublin. Because of the fine quality of his produce the merchants at market would await his arrival. And then cycling back, this wiry battling self educated and intellectual man would go for a swim in the cold sea and walk there by my studio chewing a raw carrot. Hearing my typewriter one day he made me a present of an old dictionary in which among other things I found the word 'Papaphobia'.

It was here on a June day and in a sun porch I'd built that I started to write *The Ginger Man*. My occasional visitors being James Hillman, Douglas Wilson, John Ryan, Tony McInerney, Anthony Cronin and last but not least, my first literary protagonist of all, Brendan Behan. But the latter's first arrival had been on one of the rare occasions I was away. I returned to find the oil stove blackened along with every pot in the place. And was confronted by disarray on every side as if a robbery had been committed. Which it seemed it had for there was the mystery of all but one pair of my twenty pairs of shoes gone. It did not take long to find out who the culprit was who'd unlatched a window and climbed in. Stepping out to my studio, I found there on my makeshift desk, a manuscript lying next to my own manuscript copy of *The Ginger Man*. Picking up the crumpled, stained and wrinkled sheaf of pages and in just turning a few I could see from words such as peeler, nark and screw that the setting was that of a British correctional institution. And as I was holding in my hand the manuscript of *Borstal Boy*, I recalled that day outside Davy Byrnes, Behan's proffered hand and his words 'Sure I'm a writer and you're a writer too.

> And fuck the
> Ignorant bunch of them
> Back in there'

X

With my then wife Valerie away, I proceeded on my own that day at Kilcoole to clean up the shambles of used pots and strewn furnishings. Then later that afternoon covered in dust and sweat I heard whistling coming down my long entry lane. And I went out to my front gate to see Behan in his shambling duck walk approaching me. Sockless as usual, and sporting an unlaced up pair of my shoes. I asked him where were the remaining pairs.

'Ah Mike, now I hate the countryside. I hate cunning country ways. I hate country people. And I nearly hate getting my feet wet just as much. Sure I knew you were already out somewhere in a pair of your own shoes yourself. So I took a bag full of the rest of them you weren't needing and wore a pair till they got wet on the way to the pub. And a bloody soaking wet walk it was too. As I went along I had to fling the wet pair into the field and put on a dry pair. You'll find them with no bother. Start there just over the fence is your first pair. And the rest every fifty yards or so up to the pub.'

Behan always had a favourite question for Valerie. Asking her to think of who she would rather be married to, himself or Gainor Stephen Crist. Behan although conscious of Valerie's English and finishing school background was at ease with her clearly unaffected ways, and he always felt free to make his visits out of the blue. Although one wouldn't encourage Behan to do your housekeeping, his own background in English Borstal and prison was treated by him as the same as having been at Eton or Harrow. And despite his expressed distaste of the countryside he enjoyed to come to this strange isolated piece of land. Where you could shout, cavort and sing. He had already read most of my then manuscript of *The Ginger Man*. Taking out his pencil as he did so and marking suggestions and corrections in the margin as he went along, finally signing the page to which he had read. He said it was a funny funny book but his voice

Valerie sitting with her favourite cat in front of my first improvements to provide a painting studio and later a study where the first chapters of The Ginger Man *were written. The window and the primitive wall above and below it, built by me.*

grew grave and serious as he spoke of my reference in the manuscript to the white death, which is how I described that resulting from tuberculosis. In reading bacteriology at Trinity and attending pathology lectures in the medical school I was at the grim autopsy performed on a young Dublin girl. And as the pathologist pointed out these various internal tubercular lesions and spoke of this disease I became aware of how rife it then was in Dublin, especially among the slum poor. I could see that my all enveloping mention of it, if not in a harsh and clinical manner, was nevertheless upsetting to Behan, who talked so openly, albeit privately, about his other medical and even venereal problems but who regarded this disease with a phobic concern. And he said I should play down the mention of it.

Behan as a visitor was uncomfortable stopped too long in one place. And he was anxious to progress further afield, especially if guaranteed to keep his feet dry while being transported on wheels. Mechanical devices had already begun to play a disastrous role in one's Irish country life. In America one had never even looked in under an automobile hood at its engine, never mind trying to join up

The author with his motor car formerly owned by the Bishop of Meath and striking a pose of the artist as a bohemian and aggressive young man, whose family's motto had become, 'I'll thank you not to fuck about with me you low cur.'

wires and take nuts and bolts off and try to put them back on. Still existing hand to mouth I had dared just then to buy second hand a car formerly owned by the Bishop of Meath. Disposing in the process of a red unreliable and very old Ford van. Which at first I could start mornings by pushing myself and jumping in. And then had to wait for the mailman on his bicycle and later even the assistance of my extremely strong neighbour, a farmer. But my Austin Eleven had a little black button one pressed on the corner of the dashboard and as one did so the engine would leap into life. And Behan and I were soon on our way touring the countryside. Driving first to the town of Newtownmountkennedy. Behan, like a pied piper entering the village, singing and talking to everyone on every side and drinking there in a pub. Then driving up the steep hill to the brim of Kilmurry, a table of land from where one could look down and distantly out upon the Irish Sea. And feel that Ireland was the very centre of all the universe.

There was then living and writing, another author in Ireland. This one full fledged, published, accomplished, and already achieving that one unforgivable thing above all, that of being rich by it. This gentleman was Ernest Gebler. Who had emerged from the same slums as Behan and remembered this little boy who swam bare arsed as he himself had done in the waters of the Royal Canal. Gebler, a tall, slender, high domed, taciturn figure had written a book about the story of The Mayflower and that vessel's journey to America and its landing on that shore. Which when published became not only a bestseller but was bought by Hollywood. Gebler had in successive steps moved back to Ireland from London where over a period of years the book had been written. And from a house in Dublin's suburbia he had now taken up residence on an estate overlooking Lough Dan, called Lake Park. In the lee of these bereft wild heather clad and boggy hills, this commodious lodge with a porch had two large reception rooms either side of its front hall, a stone flagged kitchen and several sprawling bedrooms. Its rearmost wings nestled against a pine forested hill and were built around a splendid enclosed cobbled courtyard of barns and stables. And in its sylvan isolation it was a paradise.

I had first met Gebler whom I now knew for some time as a distant neighbour, at a dinner party given by one of the more glamorous of Trinity's undergraduates, a David O'Leary. This astonishingly handsome, cultivated young man, despite his name, was the son of a British Army General and he delighted to bring together people whom he considered were the butt and at their peak of resentful gossip in Dublin. O'Leary had flatteringly put me head of the list. Gebler, due to his recent golden literary windfall, was not far behind. Gebler had also written an enthralling novel of Dublin slum life called *He Had My Heart Scalded*. And as he stood now boss of a great estate he was bemused to see Behan. But perhaps not as delighted to watch and listen to him as he cavorted running riot chasing servants, goosing the cook and conspicuously swimming naked in the cold, still waters of Lough Dan. Gebler was then recently married to a young American lady, his first wife, who literally was of fabled Hollywood, being the daughter of two of its stars. This strikingly handsome girl was a sensation as she arrived in Ireland, and stunningly tanned in her dazzling clothes, set all the Irish gentlemen who saw her alight. With her marvellous voice she and Behan listened to one another singing songs. And we spent an alternately tense and blissfully amusing afternoon here in this rambling shadowy house so neatly and pleasantly secluded with its tea pavilion in its walled ladies' garden. And where once, as I helped pile a load of turf in a barn, a workman confided to me.

'Sure that fellow Adolph Hitler, don't be believing any of that old rubbish he's dead. He's alive and well and living in Wicklow. Hasn't he been seen yonder more than once in the pub without his moustache.'

In the abstemious Gebler household the whiskey and Guinness were not flowing as fast and furious as Behan usually liked. And our next port of call on this Odyssey was to another writer, and too, a painter and horticulturist. We drove from Roundwood to Annamoe and to the house of Uplands also on the side of a hill where lived Ralph Cusack. No two people were more opposite nor more fond of one another than the mostly charming Cusack and the frequently obstreperous Behan. As the result of some brief conversational difference they could in turn hurl upon each other foul abuse and then fall tearfully contrite into one another's arms. Cusack, a talented painter and writer, was a man of almost painful sensibilities. As a music lover extraordinary, he would hold his brow listening to the great horn of his gramophone projecting symphonies out into the room from the top of his concert grand piano. Cusack, a serious bulb fancier, grew tulips, both importing and exporting these around the world and like Gebler had a pot to piss in. He was also the author of a hauntingly strange novel steeped in the obfuscations of Ireland and Dublin.

That night there was, as there always was, a party. Leaving Cusack's in a plethora of goodbyes, of tears, and hugs we went on our way through the Glen of The Downs in my blue Austin Eleven. The night cool summer breeze blowing a smell of wild garlic in the open car windows. And as we left the whole wide Wicklow world behind Behan was talking about *The Ginger Man*. About how although it showed the Emerald Isle in an unflattering light, that the book was an act of love for Ireland.

'Mike, as many as the kicks as you give us in the arse in that book, let me tell you I would consider it an honour to be ever mentioned in its pages.'

I chauffeured Behan and as he demanded we stopped in pubs on the way, where he would sing and astonish the habitués with his quips and burlesque. Pouring pints over his head while reciting various statutes from British law. Finally we arrived in the rough, squalid streets of Dublin's Night Town. Entering pubs there where Behan knew all the inmates as well as they knew him. In the corner snugs Behan urging me to hug all his old ancient lady acquaintances, grandmothers long retired from motherhood and its desperate struggle of survival. Behan whispering in my ear as he'd push me into a cackling old lady's arms.

'Mike, she was these forty years now as dedicated as any nun, selling her arse for a few bob down the quays, to buy a bit of bread and tea for the childer and she's deserving of a heartfelt squeeze now at the end of her long ordeal. Come on, give the old girl a decent and better kiss and embrace than that.'

Entering a great Georgian tenement not that far from the summer stench of the Liffey we climbed rickety stairs to a party held in an ancient, tall ceilinged room groaning with the weight of people and dense with cigarette smoke. Behan singing a stream of patriotic songs, frequently changing the words to others less patriotic which would incite mayhem among the fervent nationalists present. But Behan, as the roaring mouths and fists approached, was always able with a quip or two and a ready sympathetic laugh to hold off such assaults. And in his best Dublin accent mollify the aggrieved patriot and implore him to see the joke of the matter. And Behan, although an I.R.A. man, had strange opinions not usually associated with the southern Irish cause of ridding the North of its border and the supremacy of the northern British Protestant. And he confided more than once to me.

'Mike, let me tell you about the Orangeman. There's no better human being on earth. And if it were a choice between me own and one of them as a friend, I'd have the latter on my side any day. A brave and noble people.'

Behan this night was now filling a pint glass full of every conceivable drink available at the party. A mixture of stout, sherry, port, gin and whiskey, which he then topped off with poteen. Putting the glass slowly upended in one movement to his lips and swallowing it nearly to the last drop. Which he hadn't quite reached as he suddenly like a tree felled collapsed backwards unconscious on the floor. Standing next to him as he did so I could hear faint screams from somewhere below. Occasioned by the ceiling underneath being dislodged down upon an innocent, recently wed couple honeymooning in bed. Blamed for Behan's misdemeanour and now surrounded by an irate host and most of his guests, I was unpleasantly requested to dispose of the body. Behan, no light weight, was lifted up and put across my shoulder and I lugged him down three flights of stairs and tipped him in upon the blue leather rear seats of the car. Driving in the early dawn back with him to Wicklow. Waking in my damp morning bed, I heard someone out around the house talking to the cows who had broken through a fence onto the lawn. It was Behan whom I'd left asleep in the back of the car. Now awake he was advancing playfully to pet an already angered bull on the nose. Rushing naked out of bed I grabbed a pitchfork kept nearby for such emergencies and ran out on the lawn just as the bull's pawing forelegs were scooping up sods and sending them flying into the sky. Behan thinking this the beast's invitation to play.

'Ah, don't harm the poor creature, Mike, he means no harm.'

The bull charged the pitchfork and with a hook of its horns into the prongs sent it flying out of my hand and as I jumped behind a wheelbarrow full of weeds it, too, promptly was the next to go skywards, the weeds raining down on Behan like confetti, upon whom the realization had also dawned that he had better run for his life. But as he always could at such dire times, he had ready a merry quip.

'Ah Jasus, Mike, for the love of the Salvation Army would you keep the horns of that ton of bloody beast away from rooting me up the hole out of which all of me wisdom comes. And wait till I get me feet back into the pair of your bloody wet shoes and run.'

But barefoot Behan had already to flee around the corner of the car as the bull charged and removed the left back fender off that dignified vehicle. Behan skedaddling knees in the air, as he went shouting curses through a patch of stinging nettles and threw himself up on top of a hedge of briars. The roaring bull in close pursuit as Behan finally clambered up a young ash tree. I followed now trying to distract the bull away, hammering its massive heaving hindquarters with a shovel as its horns tore into the bark of the ash tree. The milling cows in their curiosity at last coming to one's rescue. Surrounding the bull and with a pair of heifers one on each side of him I was able to drive the bull in the herd, away. Behan, a devout proclaimed atheist in conversation, was on this occasion perched up in the ash tree, praying loudly to the Almighty for deliverance.

'Let me tell you, Mike, for a moment there, I did not think that my redeemer liveth.'

When things had calmed down later in the morning, and the sweat of Behan's anxiety had dried he suggested we go down my boreen to the sea. Old Mr and Mrs Smith who, hearing this singing, roistering voice coming at them across the fields and seeing Behan before seeing me, fled into the safe confines of the hedges around their cottage and locked their gate. It was only when I caught up and stood between them and Behan that they would show their faces. And, as I introduced him, Behan who could be charm itself when he chose, made his boisterous overtures to this dignified elderly couple.

'Now it's no mystery to me eyes that the handsome pair of you find the country living for all the bogs, the mad bulls and bats at night, much to your liking.'

When we reached the beach upon this cloudy, cool, grey day Behan took off his clothes and, running down over the stones and pebbles, plunged into the white, foaming, freezing waves. His great black shock of hair bobbing about as he frolicked like a seal out beyond the pounding surf. Leaving me standing in terror on this treacherous shore that I might at any moment have to jump out of my shoes and dive in to rescue a suddenly drowning Behan. And the sound now of a faint whistle reaching us. Far in the distance down this bereft coast I could see the tiny emerging dot of the train from Wicklow town. As it grew louder and closer it was a signal for Behan to come up out of the waves. And charge up the beach to stage centre on the pebbly sand. Legs spread wide, he took up his position, at the side of the tracks as the train approached. Arching his shoulders back and projecting his belly and privates forward. Penis in hand, he waved and shook it at the train's passing windows. Where I could see an occasional newspaper raised suddenly up in front of a lady's face and be just as quickly held aside for an eye to peek out. But not to say that among the wagging fingers there weren't also some laughing faces.

'Ah, Mike, I am showing them me scars of war.'

The site of Kilcoole station which was not much more than a piece of raised ground so designated. The tracks go towards Wicklow town and the beach on the left was the one upon which Behan nakedly cavorted after a cold dip in the sea, to entertain train passengers on their way to Dublin.

Behan was fond of describing and demonstrating venereal evidence of his penis having undergone wounds and mends. I did tell him that with my beard, the only one at the time in the whole of Ireland, I was known all over the district not to mention in plenty of parts of Dublin. And that there'd be a train soon coming in the other direction chock full of members of the Legion of Decency with coils of unanointed rope to string the pair of us up on the cross piece of a telegraph pole. And Behan always quick to accuse one of any sign of petty provincialism rounded on one.

'Now, Mike, if I had an erection, you could say I was being provocative but the fact that I was in a natural state of me own flaccidity, sure what bloody harm is it to wave me flag of procreation and stimulate the conversation among the passengers. Coming up this coast all they're able to look at on one side is the sea and the other the bog. And sure most of them anyway wouldn't know what it was I was waggling in my hand a'tall.'

Behan coming back up the fields came into the cottage with a roaring appetite. As I looked about to see what there was to eat Behan asked would I mind if he were to look after himself. Requesting only to have a big bowl, which he then spied, taking it down from the shelf and with his soiled sleeve, wiping its foot deep and foot and a half wide surfaces rim to rim with an elbow. Busying himself around the room, he collected various ingredients beside him on the table. Pouring in flour and baking soda on top of eggs he cracked then crunched and dumped in shells and all. Next came cornflakes, oatmeal, left over mashed potato, spoonfuls of marmalade, and strawberry jam, a banana broken in pieces, and tomatoes. And still the ingredients were added, a pint of milk poured on, slices of bread crumbled up, salt, sugar and ketchup, cocoa powder, a gobbet of honey until Behan turned around.

'Mike, what's this in this jar, I don't want to use anything that would ruin the flavour.'

'That's Horlicks, made of your pure pleasant ingredients.'

'And you don't mind if I take the rest of this tin of peaches here.'

Behan spooned out half the jar of Horlicks, shovelled in a spoonful of beef extract, sprinkled on vinegar, poured olive oil and over all squeezed a lemon. Taking a large wooden spoon he stirred the mixture to a paste, pouring in milk and water as needed to make it nearly liquid. Then as he had with his pint mixture of drink the evening before, Behan lifted the bowl to his mouth and with three brief interruptions for breath, swilled down the entire lot. Finally smacking and licking his lips as a beam of sunlight shone upon him in the window. And Behan turning around and seeing the astonishment on my face.

'Mike I always like to look after me health. And I'm a great believer in the Irish principle that more of something is better than less. And that if variety is the spice of life then why not have plenty of that as well.'

Behan disappeared off to my studio to collect up his manuscript of *Borstal Boy*. In which many songs and verse appeared. Behan maintaining the advantage of such was the space you could leave before and after each, thus with fewer words necessary to write to fill out the page. Behan always, as he did, would heft a manuscript in his hand, estimating its weight and then would proceed to calculate the number of words, choosing a page and with his little stub of a pencil, counting down the lines and then the words across and then his fingers flicking over the pages to the last one upon which he would scribble down his figures and then frowning in his act of multiplication would with satisfaction announce the result just as a farmer might, assessing the number of bales of hay stacked safely in the barn. An analogy, alas, which was as near as ever describing Behan's associations with country life. On this late afternoon standing at the corner outside my studio, and as Behan would in such profound moments of written words tabulated, he out of the blue became serious on another serious subject.

'Mike I regret as others might not that I have been sentenced to death in my absence by the I.R.A.'

'I'm sorry to hear that Brendan.'

'Well it's not as bad as it would be if I were sentenced to death and it were carried out in my presence. I have this little bit of the present geography situating me here to be thankful for that I'm not in my coffin. And now I'll tell you another thing. To your credit and not mine. I was behind your back complaining to McInerney that there you were bringing him bags from this place of old dirty potatoes and cabbages for him to use to feed his kids and that you wouldn't be that fast or generous when it came to buying a thirsty man a drink in a pub. And McInerney turned on me and nearly tore my head off, saying it was more than the fucking likes of me or anybody else had done.'

But such was Behan's concern for my present safety that it was only as he was leaving after four days, and singing me a small bit of commendation if not praise, that he made his announcement about the I.R.A. and that they were presently in search of him in every nook, cranny and pub of Dublin and might have already drawn their own conclusions that he was out peacefully sojourning in the countryside. And so informed, would acquaint with the friends he knew there and might now at this very moment be advancing belly down from every direction across the fields with Thompson sub-machine guns and gelignite ready to spray bullets and blast me, Behan, the whole place and both our manuscripts to kingdom come.

I had in those country days periodically gone to Dublin, arriving off the train at Westland Row Station and walking down its ramp into the city's dust and grit and the puddles of rain on its dark grey granite pavements. Often to call upon the sprinkling of people one still knew holding out in their various redoubts. And especially McInerney whose number of children had increased. And as often, too, one would take a solitary walk as I had done many a night out of my rooms in Trinity. Heading along Tara Street and turning down the Quays of the Liffey. Finding now that Dublin's sad, strange loneliness could overwhelm one. Making one recall the earlier days when occurred respite from the grim chronic poverty and hardship abroad in this city. The most memorable interludes being the arrival of the odd American coal ship in the Liffey river. With on board, its pouring hot showers, clean sheets and American accents and bountiful amounts of food. And Ray Guild, a former Harvard football star and scholar, who had accompanied Donoghue on a whim to Ireland and who was writing a doctorate when not freezing in the damp cold, managed through his and Donoghue's abilities as cooks to temporarily serve in this capacity while the ships were in port. And upon one vessel, its Greek cook confidentially whispering to Guild about Donoghue.

'Hey, who the hell is this guy you brought with you. He speaks aristocratic Greek, like he was a prince from a royal Greek family or something.'

At such times, knowing that one was being slowly driven out of this land, one could overwhelm with homesickness for America and its fabled prospect of plenitude. On these ships then arriving its officers would prove to be great hosts, providing food and drink for parties arranged in Dublin. To which myself, Donoghue and a handsome lady attracting Ray Guild would go. And where one could listen to a Shakespeare quoting black ship's steward who when asked how he was liking the city was quick to sum it all up.

'Hey man, there ain't no action here.'

But then just as quickly he would wax lyrical about his dream to one day transport a little package.

'Man. Just ten pounds. That's all it's got to weigh. Then one night after we've docked in the States, I just walk off the ship with it. Just one little package of that stuff they call heroin man, and I'm fixed for life. And then I'll just be able to sit back and enjoy this guy Shakespeare.'

But now out in the Irish countryside the freedom of being without a fear of reptile fangs strolling through tall, sunny, flowering meadows was to be enjoyed. Or the unworry of bears lurking in berry patches or awakened in their lairs in the outcroppings of rocks. And even

In my studio at Kilcoole. One found painting a much more congenial way of life than that of an author although it was the latter calling which I found necessary to indulge to get recognized in the first. And of course ended up persisting in the second.

where in America as a boy, once lost in the woods, it was a great old, giant, shaggy, grey Irish wolfhound who led me back to civilization again. Dublin now became dingy in contrast to one's growing affection for land and the clean aired countryside. And a growing distaste for the smoke and grime and falling down walls of that unnurtured city. Finding, too, that the love of Ireland lay under its grasses in its ancient bogs, and across its heathered hills. Upon which a man could walk, smell, touch and cherish their colours and textures. Unlike those I had known in America where one was always conscious of lethal things like spiders in dark corners and venomous snakes in tall grass. Here a safe Wicklow morn arose out of sweet mists off the sea and turned clouds pink high over the hills. The cock crowing. Swallows and swifts streaking the sky. The sound of a drip of moisture from the cottage slate roof hitting the ivy leaves. The ground silvered with dew. The air softly damp and cool and the first bee of the day buzzing.

My second summer at Kilcoole there came a crop of bountiful hay which my local farmer Farrell cut for me and which by hand I raked and put in cocks, trying topsy turvy to make and sculpt these as I went. And then an old established auctioneer advertised and held an auction. To which only one old, shrewd, nearby farmer came sourly denigrating the quality of my hay as we walked from cock to cock. Sitting then on the first stone wall I'd ever built waiting patiently for me to capitulate my reaping into his hands at a giveaway price. Which, in my crushed desperation following all my sweating hours, I was nearly on the verge of doing. But the wise auctioneer advised we not sell and hold the auction the following week. And when I told my farmer neighbour Farrell that the old farmer had said my hay was poor he commented.

'Well you'd soon find the hay would be good enough after he bought it.'

And the elder farmer Mr Farrell then showed me how to rake down and restack my cocks to a rainproof peak on top and how to pull away the hay from the base to make an eave and keep the bottom of the cock dry. Reaching then underneath and twisting the hay into roping to which could be tied a string that went up and over the cock and was joined the other side. This done, north, south, east and west to prevent the cock falling or being blown over in any wind. Telling me that any farmer, seeing the cocks firmly held down and sitting dry and safe, would conclude the hay was well made and could survive the rain and he could come back in his own time to collect them.

When the next time of auction arrived the old, shrewd farmer from up the road waited back on my wall again. And fortunately two more customers arrived. To whom I was now able to give an erudite guided tour. Demonstrating the weatherproofing of these now neatly raked and tied down cocks. And finally the bidding was begun. As usual with no bids. But then following the auctioneer's voiced impatience a bid came and the escalation was swift and furious and the price rose to a dizzying delightful figure. And somehow one felt one had won one's first great victory over struggle and adversity on this verdant isle.

And the lesson
Never while you breathe
Give up

My paintings prior to being transported in for an exhibition in Dublin. Probably some of these just completed, are drying in the sunshine. The stack of cement blocks were to form the walls of the sun porch I was to build on the cottage. And there can be no doubt that I did bitterly struggle to survive on the ould sod.

XI

My love of land came out of Wicklow. Growing up in America its terrain always seemed wild and anonymous and that you were always exploring but never lingering, and where in wandering you might get lost. Whereas in Ireland land was something you knew, touched and felt belonged to you, and into which one would one day melt away.

The village of Kilcoole was by laneway about three quarters of a mile distant or a half mile as the curlew flew. With its great looming rock jutting out from the hill on which the village was built. It was said to occupy a point at which tinkers had gathered camping on a common over the centuries. Beneath the rock in a small graveyard with ruins of a church, a vampire was reputed buried and upon whose grave the grass never grew. In the same way a forlorn air of mystery seemed to hang over this village and the countryside around. Where on the verges of the narrow sheltered lanes tinker families erected their tiny tents under which they slept. One day walking to the sea, I saw a small child playing along by the bog, on an embankment alongside a stream. As I walked by a little distance something made me turn and look back. And now suddenly the child was nowhere to be seen. I ran, returning to where the child had been, to find it was now face down immersed in the stream. I lifted the child out and emptied its mouth of water and it seemed unharmed, carrying it back soaking to its tinker parents who were some hundred yards away squatting on the grass around their fire, eating. I was referred to and thanked as the man with the beard. And long afterwards and even many miles away from Kilcoole in another county, wherever I would pass tinkers on the road, and they would see me and my beard, a greeting and blessing was always saluted to me. A reminder of how good tidings as well as gossip could travel and be remembered far and wide in this land.

On the brim of the Kilcoole hill there operated a local grocery store with a pub in the back. A Mr Poultan, a genial gentleman and his wife had bought this business and settled there. He was a ranking officer in the British forces who'd survived the Burma death march and had vowed then that if he lived he would go back into the world and be just the simplest of men for the rest of his days. And it was a strange atmosphere indeed to enter his village pub and have this pukka sahib serve one from behind the bar. But, as many other older and similar stories sprang from this curious coastal land. Towards Greystones one of my favourite walks was to Ballygannon across this flat low stretch of terrain. And along this empty seashore was the most haunting of all places. The outline of an avenue from the beach still remained where it was now half covered in bog. Leading from where a shipwrecked gentleman had made his way to the spot upon which he'd built a bijou redbrick strange, now a remnant, of a manor house with its exquisite redbrick barns and its vast overgrown walled gardens of boxwood hedges where cattle now roamed. One would return over the fields again with the plaintive curlews flying in the evening dusk, sounding their long lonely whistling cries, and feeling as if coming back from 10,000 miles away in another world. And somehow more contented to continue the days and weeks of one's solitude.

Ernest Gebler, who owned 200 acres to my four, and was an eccentric farmer to say the least, was my nearest erudite neighbour. And my isolation was occasionally broken by visits to this fellow recluse with whom one would talk half the night away over tea and the odd whiskey in his sitting room. Driving there up the steep hill to the windswept tableland of Kilmurry from where one not only looked down upon the fertile green of Ireland and its grey sea but up out of it into the universe. And beyond to this remoter wilder moorland countryside. Turning down a narrow dirt lane through gates and into a grander drive to sweep up in front of this sprawling house sheltered in the trees. Once as Gebler and I were standing in the forest upon the side of the hill looking down on the roofs of Lake Park, I asked him what he felt about his extensive tract and if he felt a sense of ownership over the large whole of it. And Gebler put his fist up against the nearest tree.

'Every bit of this bark, tree trunk and the branches. And all the shrubs and blades of grass that grow anywhere on these acres. I feel every particle of it as mine.'

An aerial view of Ernie Gebler's former estate as it was in 1951 overlooking its Lough. The house sprawlingly comfortable and nestled in this stunningly lonely beautiful spot, was the setting for many an all night conversation with Gebler whose writing efforts would begin following a midnight milking of cows and our discussions which ended as I retired to bed usually at three a.m.

Over my tinier piece of land my own feelings were the same as Gebler's. And although he was smiling at his own words, I knew Gebler meant what he said. Even to lying prone on the red, white, and black colours of his Meshed Beloudj rug in his front hall, the door open, and his high powered rifle aimed with its telescopic sights at distant sheep of a neighbouring farmer's who, when their noses were ready to go breaking through to dine in Gebler's greener pastures, they would feel the breeze of a bullet pass their nostrils, fortunately for them, triggered by a brilliant marksman.

Gebler being a night writer had organized his cattle and cows on the same lines. Sleeping till late morning or into the early afternoon when he would then take his leisure tinkering with his classically elegant cars. Their engines tuned to such superlative perfection that one or two were only started when he removed their spark plugs and with an eyedropper squeezed a preparatory oil into their cylinders. Or we might go walking the hills, shooting, and after late supper, approaching midnight, go with a lantern out to the barn to milk his cows. In the ancient mustiness talking of every subject under the sun and the moon, even to the then unheard of possibility of transplanting mint condition livers, hearts and eyeballs in place of those become the worse for wear. Confronting only a problem when considering the brain and the close to home prospect of new for old testicles. And standing once while the milk was singing in the pail and the moist wild Wicklow winds howled outside, I was telling Gebler that some of my favourite reading came in the matrimonial columns of the evening newspapers. But that my most favourite perusement of all was the lyrically saccharine In Memoriam poems of the obituary column. And on this thunder rumbling, stormy night in the white light of the Aladdin lantern, Gebler turned to look up at me, a smile slowly coming across his face.

'Mike, you're looking at the author right now. I got seven shillings and six pence for each one of those I wrote. They were put in a book so that the bereaved could select one which was then printed along with the death or remembrance notice in the newspaper.'

And in nearly the same practical way Gebler's career had begun. His Czechoslovakian born musician father had, when he was early growing up, prosperously written and played piano music in cinemas to the silent films variously in Ireland and England. Although travelling from place to place in a Rolls-Royce, young Gebler never attended schools and ended up having to teach himself to both read and write. As his father's occupation ended with the coming of talking pictures his parent now poorer became a musician with the Radio Eireann Symphony Orchestra and the family ended up in the slums of Dublin. In the big, old, Georgian tenement house where they lived, Gebler came across a pile of old magazines in the hall in which were stories he found he could imitate and then send and sell for a pound a piece to various religious periodicals. When his supply of inspiration stacked in the hallway finally ran out, he was driven to having to entirely invent and write in a new genre himself. As his recent found profession widened and flourished, his stories getting longer and his plots thicker, Gebler as a budding author became more ambitious, deciding he would now write a novel. Having meanwhile got himself a job as a movie projectionist, he took up part time residence in this tiny cubicle in the back of a cinema in Camden Street. Not least because, in setting to work on the landing outside his family's tenement flat, and as the months passed and no money materialized, Gebler's mother walking along the hall would, as she approached and passed, growl down upon his back.

'You'll never make a penny out of doing the likes of that.'

Removed to his black, airless nook Gebler continued his work, writing on sheets pinned to the inside of his coat which were then laid over his knee. As a reel of cowboy picture would run out and screams of protest would erupt from the audience Gebler knew it was time to change the reel on the movie projector. But often not before an irate manager burst in upon Gebler who would then stand up, closing his coat with his guilty manuscript disappearing under his jacket. Gebler shaved, washed and sometimes slept in this tiny projection room. Till one afternoon a letter from a London publisher arrived containing an advance of one hundred pounds for his first novel, *He Had My Heart Scalded*, a sad vivid story of Dublin ghetto life. Gebler packed up his shaving gear, slivers of soap, his dictionary and a few possessions, buttoned his coat, put on his cap and walked out the door. Leaving the fans with the first reel running of a Tom Mix cowboy film but which upon this occasion would not be changed when they shouted and stamped their feet to send the irate manager charging into the projection room.

Gebler was a disciplinarian for himself and those who chose to share in any way in his life. An early impecunious friend was once allowed a bed in a Dublin tenement room Gebler had rented. A chalk mark being drawn down the centre of the floor where Gebler ruled that his paying guest scrub and clean his area up to the line. And following his first novel's publication and the subsequent going out of business of the publisher, Gebler in his exacting orderliness immediately set to in the direction of another goal. One day an old book fell open at his feet and he saw on the page the word Mayflower. He discovered no historical novel had yet been written about that voyage, one of the most momentous events in America's history. He decided he would now write something which could become a bestseller and make a lot of money. Gebler boarded the night mail boat from Dublin to Liverpool and took the train from Lime Street Station to Euston in London. Down a basement in Kensington and at the British Museum, Gebler now embarked on years of work. Then one dawn morning, having had for sustenance to borrow a bottle of milk from a neighbouring front stoop, an hour later, gnawing on a crust of bread, a letter arrived. From an American publisher and containing a cheque. This time for 1,500 dollars. He climbed up out his dark room into the street, and every twenty or so yards, took the cheque out of his pocket, looked at it and threw his head back and laughed. He did this circling the Round Pond in Kensington Gardens till other park users brought him to the attention of the keeper. It was the first drop in the bucket which was to fill to brimming and make him a rich man.

But also such riches, as they did then and still do, brought many an Irishman with a pot to piss in, back to Ireland. And soon Gebler was in residence on his estate of Lake Park. This brooding windswept Wicklow hill which descended down through an ancient oak forest to the shore of these glisteningly black waters of Lough Dan. The tyres of vintage Bentleys, Bugattis, Delages humming on the pebbles up the drive. Roses perfuming the walks of the ladies' garden. Neat rows of potatoes, carrots, turnips blossoming. While Gebler sat at his typewriter in his study, a blazing turf fire burned in this sprawling lodge to shun away the damp and chill. And his mother had come to stay. Whose footsteps he now heard coming along the hall at the nearing of midnight just as he had settled down to work through till dawn. This sound approaching made the hair stiffen on the back of his neck as he awaited, hearing again those words hammered down upon him those many poorer years ago, 'You'll never make a penny out of doing the likes of that.' And which words now never came as his mother shuffled off to her sumptuous bedroom where a servant had lit the candles and had laid a hot water bottle to warm her feet between the linen sheets.

Gebler, voluminously read, was self educated in spheres that would astonish a Trinity College scholar. He was readily possessed of a knowledge of the world's everything from chemistry to physiology and from astronomy to astrology. But he had an irreligious disrespect for other areas of the fine arts. Which alas may have only been confined to one's own exhibited wet paintings. Two finally dry ones of which his first American wife actually bought. But which were both not long after used by Gebler to stop up gaps in his hedgerows to save his having to use nose tickling bullets to keep his neighbour's trespassing sheep out. But Gebler in the hard solitary world of writing remained much better disposed. When I, a year or two later, having gone to the United States and returned with the unpublished manuscript of *The Ginger Man*, Gebler upon reading it offered to support me till I'd completed some of its rewriting and the book found a publisher.

Despite the Irish being a highly disobedient race, an advantage when you yourself, a law abiding citizen, wanted to break a rule, it was nevertheless during these days that the other smaller and meaner spirited world of Ireland was then beginning to press upon one with its narrow minded, bigoted and bitterly resentful ways of its banned books, banned films, papers and periodicals. With much less money than Gebler to sustain me I was confronted with the wisdom of escaping the desperate sour restrictions of this isle. The manifesto foreword to my last exhibition ringing in my ears and the dream of America, land of one's birth and upbringing, growing brighter westwards over the ocean. It seemed that Irish born and reared men like Behan, Gebler and Ryan had antibodies in their systems to fight the spiritual afflictions and diseases of Ireland where you cannot fly off the handle or you'll be doing it all the time. But I was, too, to be a father. Of my first son. And Ireland had a fear. Always of bungling. That comes of dumb indifference. And my first wife Valerie had already removed to the Isle of Man where my eldest child Philip would be born.

My last act was to pack up my paintings in a great black box and deliver these to the station at Greystones. From whence they would solitary go on that lonely train ride along the coast where Behan might still haunt, shaking his prick at them as they passed. Meanwhile Gebler came down from his mountain lair. And we spent an afternoon haggling over my possessions which he bought one by one. I had sold my few acres at Kilcoole for nearly three times what I had paid for it. But had spent upon it three years of work. The sadness of selling lessened when it was bought by a pleasant, charming couple, a then Wing Commander Towell in the RAF and his Trinity educated doctor wife. I was astonished to see an odd tear in a couple of my neighbours' eyes as I said I was going. Leaving this land upon which one had scratched in the soil and where one had found it so hard to stay alive and finally realized one couldn't.

Gebler and I dined sumptuously at the Grand Hotel that evening following our bargaining session. And having so niggardly beaten down my prices all afternoon, he was now contradictingly generous, dissipating his potential profits as host on the splendours of our meal. Which we took amid the refined, mostly grey haired habitués

Kilcoole as it is today. The old stonework and my later building efforts merging as they return together to the Irish landscape, into which one can sink more gracefully than into any other on earth. And with unnoticed speed.

of this place. Who strolled the sea front, took lunch, tea, dinner and sat knitting or watching croquet on the lawn. These enviable Protestant married couples repeating their few words they had already without effort said to each other ad infinitum times previously. Gebler and I taking the house's oldest palest brandy to drink, toasting my departure as we sat back in the cosy comfort of our chairs.

'Mike, you'll be back. One day. Don't worry.'

But one is not finished yet with Greystones. Where now stood my mother's house. For there was Josie the barber in a tiny little kiosk of a building near the train station to whom I many a time went to have my hair cut. And great tonsorial artist that he was, he always knew if someone else meanwhile had touched or meddled with my hair. And nothing passing his window ever missed his eye. And after I'd long left, my brother T.J. came to live in my mother's house and winter there four winters. Testing the warmth as he moved from room to room behind its shutters on the sea front, being battered by the waves. The bellowing wind and flying spray shaking the windows and flapping the slates on the roof. And T.J. one day in his polite conversation getting his hair cut inquired about Josie's after hours' activities and discovered that as well as downing a pint of stout or two, he often did a barbering job on the recently deceased who were in need of sprucing up with a haircut. And T.J. thereafter, not taking any chances and not wanting to seem too particular, bought a set of clippers and scissors and comb to be thereafter reserved for sole use upon himself while still alive. And T.J., after many long talks and discussions, asked him once what he wanted out of life. And Josie said.

'I just want one simple little thing and I only want it after I'm gone. And that is for somebody somewhere to just remember me once and raise their glass to me in a drink, and say this one's for Josie.'

And it is in the same easygoing nostalgia that I now recall another Irish gentleman whom one had known these years and who was last to see me off to the Isle of Man at the airport as I was leaving Ireland. Ubiquitously brave, and without an ounce of literary or artistic ability or indeed even an interest in appreciating such, he was of such cocksure nerve that could enable him to sell a dozen grains of sand to a man who owned a beach. His Christian name suitably was Valentine and his surname Coughlan. And as many an Irishman can, Coughlan could simplify the whole story of his life in just a few sad but unselfpitying words. Always full of cheerful fight, he would weather all embarrassments at my wet painting exhibitions. In the case of someone sticking their fingers in my cobalt blue he had a turpentine hanky ready to cleanse such grasping organ. He stood faithfully by my little pile of exhibition catalogues assuring that a sixpence was deposited in the plate on their purchase and that few would escape buying one. This boyhood friend of Tony McInerney's was an Irishman who could serve as the symbol of all Irishmen, stage or real. We had become fast friends having begun such friendship at the end of an almighty fight in the middle of Duke Street outside Davy Byrnes on the same spot where Behan and I had confronted and first shook hands. The battle having resulted from my having caused his life to collapse in an almighty shambles.

I had met Coughlan on what was an attempt at having a polite gathering after pub closing one Dublin evening which had all begun innocently enough. With John Ryan in attendance who was at the time still of the status of a much sought after bachelor. Coughlan knew of a large prosperous pub in the outer environs of the city where in convivial musical surroundings licensing hours were stretched. In the always highly optimistic company of Gainor Stephen Crist we set off. And after an extended evening at the bar downstairs with many a song being rendered by the company, the publican who lived in an elaborate establishment above issued an invitation at closing time. Ushering us all carefully selected to the back of the premises and up the stairs. And in a large, heavily furnished Victorian room we were plied with trays of drink and food aplenty by the publican and his eager to please hefty sons. Suddenly out of a door there appeared four attractive ladies in their crinoline décolleté party dresses, each upon introduction taking up a position beside a gentleman. Crist, ever the man to be well behaved unless finding it urgently incumbent upon him to be otherwise thought that at last he was being introduced to a world of Dublin of which he had heard rumours but was always too busy in other activities to take time out to investigate and he very much warmed to the occasion. Concluding that he was at long last comfortably ensconced in his first real Irish house of ill fame. Aided and abetted as songs and music burst forth and John Ryan danced with one of the prettiest and bosomiest of the ladies. Crist leaning over to me to confidentially confer.

'Mike, I think tonight we're on to something entirely new and different.'

As was my wont on selected occasions I occasionally called a spade a spade and I affirmed to a purringly contented Crist that it would appear we might be there to entice to bed for payment. And to show we were not reluctant sporting gentlemen I announced over the loud sound of the music.

'Yes, it would appear that tonight's the night for fornication.'

The latter word which I had regarded as being discreet in the circumstances had not left my lips before there occurred four seconds of absolute silence instantly followed by roars as the first lunges were made and blows struck. For these were the four attractive respectable daughters of this publican who were by an hospitable host being brought forth from their purdah to delight and enthrall us, representing as we did unattached males, the only true one of whom was John Ryan, but who was at least better known than most to have one of the finest pots in the country to piss in. It was only the miracle of

Coughlan's split second brilliant diplomacy and strong arm intervention that a death or two did not take place in this house that night, and only an aspidistra in a pot crashed broken on the floor.

But it was following the publican's daughters' discreet retreat and our departure that the real trouble happened. Having so disastrously blotted my copybook and disgraced my dearest friends and had all of us thoroughly embarrassed and ushered forever out of that house, and having thereby had Coughlan take pity upon my mortification, he hospitably invited all of us disappointed back to his flat situated in a highly respectable purlieu of Dublin. Coughlan newly and recently married to an attractive lady, was a product of Ireland's best schools and came of its best society, having taken up a modestly important position in a large draper's. An outstanding bridge player and Ireland's champion whistler he had long assumed respectable membership in Dublin's professional class. However, despite being straitlaced, he could be irreverently honest and surprisingly outlandishly generous. But, as would happen on these occasions, Coughlan arrived back at his flat to find that a gathering of well bred lady bridge players invited by his wife had not yet departed. Viewed as a happy occurrence as two of them tended to be jolly and stunningly attractive. But Crist, as he was wont to do, had already attached to our little party two ladies and their attached fancyman who pretended of all things to be a Baron from Liechtenstein albeit with a thick Dublin accent. But all three were clearly of doubtful character and intention and had been picked up on the street just outside the pub of the recent gross misunderstanding. It was not long before one of these tough latter ladies attempted to stab yours truly in the eye with a lighted cigarette with some accusation of impropriety usually deserved while I was enjoying my higher spirits. However, as one did not strike ladies, and taking umbrage, satisfaction had to be exacted from their fancyman who had provoked the attack in the first place and was already calling me unpleasant names. The battle among us began. Gainor Crist, always a stickler for fair minded justice, could also be mediator and peacemaker, but on this occasion decided instead to be referee. Knowing somehow that peace was not to be had at any price nor at this particular time, he announced.

'Make room please. Please make room for the combatants.'

Crist had astonishing faith in my fistic prowess, nearly to the point of acting as my manager on the edge of any fight and even taking side bets. He was himself one of the strongest people I'd ever come across but rarely had I ever witnessed him engaging in fisticuffs when it was simpler to just shove me out into the fray while he saw to it he got the best odds and saw that no one was undeservingly hit in the haggis. The thunderously noisy mayhem having begun with furniture flying, windows perforated and ladies screaming, it was not long before the attentive landlord of the building heard the uproar two houses away down the street where he lived. And he promptly came rushing in voluminous dressing gown and slippers and tasselled nightcap through a downpour of rain to knock on the Coughlan door. Which was opened by the impeccably polite Gainor Stephen Crist to whom the landlord now addressed his inquiry which suddenly became hysterical for just at that moment the body of an entire person came bursting through an aperture that had once been a glass window in the front elevation of this neo Georgian building.

'What's going on in my house, stop this immediately.'

Crist in his grey herringbone tweed jacket, grey flannels and other if well worn respectable ivy league garments, stood as he often did in the attitude of a saintly seer which, of course, he was, and replied to his anxiously overwrought inquirer.

'In exactly five minutes you are not going to have a house.'

To this now stunned person in his wetted nightwear whose mouth was speechlessly very wide open, Crist bowed and quietly closed and then ominously locked the door. For this innocent gentleman in his present inclement nightmare and shut out from his own building, was merely attempting to get a fair return upon his reasonable investment. But such folk, no matter how honest and just they might be, I heard often called a gombeen man. A term which I learned was used over the length and breadth of Ireland, to refer to a tolerated but unliked and sometimes bitterly despised species of individual usually engaged entrepreneurially in a small business and who in running a shop or renting a house became the creditor of his customers and tenants who in the purchase of bread, butter, milk and eggs or in accumulating unpaid rent, went ever deeper into debt. And it always surprised me that such usurious but hard working and meticulous folk were by the Irish at large invariably regarded as fair game. And on a night like this when, slightly sooner than it was precisely predicted, the flat, its bathroom, kitchen, bedroom, drawing room and its flight of ceramic ducks ascending across the wall and other sitting room contents therein, were demolished, it was considered that any property owner had this coming to him. Crist especially being one long practised in aiding and abetting débâcle befalling landlords. And the respectable blameless Coughlan was subsequently swiftly evicted and sued.

As I was the accused prime mover in the event, Coughlan went looking for me in every pub all over town. Reasonable enough as, through no fault of his own, except his generous hospitality, he had been deprived of his happily married nest and most of his breakable chattels which had previously perched decorously under the roof once upon a time over his head. Rumour of the impending fight as it did in Dublin spread rapidly and far, now taking on the proportions of an eagerly awaited world heavyweight championship. Crist taking bets at seven to one that Coughlan would not last through the first ten seconds. The height, weight, reach and wins, losses and knockouts of the contenders in previous fights being discussed in every pub within crawling distance of Grafton Street.

However for me, a fervent peacelover, it was quickly becoming a nightmarish prospect as Coughlan, not meeting up with or finding me, was now planning a late night assault upon my college rooms at number 38. My difficulty there being that I had in another melée, already smashed the lock and half broken down my front door through which free entry to my chambers might now be made. And as I now expected any time past pub closing for an enraged embittered Coughlan, who was indeed a heavyweight and a schoolboy boxing champion, to come thundering like a bull into my hall, and charge across my sitting room and splinter in my bedroom door, I resorted to the expedient adopted by the Princess of Charnelchambers who secreted her dagger near her through the night. And I stuck my sharpest dissecting scalpel in the side of my wardrobe in ready reach in order to at least have someone else's blood flowing along with mine, in case I were jumped upon while my legs were immobilized under the bed covers. This in the Emerald Isle being a favoured position in which to catch an unwary adversary. But, alas, attempting to sleep with one eye and ear open and freezing with my blankets half way down, only resulted in entirely sleepless nights and on the third when morn came I got up enraged and instead went looking for Coughlan.

Dublin in this respect was a turn of the century cowboy town of the

American West. Where, with your fists as six shooters, you headed along Grafton Street, wondering which one of the sidestreet saloons into which you might go might have you confronted by the fastest gun. And indeed if you were at all known as being such yourself there was no shortage of those growling nearby sizing you up. With my singular beard and resembling a sad faced Jesus Christ I was a marked man all over the city. And wherever I went in my holy conspicuousness, inevitably I was accosted, at least by someone brave enough to mutter under his breath. But more than just frequently someone would come roaring into my peaceful presence shouting, 'Are you him.' But with Crist so eager to take bets biased in my favour many an occasion was settled by being bought a drink. But upon this midday I found Coughlan in Davy Byrnes. The two of us retiring to the gents where I pronto requested him out under the sky. And all finished peeing and then without a single soul in witness except dumbfounded passers by, Coughlan and I had it out up and down the centre of Duke Street.

In the interim of spending his days searching for me Coughlan had also lost his job. But no man anywhere was as adept as he in surviving or, as he ultimately would, in prospering. But in these days he took up residence in the faded redbrick hostel of Iveagh House down Bride Street. Refuge of the male indigent where a cubicle for the night could be had for one and six pence. And whose noisy, boozy, cigarette coughing inmates were chastised by Coughlan to keep up their self respect and 'don't go out looking like that and giving our city a bad name to the tourists'.

And as all good things did in Dublin then, as they still do now, the latter establishment had its origins in Guinness and the profits of that great brewery. But Coughlan being attractive to the ladies had several stationed around Dublin supplying him with porterhouse steaks and other accompanying edibles. And nothing him dismay as he would entreat me not to waste my time worrying. But his most wonderful attractiveness was his calm indifference to painting, sculpture, music and literature. All summed up in one remark.

'Guff from eegits.'

Never without his gents' natty suiting, and white detached collar over his vertically striped shirt and enclosing his neatly knotted tie, Coughlan could enter any establishment and brave his way past any human obstacle. At a word, nothing was ever past his being able to get, or at a request, see a deed was done. Among his personally favoured accomplishments in derring do was his expertise at, as he called it, honest smuggling. For whenever there existed a profit to be made from one land to another, Coughlan was within the hour in transit with a roar of laughter. Once, with a large brown leather valise in his hand, approaching a customs man. Coughlan pretending he was carrying a great weight, which he was, struggling to get the piece of luggage up on the customs man's counter.

'There are 2,756 watches in this valise and because I wouldn't want you to think I was importing 3,000, I would be pleased if you would let me open up for you to count them for yourself.'

'Well that's fine now. You just move along there now, we're busy enough counting. '

The customs man chalking his mark on Coughlan's case, as he light as a feather now lifted the great weight down from the examination table and waltzed out on the terra firma of the docks with his declared 2,756 watches in tow, duty free. And the selling of which would make him many the thousands of pounds richer. Deservedly was Coughlan later to become one of the greatest of charming villains ever to antagonize British justice.

And I can

Hear

Him now laughing

Even as deeply

As he may be

Safely

In his grave

Counting his coins

XII

Starting on my long journey back to America I had gone for my last and favourite walk in Dublin as I had done so many evenings from my rooms at Trinity. Heading out along Tara Street where the opening words of *The Ginger Man* began, and past the baths where many a Dubliner repaired behind these dirty red bricks to get rid of his bodily grime in the big steaming hot tubs. At Butt Bridge turning down George's Quay and City Quay past the Guinness boats, and the chug chug of their barges and the mountains of barrels stacked on the cobble stones. Gangways up to the moored ships. Always thinking the pubs looked bereft and lonely but knowing by their steamed over windows that inside they were alive with dock life. Past the church indented discreetly in from the quay where a Dubliner might go to confess the worst sins of impurity.

As one reached Britain Quay ahead lay Dublin Bay. And here I would then cross over the top of the locks of the Grand Canal basin and come to where the Dodder river emptied into the Liffey. In the water always several floating dead cats or dogs. Attesting to the more than occasional Irish ambivalence to animals, which alas I admit to inheriting. Walking along the Dodder banks these waters flowing with such sewerage always reminded of the death and penury in Dublin. Now one would climb up steps to Ringsend. Where near the bridge the elegant name of Shelbourne was up on a pub. If one were to sail out on the mail boat to Liverpool it was this isolated south bank of the Liffey along Pigeon House Road that one would see. A sad empty loneliness and the last vestige of Dublin before reaching Liverpool.

Sometimes I would instead of crossing the Dodder, walk past the gas works and along a street called Misery Hill. Where in my college days I would stand for many long minutes peering into the stygian interior and watch a man perpetually there illumined by pink orange flames, shovelling coal in a furnace. I ventured here, a solitary pedestrian, and never encountered another lurking soul. But once, as it was growing dark one evening, I was nearly murdered. When instead of crossing to Ringsend I walked back along Hanover Quay beside a wall of high coal bunkers. Suddenly something made me look up. And there, a few feet above my head, standing on top of the bunker, a figure loomed with a stone raised to throw down on top of me. Who may have ended up dropping on his own head for, as I looked, he lost his balance and disappeared falling back into the coal. But it was always after such excursions out into this barren bleakness of Dublin that one would come back again into Trinity's academic cloister, the gas lamps faintly gleaming, and the choir's music from the chapel chasing away the winter damp air. And know that one never ever wanted to leave this peace and serenity.

Departing at the airport to Coughlan's waves, I flew away to the Isle of Man. Which, like the moon is to the earth, this Manx island outpost is to Ireland. A neutral independent place where the Irish need not feel they were among the British and where on holiday they

Myself having breakfast with Michael Heron on the garden terrace of my mother in law's house where she lived until her death. Life in this house, with my mother in law a brilliant hostess and Michael Heron a connoisseur of wine and food, was possessed of considerable bliss and would always turn my greying eyeballs glistening white. Tea at four, sherry at six thirty, dinner at eight and the sound of the sea round the clock.

Philip Donleavy and Valerie on the road outside the house once lived in by my mother in law at Port e Vullin, Isle of Man, and the wall below which lay the tea garden. Philip, always an acute observer of life, being about eighteen months old at the time.

could feel unwatched and freely breathe unshackled from the wagging finger and whispering voice of crut. Coughlan saying as we shook hands.

'Mike, the only thing wrong with the Irish is they think they own the country. But they're quick enough to get out of it when it suits them in the pocket book. And return only when the mother or the father is dying. But then after the funeral a few of them get stuck for months and years afterward like some lost, wet fly stuck in the gluey sap of a tree.'

On the Isle of Man after a picnic on the edge of the high cliffed headland Niarbyl Point, where one looked out across to the Irish mountains of Mourne, my son Philip was born following a quickened journey back over the mountain road to Port e Vullin in the north of the island. Relieved of my struggles on the land, I now reverted back to my former undergraduate ways and collapsed pleasantly into luxury and leisure, courtesy my now widowed mother in law who always bravely bought one or two of my drier paintings. One breakfasted in a terraced alcove under a palm tree, the sea breaking upon the beach beneath the garden wall. Late mornings motoring for fittings to Kaighen, my Manx tailor. Gâteau and Earl Grey tea at four, sherry medium dry at six thirty. But soon from this temporary easeful civilization, I was to return to Dublin. Flying from this Manx small airfield to sojourn a couple of days at the Shelbourne Hotel before taking the train to catch the ocean liner *America* at Cobh. Thence to cross the Atlantic to New York as my own parents had done. And of which my mother had said.

'One minute I was but a barefoot girl in an Irish field and the next I knew I was on Park Avenue.'

And now with an heir, arriving back in Dublin. Where it was always an eager Irish inquiry to know of children and especially of how many you might have. In from the Wicklow countryside Ernest Gebler arrived in his fur collared, long, leather motoring coat to take tea at the Shelbourne Hotel, his MG sports car parked across the street. I could sense that even he, in his own professed love of this land and despite his entreaties that I should not go, hankered himself for the promise of the New World which had already bestowed upon him so many riches. On that morning's walk in Dublin I kept thinking that around each and every corner I would find again some trace of the faces, laughter and voices which made life live in this city and whose buildings and streets had a way of making you feel it was yours. And that the streets would speak. The granite paving tell of the feet trod there. Alleyways whispering out their sad sorrows of cold embraces. Pub walls repeating all their tales. The calumny, backbiting and lies that begrudgers spoke. The scheming revenges keeping alive energies that would otherwise die. The envious burdened by their resentments, shuffling through the city avoiding looks and eyes. But all of them even more than the buildings and streets, were part of the sad and betimes glad soul of Dublin.

Crossing the ha'penny bridge from Bachelor's Walk over the Liffey, swans cruising beneath, I walked towards an old granite archway, realizing suddenly that Ireland was a state of mind I now carried with me where e'er one might go. Of words said and listened to and dreams promised. Then as had happened in all my previous years abroad in Dublin I met coming around a corner Randall Hillis, a brilliant law student now graduated and Gainor Stephen Crist's brother in law. He was on his way to the hospital to attend upon an old army friend who had come for the first time visiting to Dublin and who had suddenly taken ill and died the previous day in hospital. The deceased gentleman without living relatives had known no one in Dublin but Hillis who was now having to arrange his funeral. Planning to meet that evening for a drink, Hillis said he would later be going to keep his friend company in the hospital chapel where the funeral director had arranged for the coffin's vigil. That night I walked with Hillis in the wet, cold, winter darkness to this lonely death through these bleak back Dublin streets. And already one saw the sad desolation in the pale light of this hospital's window placed in their chill walls of grey stone. Inside, a black habited nun whisperingly directing us along the bare halls to the stained glass windowed chapel door. A low murmur of voices from within. And a startled Hillis entering to find the chapel full. Mourning figures kneeling and praying and votive candles burning. In the wax scented air we knelt at the back, watching these strangers pay their respects to the coffin. And as one of the old ladies blessed herself from a font of holy water nearby, Hillis, as she was leaving, inquired of her if she were a friend of the corpse.

'No, your honour, but whoever he is his soul couldn't be the worse off for the saying of a few of my humble prayers.'

Hillis was quietly pleased with the befitting event of this lonely friend who had come half across the world to see him, and had, as he wouldn't anywhere else, grievers to escort his final parting this earth. And next morning in this other world of Ireland, where gaiety, feigned or real, reigned and elegancies formed settings for another way of Irish life, I retired to the lounge of the Shelbourne and resting back in its flower decorated, deeply soft chairs, one ordered from an always slightly distracted flowing, grey haired waiter a bottle of champagne. To toast a bon voyage to Hillis's friend. Whose funeral was then happening at this eleven o'clock on this hotel's busy morning. Where folk arrived from foreign parts scrutinized foxhunting fixtures posted in the hall to which they were en route. Their monocles flashing as their haughty voices cut the air. Strutting and striking superior poses in their tweed suitings. Boy pages with their slicked back hair singing out names through the public rooms. Lunch aromas wafting from the kitchens. My old pal of the 200 mile an hour tennis serve coming to call. Keeping his life a secret as he always kept it. His magnificent vowels explicit and shy. Keeping his sentiments away from alien listening ears and prying eyes he knew so well were

Randall Hillis at Kilcoole aseat on the running board of the Bishop of Meath's car. This steely nerved gentleman who had fought the war in the Canadian Army had survived days of bombardments trapped above the beaches of Normandy, was responsible for doing the first proofreading of The Ginger Man *manuscript.*

eavesdropping and watching all over Ireland. These citizens so full of curiosity just like their cows and horses. To find out what you're up to. And then to see if there is any hope of making you fall flat on your face. But then later rushing for the train as it was about to leave for Cork, one's dire thoughts concerning this land were again retracted. The station master was about to sound his whistle and drop his green flag which, upon seeing us, he now held waiting behind his back.

'Ah, now, take your time we wouldn't let the train leave without you.'

But however briefly, one was soon to know too, in the obtuse sense, that one was back in Ireland. For following this long train journey on a rainy dark day on the Irish five foot three inch gauge railway track to Cork westwards via that strange stop Limerick Junction outside Tipperary town, we arrived at our hotel and had repaired to the dining room. To there, upon the white table cloth, unavoidably have tomato soup, mashed potato and stew, strong tea and custard. The well meaning waiter, in his stained, soiled white jacket, the sleeves rolled back from his wrists, hovering at the table and dipping back and forth several times like a cobra ready to strike before he would put a plate on the table. And then suddenly, just as we were about to begin our meal, Valerie sensing something amiss suddenly got up from the table and rushed back to the room. To there find that the maid had laid a raincoat over a sleeping Philip's carrycot. Had it not been for Valerie's premonitions and having not wanted to leave him alone, Philip would have smothered.

It was a departure now after seven years in Ireland. And in the soft mists, the drops of moisture streaked the train window as we rumbled along the coast of Great Island, from Cork to Cobh. To this town of steep cobbled streets and its old weather worn houses. Gulls squawking and alighting in the sea breezes as we took a tender out to the great black hulled liner *America* sitting majestically high on the water. Climbing aboard into its bright lit warm corridors. All shiny new and spic and span in its cabins. And with a trumpeting horn of the ship echoing back from the surrounding hills we sailed out upon heaving swells of the Atlantic Ocean southwestwards down past the old Head of Kinsale, past Cape Clear and the Fastnet Rock. And knowing that northwards was passing the last point of Ireland. Slea Head of the Dingle Peninsula.

On board the ship to be thrown instantly back into America. And the slow awakening to the shortcomings of that land. Where, returned isolated to the wastelands of my own romantic Bronx, I was soon to best get to know the Ireland I was leaving. Which before the next year was out became the only place I wanted to be, again under its rain and again feeling upon my hands its enduring loamy soil. Arriving, I met and talked with previous American born friends of Irish origins, and could see that the succeeding generations had never erased in the New World that indefinable look, skin, and cast of face that still reflected under their quizzical countenances the ancient suffering of this race. One did not know how scientifically explicit to be to their curiosity as to what it was like over there. Unable now under the weight of seven years of moral shock to repeat my first rose hued impressions. Or to tell of Ireland's uniqueness. The prevalence of vaginismus, among the female population. Namely the painful spasm of the vaginal muscles which in Irish women prevented the penetration of the penis. And thought to be the greatest cause of non consummation in the land. Attributable to a combination of raging tyrannical fathers, the Irish Catholic religion and the taboo of the body's sensuality. Yet one had, in one's moral American innocence, come upon, in just one evening down in the latter day Charnelchambers, more penetration and more fornication than you could wave a crucifix at. Such observations were, of course, always subjects for Honesty Night back in the old sod when the drink had stirred the passion to spout truth aloud and instead of singing praises to the sparkling silver streams, shimmering rainbows and green boreens, declarations were made as to the god awful crut encrusted misery of that bloody country.

As this year passed, having returned to the United States, with the manuscript of *The Ginger Man* growing thicker, one became increasingly homesick for the land that gave this book birth. But who should one day turn up out of the blue, but the man who had in the first place imported honesty to Ireland. A. K. Donoghue was back in Boston now prospering giving accent lessons among other things to those who wanted to speak the King's English. His inspiration in this pursuit coming from Trinity College's Anglo Irish who, if they were not in the squares of college conversing, would then be wielding such superiority out in the wilds of Ireland high up, boots gleaming upon a horse. And in this latter recreation Donoghue was already daily taking riding lessons. Meanwhile I was branded everywhere as an Englishman. My father telling a friend that any day he expected the Union Jack to be flying from a flag pole top of the house. But then not many days later I was reassured to overhear in a downtown Sixth Avenue bar a self proclaimed authority maintaining that the best English in the world was spoken by those at Trinity College Dublin. As my accent was just about the last asset I had now in the world, I was cheered. For the dreams of America were turning rapidly sour by the hour. Ireland for all its impoverished liberties and encrustations of crut that one had railed against, now loomed as a heaven beyond heaven. And if I could not as it now appeared, survive America, Ireland was the place where I would rather most go to die.

And lo and behold, hot on my heels and the growing holes in the backs of my socks, who else should arrive but that traveller most intrepid, and the eternal patron saint of tourists, Gainor Stephen Crist. Deposited upon this North American shore with his own débâcles in tow. And carrying recent tales of the old sod, convoluted and entangled as only Ireland's embellishing gossip could make them. There was in his life now a new lady Pamela O'Malley, later to be his second wife, who from a family in Limerick was a foxhunting equestrian as handsome as she was elegant. And a lady who exemplified the best in Irish women, that of braving and surviving the foible strewn paths taken by foolhardy men. Crist arrived, too, with the essences of Ireland, its familiar names, and long unchanging land and cityscapes to which I was now clinging to hold afloat one's spirits on this continent so massive and anonymous. That crushed from you not only your voice but every vestige of your pathetic identity. My father telling me that getting on television would get you somewhere, and as I hardly had car fare to get on a bus, I had to dismiss this unlikely prospect. But one suspecting and even knowing that if you were able on the airways to scream coast to coast into every American ear and stand stark naked on your head clapping your feet in front of every American eye, you still would be erased from every American mind a few seconds later.

And yet, America did have some pockets of tranquil repose. A. K. Donoghue, in early childhood growing up in this land with his Irish born parents, thought then that he was alive and well in Ireland. Overhearing his mother and father referring to Paddy over beyond in the meadow milking the cow and Bridget barefoot braving a muddy ditch collecting eggs. Donoghue was nearly seven years old when suddenly he one day discovered from his taunting friends that he was in fact in Boston, Massachusetts in the U.S.A. Nevertheless he was able to reply to his scorners with 'Pogue ma hone', which was the Irish for 'Kiss my arse'. It was this same recalled world of Donoghue's Irish parents to which Crist and I found ourselves holding in this nightmarish land. We both of us American born and reared were now indelibly attached to that country where we had only spent a handful of years. My own mother whenever reminded of the day of her departing Ireland, her eyes would fill with tears. For she was suddenly chosen from among her sisters and brothers to travel to America in the company of a rich Australian uncle. Her family gathered on the platform of the tiny train station enacting a scene repeated so many times all over Ireland, leaving those remaining behind red eyed with their grief as another young one among them left for the New World. Years later my mother saying, 'Never feel sorry for me, that I left.'

But in my own sadness now my whole being was yearning for the hills of Wicklow and the shafts of sunlight slanting out of its low skies along its coast. Instead of where I now languished, holding up both head and fist to the then raging coast to coast witch hunt to ferret out communists. My beard automatically proclaiming me one, despite the most fervent of capitalist souls purring within my impecunious person. Both Crist and myself felt isolated. He more by the loss of his glasses and his impatient demands of strangers to read signs. On buses and trains there invariably came mutterings in my direction and sometimes even remarks shouted back from the safety of the subway platforms as the train doors were closing. But I was not that long suffering due unexpectedly to a disquieting event. A gentleman, Willie 'The Actor' Sutton, a number one wanted famed bank robber was indentified on a subway train, and a few days later the identifier was shot down dead. Not only was I no longer muttered at but I had now merely to step into a crowded subway car, and would find it comfortably emptied out at the next stop. And any offending look requiring only a glance to send the perpetrator scurrying away.

Crist had located himself in an apartment on Long Island along Queens Boulevard overlooking the teeming highway. He had built himself a wigwam over his bed into which he now retreated for days at a time along with gallon bottles of Chianti and a stock of photographs he borrowed from me taken in Ireland and upon which he would gaze for hours in tears. As America closed in on me in ever tightening circles, I increasingly romanticized about my return to Ireland. Thinking of peninsulas found on a map whose headlands slanted out from the southwestern coast into the Atlantic Ocean and which I felt were remote and whose grasses were of soft green over which the moist mild winds blew and whose moorlands and meadows were sometimes swept with sun. And where I could taste being alive again. And if I were demising as I deeply, sincerely and self pityingly believed, how softly, how gently would the arms of that earth enfold and surely rest me in peace.

Whenever Crist's and my previous associations with Ireland became known, there was no explanation that would satisfy anyone as to why one did not have a brogue, never mind the American accents we were both born with. Finally it was simpler to merely say one was educated in England. And skip explaining all those centuries of marvellously wonderful Anglo Irish civilizing influences, and which were so intrepidly maintained within the high encircling walls of Trinity College Dublin. Where not only lofty vowels were elegantly spoken but where brollies unfurled in the rain, and bowlers were tipped in greeting and reasonably clean collars, shirts and socks were worn with only one or two holes and were only mildly disintegrating unwashed a month old. But at least now the Irish could be seen bathed spruce and fragrant in America and free of most of their chains. But there were the many still among them and who had not successfully realized their dreams in this land, who were even more blindly bigoted than the countrymen they left behind. And as a once shunned and hated race themselves, were busy hating and shunning the wops, coons, and kikes and others, who could be discriminated against as they had been as micks. Suffice to say my own father, as all Irishmen tend to do who have ever counted cattle and driven them to sell at a fair, put the entire blame for whatever was wrong in the U.S.A. on Wall Street. Ah, but nary a single prejudiced word uttered against those whose ethnic origins were English and who had perpetrated the centuries of Irish oppression. They were now the approved neighbour next to whom the Irish were glad to move and whose example of upstanding well groomed citizenship they might even emulate.

But the pace of my ebbing in this land was increasing. Just as my resolve was not to acquiesce to its witch hunting fear. Having daily to point out to all those daring still to speak to me, and who, implying political disloyalty, asked why I was growing a beard, that I was doing nothing, and that they were in fact shaving theirs off. I recalled now people like James Hillman, and Ernest Gebler who had each warned me of such a return. Ireland for all its faults and sins and lack of pots to piss in had been fatal in reawakening seeds sown by ancient peasant forefathers. Everything in America now was seen in terms of Ireland. Where gossip at least saw to it that you had ear witnessed news of eye witnessed misbehavings beyond the hill, or over in the next town or parish. In America all was the corrosiveness of the unfamiliar, of the so many faces unknown, and each disguised by resembling the other. Gebler, that sage man, had said America was a spectacular country but that Ireland was a beautiful one. He even went so far as to suggest that not everyone in the Emerald Isle was a backbiting, whispering gossip and waiting with a hook to wrap its sharp edge around the unwary carnal committer of sin. But as there was no touch or feel in America of being alive under its sky, I needed less and less convincing. And the sounds Gebler made, exhorting to

American born Irish. The old sod can always be seen upon their faces and the indelible stamp of this race never fades, not even when such sons with such faces have the biggest of all big pots to piss in.

fly back to where the wind and the rain sang a music like harp strings and where my forefathers had sprung forth, became louder and louder.

Except for the strengths lying dormant in my written words of *The Ginger Man*, my spirits were gloomy and hands weak with their uselessness. No hope to fight back against this massive country into which two centuries and Ireland's poverty and famine had poured the dispossessed. Where bullets flew by accident as much as they did when fired in murder and robbery. Black widow spiders in the shadows, copperhead snakes in the grass, sharks off the shore. And upon lonely Bronx and Brooklyn wastelands, bodies were dumped riddled by holes in rub out executions. The sound of my speaking voice was stilled. I found myself reading and cherishing every vision in Tomas O'Crohan's *The Islandman*, and Patrick Kavanagh's *Tarry Flynn*, bringing me living back to Ireland with it each day becoming more and more my dreamed of future refuge.

When I dared now to meet Crist he would inveigle me to places like McSorley's pub which emulated the Irish tradition of men only. Its sawdust covered floor and its plain interior granting some solace as one munched a raw onion slice on a slab of rye bread and washed it down with a beer. Evidence enough why so many American pubs are Irish named, albeit, this of McSorley, perhaps, originating in Scotland before it did in Ulster, but Irish enough for me all the same. To the other pubs we went, Crist and I with our Anglicized accents were invariably accosted as seeming foreigners. Having then to listen to our fellow Americans singing the praises of this land and what a great country we were privileged to be in. Unlike one's response on an Honesty Night back in Ireland, Crist brought sober silent reflection to these inquiring voices to whom he merely had to reply.

'Have you looked at the faces.'

But all was not banjaxed. Donoghue had spoken of Boston. Its bricked, paved, walkable streets. And all his lifelong Irish connections. The quiet, sombre elegance of Louisburgh Square where he'd first seen the splendours of space to live in from the vantage point of one of its kitchens where his Irish born aunt was a cook. And where a graceful lady of English ancestry patted him on the head and said, 'And whose little boy is this.' He told of Boston's West End ghetto, its family bakeries and family undertakers, and its cheap rents and food in this pleasantly livable city. And not that long later, at the end of that summer one was there. In a tiny dark flat, behind a disused shop front with windows opening out on a bleak dark courtyard, a patch of sky just visible vertically up. Little was Irish down these shadowy, narrow, garbage strewn streets. All seemed Polish, Jewish, Lithuanian and Hungarian and God knows what else.

As the weeks went by, the only Irish I met in the Irish town of Boston were Donoghue's closest friends, Lizzie and Julian Moynahan, who like Donoghue himself had Irish parents but unlike him were never under an illusion of growing up in Ireland. Products of Radcliffe and Harvard, these two handsome people with their charm and stunningly sharp intellects were the fortunate heirs to much of what was commendable in America. Having its humanity and generosity but also able to avoid its bleak bland conformity. Both tolerant observers who were not alarmed to be politically or religiously irreverent and were prepared to remain fervent backers of the underdog. Two people at least who were a reassuring flowering from their forebears who had in their coffin ships tumbled on the waves to this land.

And on an afternoon in Boston after one of my many sleepless nights I lay back in this shady sultry silence to nap a moment to regain energy enough to go back to my makeshift desk to write. For there was an Italian woman upstairs constantly day and night nagging at her husband and son and who had suddenly shut up and must have either taken cyanide or hung herself. I was listening to my pulse throb in the space between my ear and the pillow when suddenly I was transfixed. The palest purest music seemed to come drifting in my open window. I turned my head towards a fence separating another courtyard towards which I had often looked and from where just peeked the leaves of a poplar tree I could just barely see. The strains I heard were those of 'The Lark in the Clear Air'. Last listened to as I sat within the brocaded finery in the music room of Burton Hall. When John Ryan played it for me. And whose own windows looked upon those soft green acres of parkland. And not upon a bleak sewer sour courtyard. I thought I'd finally cracked, unable to take the struggle any more, and had been long gone upwards somewhere floating in the infinity of the celestial blisses. But as this unbelievably welcome soothing sound continued to reach my astonished ears, and then came the music of 'She Moved Through the Fair' with its sad words singing of death and disappointment, I knew somehow I was not deceived. And with my eyes closed, never did such a glow of hope give light so bright down in that dark tomb where no sun shone and bedbugs scurried across the floor.

My sensibilities in this ghetto enclave were not entirely alone. I had often passed an iron barred gate which led down a narrow passage to where a tree grew in a tiny curtilage called Poplar Court. In the adjoining alley beyond the wooden fence was living a Harvard professor. This gentleman was never to know how he had nearly saved my life as he continued over the weeks to play these traditional Irish melodies and make my struggles during this bleak summer tolerable. For my only other small comfort was an ancient Jewish gentleman who always, as he went past me on his way to the synagogue, and as I sat taking a few minutes break on my shop front stoop, would reach to tweak my cheeks to say 'What do you do in there. What is such a good yiddish looking gentleman who speaks so fine like you and makes tap tap with a typewriter noise, doing in such

This old white house at the top of the hill in Woodlawn the Bronx, became an outpost upon my first return to America from Ireland. The three front bedroom windows above the sun porch was where many pages of The Ginger Man *were written and it was also where Gainor Crist stayed as a guest in fleeing the horrors he encountered upon his own American return and where he bathed his forehead in balm with the shades pulled down in case someone was taking a bead on him with a gun.*

a terrible place like this. You no speak. You no explain. But don't worry, I ask you on my way back again.'

Ah, but in Boston, true to its nature, a publisher in his summery shirtsleeves on another sultry day pointed at the manuscript he had placed farthest from him on the floor near the door and said 'There's libel and obscenity in that book and we would be tarred and feathered were we to publish it in Boston.' Thus did the moral overtones I had been so used to in Ireland, follow me now to this New World. And clearly make themselves felt in what was one of the most Irish Catholic cities in America. If one had to suffer such things here why not go back and tolerate them where the breezes blew soft and moist and warm and were sometimes stained with sun. With peace so wild for wishing where all is told and telling.

And I did. Return to Ireland. Even if it were as brief as only staring down into the waters of Cobh harbour. And back in New York and no longer writing *The Ginger Man*, I continued to read each day away dreaming we were already back on the hillside overlooking Kells Cove in Kerry. Even the eternally patient, long suffering Gainor Stephen Crist had had enough, escaping as he had been doing from one nightmare to another and the next always a greater one. And I was not to know as he lay upon his bed at that famed outpost of that white house in Woodlawn atop 233 East 238 Street, New York, that he too was plotting to escape. I squeezed lemon in the warm water with which he now bathed his head. People were looking for him all over New York for various misdemeanours which were always well meant by Crist at the time they were committed. In a brown paper bag he carried a length of rope and piece of cheese. And upon his head he wore his thick, woollen Aran islander's hat. In an Ireland steeped in crut they might indeed make life a fight with the heavyweight champion of the world and revive you only to knock you out again. But there, beaten though you may be, they at least let you live. Here sudden death was everywhere. On the highways, a million cars streamed ceaselessly. The nation never stopped, day, night, midday or midnight. Even an unbelieving Gebler in his hotel when first visiting New York, got up from bed every hour to look out on the highway along the East River waiting for the cars to stop. And through the night they never stopped. In a letter from Ireland he wrote now speaking yet again as he always did, of weather, of colours, of the warm waiting stillness, and the soft heathery hues under the grey grey of its skies. A farmer in the distance shouting at his cattle and the echoes wafting back with the coconut scented perfume of the golden gorse.

The manuscript of *The Ginger Man* was thick and heavy between its grey cardboard covers. Crist in his yellow tie and faint green shirt would open it up across his chest and occasionally chuckle. My brother T.J., taking a peek, said if that ever gets published there'll be lots of lamp cords in under suburban closet doors. My wife Valerie and son Philip had already lofted into the sky eastwards and were back on the Isle of Man. Even some Americans were now encouraging our escape. After a night partying downtown with Crist, my wrist was ripped open when my fist had plunged through a pane of glass. And I stopped speaking. To a world that was so utterly indifferent to my voice. Gebler from Lake Park was saying get out even if you have to walk on the waves. And I would do, to get my hands to touch and dig again in the ancient loams of Ireland.

It was upon a February day. A sky cold and heavy with mist. The faint sun glowing pink. Chauffered by my parents I made it to the pier. Over these last days the shades of my room were pulled drawn to the sill. I boarded this ship sailing for Liverpool, via Cobh and Ireland. With relief one stood upon this deck, the ship ready to sail. Its horn in a throbbing blast echoing back from across the Hudson and the New Jersey shore. Beef tea was announced to be served in the garden lounge. Stevedores lifting the massive hawsers from their iron capstans and the great ropes of hemp splashed down into the water, were being winched back up on the ship. Then came an astonishing sound. And a voice I knew so well. Heard now as if I were dreaming. Feet pounding down the pier. And the black coated figure, whose sudden miraculous appearance I could not believe. A suitcase in one hand and his trusty brown paper bag banging against his knees as he ran, shouting 'Wait for me'. None other than that magic saintly man, Blessed Gainor Stephen Crist, clambering up the gangway just as it was being winched ashore. For this Dutch descended, honorary Irishman had disappeared without trace days before I left. Hiding out all night on subway trains, travelling last stop to last stop with his luggage in tow all over the city. And now fleeing back towards the ancient remoteness of Ireland and to the eternal follies of Dublin which certainly upon that embarkation day neither one of us thought we should have ever left.

To come
To this new world
Land
Under a sun
Bleeding with
Sorrow

XIII

It took eleven days on a storm swept Atlantic for the good ship *Franconia* to cross the ocean. Putting into Halifax Nova Scotia while the tail of the hurricane moderated. On this seasickening journey more than half the crew were laid low but Crist, his stomach impervious to the pitch and roll of the ship, was, unperturbed as ever, striding the deck with his nervous quick walk and was sometimes the only one in the dining room golfing down plate after plate of abandoned food, especially the smoked salmon uneaten in first class. He even won the Ping Pong tournament but lost against me when we'd played chess. Passengers collecting about to watch these titanic struggles during which I would mime the disaster I intended to visit upon his various pieces.

It was early on a chill morning, a misty rain falling, when from the deck of the *Franconia* I watched Crist debark upon the bobbing tender to take him away across this grey bay to the green shore of Ireland and land upon the granite pier at Cobh. His blue Aran islander's hat brightly conspicuous on his head as he stood on the tender's stern and waved back up to me on the ship. I was not to know but it was as close as I was to get to Ireland for some time to come. Weeks later via the Irish network of gossip I heard the unbelievable tales of Crist's complicated detouring journey northwards to Dublin which took him two weeks instead of one day. Typical of an Ireland where a stranger could in moments become an ancient friend and involve you in the rest of his life.

As there had been for me as a painter in my wet painting period, I realized that there was no future for me as a writer in the small, embittered, destructive, literary world of Dublin and Ireland. In my continuing struggle to survive and parked temporarily on the Isle of Man, I finally moved to London. But not before there had been a considerable imbroglio with the self elected protectors of a young Irish girl with whom Gebler had taken up. This new attractive lady, full of laughter when not full of tears, had broken away from the Irish

Son Philip in the front garden where a hammock swings and where tea was being taken under the palm trees when interrupted by the arrival of the Irish vigilantes looking for Gebler. When such violent incidents were not in progress the Isle of Man was an idyllic sub tropical if windy paradise.

prescribed way of life. And from behind a chemist's counter was overnight coping with her new role as the friend of an acclaimed author and was staying without the blessing of marriage as a long term guest in his manor. Edna, as she was called, was the product of a respectable Irish farming family from the west and convent schools, and arrived with Gebler at The Anchorage, Port e Vullin. This splendid house of my mother in law's perched in its gardens nearly sat on the waves. With my mother in law in India, we took tea in the garden under the sub tropical palm trees. Suddenly out of the blue a Manx detective arrived inquiring in general about the weather which was agreeably bright, balmy and sunny. Then other folk came in two more laden cars. Full to the brim with pure Irishmen. Plus a bishop from somewhere. At first it looked like the arrival of friends and a version of a family reunion and with the detective acting as equerry I decided to leave my guests with their guests and repaired back up to my study whose window faced out upon the sea and where I was writing a revision of *The Ginger Man*. Suddenly I heard screams from Valerie.

'Mike, come quick, come quick, they're beating up Ernie.'

Daughter Karen in the front garden where the door through which the author exited to defend Ernie Gebler is in the background. And Karen, who shares her mother's passion for cats, sits on the edge of an old well turned into a flower bed.

I leaped from my desk, papers flying and jumped down the stairs, taking off my jacket and a heavy sweater. I went rolling up my sleeves as I ran through a hall. Depositing my watch on the dining room table as I sailed across that room. I could hear the young lady Edna sobbing somewhere. And I increased speed out through the kitchen, already throwing shadow boxing blows to warm up my arms. I raced along a conservatory passageway which led to the front gate and a large door in a wall from which one could proceed by a slipway down along the side of the house and which sloped to the sea. At the bottom, caught between the high garden wall at his back and a railing fencing him from the waves, was Ernest Gebler battling for his life as six or so folk rained blows and kicks upon him. Above me as I turned out the door I spotted a seventh acting as a lookout on the road, and who saw me coming. I had no idea that the tongues had been wagging across Ireland over the association of Edna and Ernest. Or that those who abhorred such had banded into an army to end the relationship. But I did know that if people back in Dublin had doubts as to whether I could write or paint, the one thing no one seemingly disputed was my being able to give a decent account of myself in an affray. And the cry of warning was raised as I sallied forth down the slipway.

'It's him. It's Donleavy, he's coming.'

'You bet your bloody Irish arses I am and I'm going to kick the living bigoted shit out of all of you.'

Of course I may not have said 'bigoted' at the time. However, I remember trying to be positive sounding in my purpose as it at least would deflect some of the acrimonious attention being paid poor Ernest Gebler. And I knew by the expression, 'It's him', that my violent reputation had preceded me. But even as I approached Ernest who was as strong as an ox, and could snap his sinewy steel muscles like a whiplash, he had already flattened prone one of the six on the slipway and had just sent a fifth with an uppercut hurtling skywards, arching head first and feet last over the railing into the sea. And as I reached them I was able, in an authentically Irish manner, to level one more with a grossly unsportsmanlike blow just to the rear of his right ear while this victim's back was turned. One of the three remaining, turning to scream.

'Don't hit me I'm an old man and I've a Friday left to make of the nine first Fridays.'

As the latter gent, who admittedly wasn't in the springtime of his prime, was trying his damnedest to gouge one of Gebler's eyes out, I had no hesitation in unleashing an almighty boot up his backside to send him pitching forward on his face as he was scuttling away up the gravel slipway to escape. This seemed the signal for the two gents remaining and facing the two of us, in what now could have been a fair fight, to promptly speedily depart. One having to proceed hopping on one foot for Gebler had firm hold of the other. It was at this moment that I spied two more figures who were all this time lurking behind a wall in reserve but now thought the better of leaping into the breech as their cohorts limped, hobbled and crawled as fast as they could to their cars. The rear being taken up by the chap Gebler had sent flying into the drink who with the copious amounts of seaweed hanging down around his ears, now resembled a female impersonator transvestite. Clearly the intention of these unannounced visitors had been to beat Gebler to within an inch of, if not entirely extinguish, his life. And in the present rout of this gang of Irish beating it up the slipway, and me still outraged by such bullying behaviour, I had no hesitation in landing further kicks here and there on the various backsides. On the road at the top of the slipway and in the blazing afternoon sunshine and peaceful buzz of the bees in the honeysuckle, the bishop from somewhere stood with a crucifix and rosary blessing himself and declaring I thought, most unfairly and inappropriately.

'O dear God, I pray thee to deliver the pure and innocent of us from evil.'

As the culprits of the attack leaped back into their cars and disappeared up the road and over the headland in a cloud of exhaust, and Gebler finished thanking me for saving his life, I counted six teeth on the slipway and quickly ran my tongue searchingly back and forth in my mouth. Happily neither I nor Gebler were missing any. And Ernest, a genius with home remedies, bathed his cuts and bruises while comforting this pretty and entirely innocent girl who, sobbing before, was fortunately now, as I gave ringside descriptions of the infighting, able to see the amusing side of the matter and was half falling off her chair laughing and adding her own embellishments with her lilting brogue which could so melodiously coin a poignant phrase or make observations in fresh new words in her inimitable Irish way.

Of course, the young lady Edna was not only charming but also innocent of the culpability being alleged by the ostensibly well meaning vigilantes out to save her good name and to prevent her from being led astray by an international author and to put her back on the previous good path laid down for all well bred Irish country girls. In any event, Gebler was, for all his sometimes dour qualities, one of that rare breed, a consummate gentleman. And fully deserving of the battle fought to save him from the unjust punishment intended. But the Irish in revenge never give up, or at least not until you marry the girl. Which Gebler finally did as his second wife. And alas, another talented Irish writer came into being and to ultimate acclaim. Years later it did make me remember how, before the latter lady achieved her recognition, she had been made to suffer obtuse ridicule at the hands of some of Gebler's contemporaries, pretenders to artistic sophistication who, ready to pounce, lurked resentfully in the bitter world of Irish letters. And to whom I once announced.

'You are making fun of a young lady who will one day be the literary queen of England.'

Of course, the young lady could well take care of herself and certainly needed no help from me but I was full of such bizarrely grandiose predictions and never wasted an opportunity when I felt they could be expressed, not for a second thinking that any of them could ever come true. As indeed a few did. In any event as Gebler was already a literary king it was easy enough to throw titles about. Especially as I was pretentiously as possible readily assuming them myself. One never knew for sure who all these volunteer vigilantes were who landed out of the blue on the Isle of Man, but they did represent a faction and a mode of action frequently employed to stamp out any carnal impurity that might be thought afoot and publicly affecting the morals of the female citizenry of that land. And one knew such contingent could be gathered in a thrice by merely a whisper in an ear in any pub, especially if the perpetrator of such alleged debauchery had a foreign sounding name. And so had I come, in my little interim, away from the old sod, into contact with Ireland and the Irish again.

Not long after this event I debarked from this pleasant little island to London. Former denizens of Dublin like Desmond MacNamara, and Valentine Coughlan were there from whom one would hear the usual recent Dublin stories. Such as the news that modern criminal methods were being introduced to Ireland. And a couple of apprentice criminals with a bomb timing device were robbing a bank. And had this night driven their car around the block again and again awaiting the explosive charge to detonate. But then seeing nothing happen they then parked. And, lo and behold, who should come walking along but a member of the Garda Síochána who, viewing this suspicious pair three a.m. in the morning sitting in their vehicle outside a bank, ventured to inquire as to what they were about. And as they were explaining that they were merely deep breathers, out taking in the night air and minding their own business, the bank's windows blew out in a blaze of flying glass.

But now, settled in England I was as far away from Ireland as you could be, down a working class Fulham street where nary any soul thinking of the betterment of his social position and future, would dare to venture. And a young British élitist, son of an Oxford don, once walking with me through Kensington suddenly stopped in his tracks.

'I'm awfully sorry, my dear chap, but I cannot proceed farther, you see we are about to enter the borough of Fulham and I never walk there.'

There were other snobs but it was now left mostly to the Irish and those of past Irish association to visit me. The most consistent of whom were a Glin Bennett and a Davy Romney, both former Trinity medical students who'd become physicians, and were later to distinguish themselves in that profession. Desmond MacNamara came by bicycle bringing his own pillow to sit on my hard chairs. And Randall Hillis, with whom I waked his lonely friend, not only came but even moved nearby with a stunningly beautiful, genuinely Irish wife.

But there were other Irishmen, too, with their own special brand of snobbery. And on a Christmas day, holed up down my grim street in Fulham, where instead of fresh westerly winds down from the Wicklow Mountains I had now the tall chimneys of the Fulham power station looming, unleashing their clouds of smoke. Valentine

The author in his former Fulham sitting room as a first settler and social untouchable long prior to Fulham becoming fashionable and its residents acceptable. One former Trinity College friend at the time remarking upon discovering where I lived, 'Ah we've all changed. But he hasn't.'

Coughlan, full of his usual optimistic bonhomie, had come for this festive day's dinner. Which was not of your usual goose or turkey but of rabbit. For the occasion I had invited another single male Dubliner to my table and whose arrival we awaited. As nearly an hour ticked by, and my hungry son Philip, and tiny daughter Karen and wife Valerie were growing anxious to eat, Coughlan asked me did I by any chance at all tell this awaited guest, as I had told him, that I was having rabbit for Christmas dinner. I said yes, I had. And Coughlan drew his chair up to the table and gave a grunt of contempt.

'Well tuck in your napkins now and dig in your forks and start eating for you'll be waiting till beyond next Christmas before the likes of that bloody snob looking down his nose shows up.'

Then I recalled that this person of an Irish name and ancestry had been born and raised in England. But certainly there was a true Irishman arriving when Behan would occasionally show up. The two of us often setting off on a walk covering miles and miles, meandering in any direction across London, discussing as we went all matters pertinent and impertinent to our world, and to the world's world. Behan often, as my own father did, stopping to talk with anyone along the way digging a ditch or building a wall. Inevitably by evening we were in some pub near the London offices of some Irish newspaper. And on one such occasion we finally did have a fight. In the middle of Fleet Street. Battling back and forth and stopping the traffic. And finally being temporarily arrested. Behan, as an ex inmate of Her Majesty's Prisons, already persona non grata in the United Kingdom, seemed to know how to placate a British bobby and not further compound our felony, and ten minutes later up a Fleet Street alley the two of us were let go. Next morning while I was out, Behan with a red swollen nose and black eye turned up at 40A Broughton Road with none other than Lead Pipe Daniel The Dangerous in tow. But first the two of them had already visited my local library where they pretended to inquire after my address, the librarian telling me later in hushed tones of the incident.

'I didn't think, Mr Donleavy, that you would want me to release your address to these two particular gentlemen.'

In true Dublin style Behan wanted to borrow my typewriter. And Lead Pipe Daniel The Dangerous clearly intended to pawn it. My wife Valerie resisting their supplications. But Behan did help *The Ginger Man* to at least get published in France by telling me on the night of our fisticuffs, of The Olympia Press in Paris. Later, when the book managed to get its first reviews with its publication in England, and just as one's Irish associations were slipping, and over those particular long months when I was nearly more banjaxed than ever with litigation looming with The Olympia Press, Paris, over *The Ginger Man*, there suddenly came out of the blue a letter. The theatrical critic Kenneth Tynan, who was also a film script editor for Ealing Films, was writing to say he'd thought *The Ginger Man* a marvellous book and did I really hate films as much as Dangerfield suggested and that if I would think of something that could be put on celluloid my dialogue would be a godsend to British films. These were ecstatically encouraging words to hear while impecuniously tightly squeezed down this small Fulham side street. And there were no doubts in my mind that I had in the last five minutes entirely revised any previous loathing I may have had for films or Hollywood and was now, if I had not ever been previously, a fervent lover of tinsel and celluloid. At our meeting in his lavish Mount Street flat, Tynan, a cigarette dangling between his ring and small finger, admitted some possible Irish ancestry, and said, just give me an idea, tell it to me now or write it on a match cover or back of a postage stamp and provided you have no aversion to large sums of money we'll drop a contract through your letter box.

My mind, quicker than it seemed to have ever worked before, duly conjured a story concocted out of one I'd heard of a returned American making a trip to the west of Ireland to recover money left in a will. This idea, as Tynan had suggested, was duly scribbled on a match cover. And along with my dreaming of the free openness of Ireland and a film to be set there, a cheque came. Once more I was on my way back to that island land bringing with me a new pot to replace the old one I had been pissing in which had incurred so many recent leaks. Much needed, especially in a nation where, in the history of pissoirs, you will never find any so dismal.

I had answered an ad in a London Sunday newspaper, to rent a house in Connemara. Setting off from London with Valerie and a family of my two children, Philip and Karen. Arriving at evening after a long day's journey by train and boat, to at last come between those familiar enfolding arms of land around Dublin Bay. Howth to the north, Dalkey to the south. One's memory ringing with other names. Clontarf, Blackrock, Rathmines and Booterstown. And there was Dublin, dirty and grey. And now changed forever because A. K. Donoghue, purveyor of honesty and Blessed Gainor Stephen Crist, patron saint of tourists in Dublin, were both gone. Yet if only as pale substitutes for these two eminently volatile gentlemen, one did still see a few familiar faces passing like moveable landmarks upon the street. As if one were opening an old favourite book, the pages faded, but the words still there saying exactly the same.

And there were those other faces of sadder men, the poets, the novel writers, lurking figures who made their solitary excursions through their city. Casting an eye perhaps at a Jewish gentleman, inspiringly insane in the middle of Grafton Street who over so many years so benignly and brilliantly directed rush hour traffic. He was still there on this day as we took the train from Westland Row Station to cross the midlands to Galway City. An even bleaker place than Dublin. Where we were met and taken to an hotel and given dinner by my hospitable landlord. Who insisted on paying the bill and then drove three hours, mile after deserted mile over the curving road through a lake and pond dotted boggy Connemara. Its moorland landscape strewn with stone and grey granite outcroppings. My intrepid landlord leaning over his steering wheel to see ahead in the lashing rain drenching this endless loneliness. And to my question had we much further to go.

'Well, it wouldn't be much further now.'

Beyond Clifden and finally, over a dirt and rutted road and in an even more deserted landscape with the bleakest of darkness upon us, we arrived in the downpour to an isolated house in the wildest of wild places. Indeed, it was out on a peninsula reaching into the Atlantic Ocean, such as I had dreamed about. And stepping out of the storm swept black night, one was suddenly standing in the hall of this cold massive Georgian edifice. One's breath white on the air. Where nothing seemed to matter now except remaining warm and fed. In the gloom a staircase rose up to these giant bedrooms. One already felt a little haunted by the space enclosed within these thick walls, and the large brooding Victorian furniture. My imagination measuring a dining room fifty feet long, thirty feet wide and twenty feet high. Our exceedingly courteous and solicitous landlord promptly lit a fire or two to drive away the damp and cheer up our spirits. But none the less in my worry I fell asleep thinking that one's children could be found chilled dead in the morning. That is if I weren't found first. But when I did finally fall asleep and awake again, a surprisingly mild morning sun was streaming in the window. I could hear singing elsewhere in the house and I went to investigate. And there across the hall, was Philip. Already having the circus time of his life jumping with cliff hanging daring from one bed to another in his room. Later the two of us were happily playing soccer together in the cavernous front hall.

I set up a desk to write upon in a large sun porch that jutted out over the front door. Able to stare out miles over this windswept wild countryside. Where tracks led over the stony little hills to magically golden coral beaches. I could see six mountains and what appeared to be a lake in front of the house, but was in fact the Atlantic Ocean. Looking out on this landscape I wrote the film script of *The Rich Goat*, and began in this vast silence my second novel, *A Singular Man*. No visitors, no telephone, no newspapers. And with no radio, no connection to the outside world. But occasionally up from behind hedges and disappearing around walls were human faces and shadowy figures. Someone that first day of arrival was being buried. In an anonymous grave like the others in the cemetery which were unadorned but for a slab to mark the foot and head and a pile of stones covering the rest. A reminder that here was an earth which, as quietly as a flower blooms and its petals fall, could take one back into its bosom.

One morning in my sun porch workroom while I was staring down on the small field in front of the house, I saw the neighbouring farmer come running in the gate from the road. Philip and Karen were playing on the grass at the other end of the lawn and my neighbour shaking a raised hand at the sky and pointing up as he shouted.

'There's a dog up there. There's a dog.'

And apprehensive as the wildly gesticulating farmer approached in the direction of my children, I ran out into the hall and shouted down to Valerie in the kitchen, to call Philip and Karen as quickly as she could into the house. And out of the way of this obviously insane and possibly dangerous man. Who, as he now went back onto the road, was repeating his observation about this bow wow which he thought was barking high in the heavens. Meanwhile and later that day our landlord, providing us with a radio, also arrived with the news that the Russians had put a dog up in a space capsule orbiting planet earth. And isolated out in the bleak beauty of this ancient land one learned that the rest of the world had entered the space age.

And it was here that one came back to Irish ways. Indifferent to time, stoic to discomfort and calamity. A newspaper ordered from town came. It would at least be of a recent date, and at most, maybe a month old. But on the outside only. For inside, fattening the thickness of the edition, were other pages of some ancient date and from a newspaper of a different name and even of a religious or sporting nature. To me who did not want to know any recent news if I could help it, such random assembled out of date newspapers were a godsend. However there were other drawbacks of a different nature. A piece of pork ordered came delivered dipped in methylated spirits to disguise its very high and smelly nature. So too did come last year's biscuits and last year's coffee. But it was nothing to kill you as the natives thought a tomato, onion or fresh vegetable might. Ah, but why be fussy when one felt absolutely and contentedly at home. There was salt fish, potatoes and cabbage and the squirt of a bit of milk out of a cow and cream churned into butter. Not a stone's throw away there were the clear, clean Atlantic waters tumbling their foaming waves on these golden shores. To which one strolled each day. A local recluse always following along jumping behind stone hedges and outcroppings to hide and watch. There was, too, the strange phenomenon of excreta precipitously deposited on the peaks of stones in salient places such as forks in the road and especially along paths and lanes where it would confront the traveller and where villagers were sure to pass. Obvious to all that such could not have been pinpointed there by dog, mule or other beast but a human one.

The postman could be seen miles away on the hillside on his bicycle coming with the mail. And one day in answer to a card I wrote to a London friend, Christopher Logue.

Connemara
Sunday

My dear Christopher,

Come and visit. There are not many blades of grass out here but what there is, is counted by the population every morning. There's not a sound of anything anywhere except wind and rain and the odd donkey. The place will give you a jolt, at least the silence. You may not have sheets or enough covers on your bed but one hopes to keep you unchilled in the heart. The most bizarre bunch of fantastic faced people are here. The curiosity in their expressions makes them look mean. Maybe some are.

But when not doing their disappearing acts or standing on their heads clapping the mud off their boots, the natives seem by their toothless grins to be friendly enough when greeted. Others, the 'queer' ones, board up in their houses and come out at night. But by day some have not been seen for twenty or thirty years. When I asked what they did with themselves locked away with their windows covered over to the light, I was told they read by candlelight. What, at first, I couldn't imagine. Except old newspaper accounts of the sinking of the *Titanic* which are abundant here. But then on the front stoop yesterday came the news that at least one of them was reading a book called *The Ginger Man*. Which may account for some of the wild riotous laughter which woke me way past midnight the other night. This morning one of them (not a reader, I'm told) was buried and the countryside was smiling ear to ear as Irish do when another green greedy mouth is dead. So I leave it to you to come if you can.

Christopher Logue duly arrived smilingly after his long travel. Already with tales of prostrate drunk bodies on the mail boat and someone leaping overboard in a suicide. But at least by that evening he had got some amusement watching me in order to amuse Philip and Karen who were being bathed in a portable bath in front of the turf fire in the dining room, while I pretended to be a Roman gladiator, mop as a spear and with a silver sauce boat off the sideboard on top of my head.

Of course, Christopher Logue with his penetrating blue eyes and eccentrically aristocratic face and who with a long black flowing cloak out behind him as he careered on a rented bicycle about the winding hilly roads, was a lot stranger looking than any of the natives. Who indeed fled at the sight of his approach thinking him a reincarnation of a poet they thought was known by the name of Yeats and was long dead. Logue creating a sensation for miles around, as he swept down hillsides like a great raven, his bike bouncing over the stony road and his cape flapping behind him as he pedalled across the countryside while his splendidly booming voice declaimed his poetry out on the winds.

Christopher asked me why people seemed to shrink back as if in fear of him. And I told him tales of the power of a poet. That such a man in making his verses could compose one of ridicule to bring down upon those causing his displeasure, a curse repeated and recited down through the generations. Logue, a man of extremely practical inclinations only smiled to indulge what he knew were my frequent highly embellished exaggerations, but meanwhile he was surviving well. Mary, the girl who worked in the house and who would walk to Clifden seven miles away on a Friday night to attend a dance and walked all the way back, was amused with this gentleman who could go laughingly booming his voice through the halls and especially with his putting unsmoked butt ends filling up a jar in his bedroom. Logue meticulously saving these to remake and smoke the remnants reconstituted in his hand rolled cigarettes and which he could puff upon during the long train and boat ride back to London. And upon the eve of Logue's departure Mary had thrown the whole lot away. Collapsing in fits of laughter when she heard why Christopher had been saving them. However something else was to happen when Logue was leaving and returning his rented bicycle to the man in the town from whom he'd got it, and who seeing a few mud spots on the fenders and alleging other damage, now stood at the top of his stairs refusing to give Logue back his pound deposit. Logue then remembering what I'd said about the power of poets in Ireland. And just as your man was standing stubbornly shaking his head no in reply to Logue's loudest demand, Logue pointed an accusing finger up at him.

'I am a poet and I shall make up a verse that will ridicule you and all those belonging to you down through the generations.'

Before Logue could turn and leave, a crumpled up pound note landed at his feet at the foot of the stairs. Clearly out there in the back and beyond, and if not among the untutored and savage, it was at least still believed by the worldly astute that ill fortune if not damnation could be brought down upon you by the ancient power of poets.

Before *The Rich Goat* could be made, Ealing Films got sold. And except for one unforgettable event, a long gap of ten years was to occur after my sojourn this early winter November 1957 in the west. But on 26 October 1959 two years later, I was to be back briefly again in Ireland and certainly sooner than I expected. This time in the wake of the London production of *The Ginger Man* transferring to Dublin. Which no doubt was encouraged by quotes, one of such was attributed to Harold Hobson of the *Sunday Times*. 'There are two modern plays in London through which blows the wind of genius. One of them is Brendan Behan's *The Hostage*. The other is J. P. Donleavy's *The Ginger Man*.'

I was on this occasion to learn something about Ireland I suspected and which I had already expressed in one of my forewords, 'In Ireland friendship is on the lips but not in the heart'. But somehow I did not ever believe it possible that the emnity would ever come out into the public light. When news of a transfer of *The Ginger Man* stage production to Dublin reached me, I was delighted but thought it the ultimate act of bravery or madness. But to at last bring back to this land, this work to where it had found its origins, seemed fitting enough, if not even a vindication. Then with a couple of verbal first night protests, the storm clouds began to gather. At the final curtain were demands to make cuts. The cliff hanging moments on the second night taking place in the theatre owner's office when the production might have at any second been called off. The tension mounting each succeeding day as the newspaper word spread of this distasteful, repulsively sordid evening which was an insult to religion and decency. As the hours went by more tickets being sold, the audience increasing and queues forming down the street in front of the theatre. The secretary of the Archbishop arriving and then departing to the comment of Richard Harris, the play's star, 'There goes a battleship'. Following the third performance the play was finally taken off. In disgracing themselves yet again, the Irish had finally done it. For the first time in Irish history, they had stopped a play playing on the stage.

I had already seen *The Ginger Man* survive its way past countless publishers' rejections and then censors in France, England and the U.S.A., almost as if *The Ginger Man* could wield a curse against all who opposed or stole or ridiculed its words. But in Ireland I was to find a vast convoluted instant conspiracy spreading its secret silent tentacles in all directions and especially to every corner of Dublin city. It was clear that no public contrition or prostrate beating of one's head on the wooden blocks of Grafton Street could assuage the emnity. Telephones went dead. Hostile glances came from every side. One was followed upon buses and upon foot. A narrow minded intolerance welled up so vast, widespread and deep that it could hardly be called intolerance at all. It was the natural condition of the people described so long ago by Gainor Stephen Crist as the Crut. But it was now more like an electric wire plugged into everyone in the nation to whom intelligence reports were being hourly made to provide a glowering sea of threat. The only antidote to which was to

(Left) *This was the poster which, all over Dublin, disappeared within hours when* The Ginger Man *was forced off the Dublin stage by the intervention of the awesome power of the Catholic authority wielded by the then Archbishop of Dublin. This single poster was rescued by Tony Walton who had the presence of mind to grab it prior to leaving for London, and which he later bequeathed to me.*

(Below) *Richard Harris as Sebastian Dangerfield conferring with Isobel Dean as Miss Frost over a choice of sausages. Harris' rehearsals were as dramatic as his performances and were full of realism, and even merely reciting his lines had been known to stop traffic outside his flat in Earls Court Road.*

get word out to the outside world. But in attempting to alert foreign newspapers all our telephone calls were blacked out to and from London's Fleet Street. Subterfuge was everywhere. Not one of these enemies would reveal themselves into the light. There was even a fear that one might be trapped and prevented escape. Except that one knew too that they would be more than glad to see one go and rid Dublin of *The Ginger Man*.

John Ryan throughout was there, a friend in need if only to be just one sympathetic voice in the battle headquarters of the Bailey Restaurant which he then owned in Duke Street. Even Behan whose destinies and mine seemed temporarily to coincide, was there drinking soda water and somehow in his strange way was making amends with me, perhaps for no other reason than our infrequent meetings these past few years. Patrick Kavanagh, himself previously the plaintiff in a libel action headlined across the entire nation, was still ready to raise his voice in the praise of the prevention of public cruelty to authors and playwrights in this land that had now practised it for a century. 'In a mini metropolis long dead, Donleavy has at last set the city alive once more.' And as I walked out of the Bailey, I did hear another Irish voice.

'No wonder Ireland has long been the loud laughing stock of Europe, full as it is of the most insufferable narrow minded eegits.'

With no bands or flags there to see us off, we at last had made it out to the airport. A slightly eccentric friend of Ryan's driving us dangerously fast, making it unnecessary to look behind to see if we were being chased. Richard Harris, as Irish as anybody and the star of the play, was crumpled up brooding in the front seat of the car. He had declared he would play the role on top of an orange crate in the middle of O'Connell Street Bridge and break the jaw of anyone who objected. And Harris, as strong as two oxen, faster than a leopard and bigger than most, had to be believed. Indeed he more than anything else may have saved the author from being strung up in the fly space of the Gaiety. And now Harris was planning to fly with the script to Rome. To either give the Pope a reading of the play in St Peter's Square or else just deliver a piece of Harris's outspoken mind. 'If the Vatican is running Ireland and the Pope is running the Vatican then by God I'm going to put in my two cents to run the Pope.'

In order that no impurity reach the natives I had suffered exactly the same treatment as many before me. But at least I could feel free of these shackles clanking and subduing the voices that had nowhere to speak and nowhere to escape. Always knowing Ireland was a country in which it was best to be a foreigner, and be forgiven not knowing of its obtuse tyrannical repressions. And being an island from which you must take a bigger step to leave than you would a country where a train takes you across the border to another land. It was one wonderful, bright and cheerful feeling of freedom to step off that plane in London. Even realizing that I might never set foot on the old sod again.

But meanwhile the first inklings were manifesting of something that was happening to the world. American culture was spreading to population hordes everywhere, conquering and changing all in its wake. And in Ireland, banned though it may have been, they were, even as copies fell apart, reading *The Ginger Man*. And news of the words 'Will God ever forgive the Catholics' was out. Television, breaking through the custom barriers, had crossed the Irish Sea and was alive in front of Irish eyes. Which were bulging with insatiable curiosity. To stare at such immoral flesh and listen to such immoral words. I had briefly travelled to visit my mother then staying in Greystones and to overnight call on James Hillman temporarily residing in a mansion high up in the hills of Co. Wicklow. In my Dublin hotel room returning from a morning stroll I suddenly came upon the maid and a porter looking sheepishly guilty. And later I found a filmscript copy of *The Saddest Summer of Samuel S* missing from my luggage. Even all these years later, the conspiracy was still alive. But then on the same visit I had strolled through Dublin. And received the first of what were to be many taps on the shoulder, following which would come an inquiring voice.

'Are you J. P. Donleavy who wrote *The Ginger Man*. That's why I came here all the way from the U.S.A.'

When I went to visit some of my old haunts, the first of which was Jammet's, I found it closed and gone for good. Then a strange and curious sight in a main Dublin street. In a shop window a public protest at corporal punishment given in a Catholic school. Photographs of weals on skin. Something had changed. Voices were speaking to be heard. I strolled then to the Bailey bar and restaurant which was still there but since sold by John Ryan. As I ordered a half of draught Guinness at the bar in this large room jammed elbow to elbow and full of smoke and din, a voice somewhere away in a corner began a slow chant which slowly spread until booming in my ears my name was chanted on everyone's lips. And here anonymously in Dublin where the eye of conspiracy was upon me once more, I suddenly found myself triumphantly conspicuous. Not as the butt of resentment and glowering emnity but in the acknowledgment that here all around me were now Ginger Men and Women. Thinkers for themselves. And maybe even grateful for the spiritual favours received from the Blessed Saint Sebastian Dangerfield himself.

However as the chant of my name continued I was only able to wryly smile and quickly depart, leaving my drink behind. Sorry that in one's long reclusive isolation I had become too timid and inarticulate to show my appreciation and shake some of these ladies' and gentlemen's hands. But aware now that at least and at last and indeed, something was happening. In these minds behind these younger faces if not brighter smiles. And if they had not newer and better pots to piss in at least they might leak less. Where now in this ancient land of saints and scholars.

Among

The zealots and philistines,

The crut

Was being crushed

And forgive

Me

If I blow my

Own horn

With just a tweet or two

For it is at least

Of my own

Melody

And sweet to hear

XIV

Back in London and variously on the Isle of Man, nearly all my direct contact with the Irish had vanished. Valentine Coughlan still stacking up his secret riches in coins and Swiss bank accounts, would telephone me for front row opening night tickets and show up at my plays in a vast limousine full of his guests. And once asked me to write a poem for him to win a poetry contest. Which I did and he lost. I tried religiously each afternoon to take tea, even as late as it might be, and to desert at least for a couple of hours, my eyrie in a tall block of flats near where the hangings at Tyburn took place. I delighted to refer in general to the building as 'Tax Dodgers' Towers'. Such name due entirely to a single inmate who one morning when his driver had brought round his gleamingly new powder blue sparkling Rolls-Royce convertible to the front entrance, had irritatingly said to this chauffeur who was about to jump out and open the door for him.

'No, not that car, you silly, the black one.'

And from the same lofty heights, I had now for some years revelled in walking the streets of London, actively taking pleasure that no Irish zealot pedestrian here would dare point an accusing finger and assert that there be me passing upon such pavement, a known defiler of religion and outrager of decency. And alas, more than frequently, I was to be found at Vespers, in many a Catholic and heavily Irish church, listening to the singing and music. But a remaining Trinity College connection, A. K. Donoghue, former importer of honesty to Ireland and previous loud advocator of cunnilingus to be practised by the Irish male in the interests of the Irish female, would occasionally fly in to visit me from his haunts in mid continental Europe. Spending long festive evenings telephoning old friends, located now across the world, like the Moynahans and a doctor pal Ned O'Rourke to whom one would sing an Irish air or two into the mouthpiece. And one night descending twenty floors I watched Donoghue at this midnight walk out and away from the building to take the underground to

The author himself in his dentist's modern 'Tax Dodgers' Towers' during these balmy days and working up his appetite for the rare vintages and rare roasted beeves ferried up from Fortnum and Mason's. Having been so low for so long in one's life the contrast of being up high, delighted one. And, of course, everyone in such buildings did pay their taxes.

another outpost I kept in Fulham. From this great height one could see over the rooftops into the deserted streets beyond and there I suddenly saw a figure weaving a block away and out of sight to Donoghue, and who then came around the corner to confront him. Donoghue pausing to listen a moment to this only other late night pedestrian, then promptly going on his way. Next morning I asked on the phone about the encounter.

'It was, believe it or not, out of the ten million in this pagan city, one of me own, a drunken Irishman asking me for a handout.'

Due to some accumulated litigations on several continents I had carefully selected the location of 'Tax Dodgers' Towers' to be certain of no such encounters and that no one unless in a passing airplane could look in my windows nor would know where I was. Nor could I, by descending deep into a garage and getting in a car, alas only a

A. K. Donoghue in 'Tax Dodgers' Towers' or 'Dentist's Modern' as he preferred to call it. Where he would come for our lavish evening meals and around the world all night telephone calls to old friends, and then depart back to Broughton Road where he would stay.

Daimler, be seen coming or going. But upon the actual day of moving in, I went into a pub, which although around the corner, I could directly see down on the street below me from my study window. In its saloon bar, I had just sat down contentedly in the bliss of my privacy when a melodious Irish voice, somewhat Anglo to be sure, erupted.

'Give that man sitting over there a drink of whatever he wants.'

The gentleman speaking was a Trinity College Dublin man, Michael Mussen Campbell, later Lord Glenavy. When this charming, welcoming gentleman asked what I was doing there, I dared not tell. For a start, not only was this Michael Campbell's local pub next to which he lived, but also a frequent literary meeting place, for Campbell was an accomplished and reputable Irish writer. For a long time afterwards I skirted this street, not to avoid the excellent company of Campbell but merely in the interests of the continuity of my reclusive privacy.

But ironically over my time there not once in the years did I ever again confront the engaging Michael Campbell but instead it was I who invaded this pleasant Irishman's privacy something awful. Being able to watch down upon his house and witness his arrivals and departures and be sure that among them there would have been some nostalgically nice face I'd known from Dublin. And always in my dull slogging afternoons I found pleasant distraction wondering what Michael Mussen Campbell was doing. Which, as I was mostly desperately glued to my typewriter to pay numerous lawyers, enabled me to keep track of the social seasons. To suddenly see him on his stoop in morning suit and top hat and know he was off to Henley or later with a bevy of friends and a limousine arriving, to know he was departing for Ascot.

It was upon one of these sunnier days when I would set off innocently south across Mayfair that the momentous moment came that brought Ireland back into my life. Mr Young of Fortnum and Mason's stopping me at the tinned soup counter with the revelation which at first I couldn't believe until I saw it imprinted in the highly respectable journal of the *Economist* whose offices were only a strong man's stone's throw away around the corner from Jermyn Street. And to which I repaired for a copy immediately following tea. There it was in black and white. This emerald green nation, the first in the history of nations, legislating to the exclusive benefit of artists. And money, if you could get it for written words, composed sounds or colours drawn, was yours every penny to keep. But of course in hearing this tax law, and once banned and twice banjaxed, I did think that it could be a ruse. Not only to get me, and others like me back there, but once innocently and securely dug in, to then hear said 'Now we've got you, you bunch of dirty minded bastards. Not only are we going to tax your filthy artistic earnings but we're also going to arrest you and put you in prison and burn all your bloody obscene books and manuscripts.'

But perhaps not. Brian Friel, the distinguished playwright, laughed when I told him this. And said that if anyone deserved to benefit by this law, it was me. There has been subsequently, an odd scare or two, but in a land which has undergone a sweeping revolution greater than any that has ever occurred to any people on earth it may be that freedom of speech and expression is here to stay. For since those days of the stopping of *The Ginger Man* and when that book was long banned, at last like a thousand other books it is freely available once more and there has been no need for Irishmen like Richard Harris to be ready on stage to give battle to an irate audience who at any moment might up from their seats, and pour at you over the footlights. When you would hear that perennial cry which put in Patrick Kavanagh's words would be.

'As a Catholic and an Irishman and a fucking eegit, I object.'

Ah, and what else did happen to the Ireland to which I returned. Besides half of it falling and being knocked down in a shambles over which many a greedy gombeen man licks his salivating chops. And where once antichrists were doomed from pulpits to burn to a crisp in hell. Where, too, there was no lonelier scene on the face of this earth than a Protestant evangelist preaching, that their redeemer liveth on a Dublin street corner. Many is the time, merely politely sympathetic, I paused to listen. These days such a sight is even lonelier, for no one is there now at all. The nation strains breaking from its shackles. Coming asunder to imitate the rest of the world. And it was the naughty amoral English, once again, who did it. Who broadcast their nudity, contraception and divorce. Their amoral words and modern ways arriving upon the innocent of this land unstoppable and unseen across the sky and descending through the antennae that reach high from every rooftop. And which, by God, you'd think might be shaking above as if copulation had only just been invented below. With hardly a mortal sin left to commit, a barrier has been raised between those former faithful and their moral custodians who have for so long been a massive power established in their grey dour buildings of Maynooth, planted on the lush green Meath countryside. But to where, too, the like of me has since been invited to say what was recently on my mind. And not once did anyone, censor, zealot or philistine, shake a fist in my face. Sad, too, now that this ancient religious culture with its plainsong, black refinements and sacred ceremony, has not been able to shield from the new inelegant gods who spawn their tastelessness and vulgarity. But then who was to know that so soon there would come the revolution.

It did sure long seem then that one would not ever again be back in this land of its now faded saints and scholars where the religiosity of the people had exchanged for garbage disposal, television and cars. I learned that my mother in America had, when de Valera was asking for money for this nation, given it, and too, that years later it was repaid with interest. And now that I was back in Dublin town fresh from 'Tax Dodgers' Towers', I, too, was looking for a loan. My bank in New York telling me they'd opened a branch in Dublin. To which I went to submit my further and hopefully better particulars. To find

Levington Park. The author's home at the time of writing in Ireland where with nine bathrooms, indoor swimming pool and eleven toilet bowls he finally has a pot to piss in.

my banker a fan of *The Ginger Man* and who, in taking a look at a picture I held up of a house I wanted to buy, said.

'Is that it.'

And I was handed a cheque book with such pleasantly casual ease that I nearly then became too terrified to use it. But nerve returning soon as I headed out once more on these streets upon which one had so often wandered previously on their grey wet granite pavements. And finding that Sebastian Dangerfield was walking everywhere before me. To begin my life again in an old familiar land. Where only in Dublin could you see a man pass oblivious to obstructions, with his nose buried in a book. And another on a park bench reading a tome opened on his knee. Who as I passed, jumped to his feet, cursing in high dudgeon and then sat back down again to peruse his page further which again incensing, had him once more up pacing in a tight circle. Where else in the world would you hope to find such serious readers. I then listened to the mellisonant, elegant voice of the estate agent, Dennis Mahony, rude in health, ready to laugh and in his stout country shoes and tweeds, was delighted I'd come to Ireland. And who, as I autographed a cheque and bought a house,

*The author and his present family who occupy Levington Park consisting of wife Mary,
son Rory and daughter Rebecca seated on her rocking horse.*

gave me a copy of *The Ginger Man* to sign. And then charmingly to protect my interests, even against him, brought me to one of the best lawyers in town. And where the monocles flash under its skylight, we took glasses of stout in the Royal Hibernian Hotel. I had a pot to piss in. And it felt warm like the feel that Dublin once had and was now felt again.

The house where I first went to live was Balsoon House, on the banks of the Boyne near Bective Bridge. With its ancient ruins and cemetery this house was built on a site historically connected to the Ussher family, founders of Trinity. And then I moved to Levington Park, a mellow stone mansion where James Joyce came as a young man and stayed to walk in its halls. But here now as Ireland is, and upon whose verdant lands so much of the outside world's tawdry has descended, there were graces still. Remaining alive even among all those past sins.

On my first trips into Dublin one still felt that sense of stirring anticipation remembered of leisurely late mornings years ago when setting off to Bewley's Oriental Café out the gates of Trinity College. In the city where abject domestic circumstances never prevented your being alive and well out in the pubs and coffee houses. But now I came upon destitute, ragged, homeless scholars slumped over their books seeking only the warmth of the National Library. In a dark, sombre, noonday pub silent habitués were sitting over their pints watching an American film projected upon a big screen, the mystification with the modern world still written across their faces and buried deep in their souls. Here and there on the streets, one could see the phenomenon of the trusted and prosperous well groomed refined Protestant Catholic. Ladies and gentlemen who on a sunny day might be seen tweedily passing into the Royal Irish Automobile Club, perhaps one of the best preserved small enclaves of privilege remaining in Dublin, where very little now endures. For the buildings, they tumble down in this city. But there remains at least the perfection of the purple dark tops of the distant Wicklow Mountains rearing at the end of many of its longitudinal streets. Upon which, wisdom is still being uttered. A swaying gentleman on a corner with drink taken admonishes the passing pedestrians.

'Who the fuck is Ireland. You'd think listening to them talk that it was one of them.'

But there was wonderfully one of them. An Irishman in an

Forty years on from the days of Trinity and coffee in Bewley's, Tony McInerney and Arthur Kenneth Donoghue seated on the porch of the author's house, Levington Park. McInerney tendering the proverbial shilling and Donoghue pulling his forelock and the conversation never ceasing.

expensive Irish restaurant who finished his meal and jumped up and got a headlock on the owner and yanked his head down and pushed his face into his just rendered bill, and said 'Now you eat that and tell me if you think you've been overcharged.' And indeed there remains wherever you go that uncomfortable feeling that you are going to be cheated or lied to, and then the strange relief and pleasure when you're not.

I went to visit Behan's grave. And appropriately enough, in view of the publicity he had while living, it was unmarked. But now there's a headstone and his epitaph is proclaimed along with that of Joyce's, Yeats's and other such giants of literature. All reared up now to become tourist attractions. Their images on sale, the houses they lived in adorned with plaques. Bringing many a foreigner's voice to be heard and their cameras' shutters to click. And at least turning one of these authors, previously obscene, into a latter day saint.

I sit at a desk sipping China tea and lemon, chewing a blend of toasted cereals, nuts and seeds in an English made crunchy bar. And where from that same country across the water, evensong broadcasts on the radio. A late summer's rain spatters against the windows. The sun comes out with the chirp and chatter of swallows. A dove hoots. No snakes. No poison insects. No death in a shadow where you may reach your hand. Just old mouldering graveyards for their dead and for the living, the heritage of chickens and pigs once running around their parlours. And where unlit bicycles and cars still go in the dark. A benign earth to which earthquake tremors and a crematorium have only recently come. Adding at least a little doubt to the belief of the people that Our Lord preserves Ireland above all other nations.

I go to walk high on a lonely deserted hill with a church and cemetery from which one looks down on Lough Owel. Protestant names here fading away on the stones. A foal gambols near its mother sheltering by a wall in a field. As autumn comes, the foxhunting élite will gallop by. The weather forced the Irish to put their hope in heaven and made their bowel movements come at the end of day. This fair skinned nation raging alive, kicking asunder its ancient chains. Where once its sour grapes were boiled in bile. Now it advertises across the world its hospitality and friendliness. This land where time cannot fly. To which the stranger comes. To be fleeced or fooled by the smiles. A nation from which so many fled, now crawling with its human race. But no more do comely maidens dance at the crossroads. Or potato diggers pull their forelocks. Yet there is more to tell. Out here nestled in these midland hills. The air scented green. Ancient friends awake out of their deaths to shake a hand. Walk together across the meadow. Keep your voice down. The grass has ears. To hear your secrets said. Beyond these eastern rainbows. Under which at last this pot. Doth be. To piss in.

Where the brooding
Heavens carry
Their veils of rain
To hide all her sins
And keep her safe in her graces